The Ocean of Grace

Tributes to Amma's All-Embracing Love

Volume 2

The Ocean of Grace

Tributes to Amma's All-Embracing Love

Volume 2

Edited by Veena Erickson
Co-edited by Julius Heyne

Mata Amritanandamayi Mission Trust
Amritapuri P.O., Kollam
Kerala 690546, India

The Ocean of Grace – Volume 2

Tributes to Amma's All-Embracing Love

Edited by Veena Erickson
Co-edited by Julius Heyne

Published by:
Mata Amritanandamayi Mission Trust
Amritapuri P.O., Kollam
Kerala 690546, India

Printed in India

First Edition December 2023: 1000 copies

In India:

www.amritapuri.org
inform@amritapuri.org

In Europe:

www.amma-europe.org

In US:

www.amma.org

Contents

“The real source of grace is within you.”

— *Amma*

Preface

A child, lost and desolate, is hemmed in by a crowd of people. In the hustle and bustle of the crowd, he had somehow let go of his mother's hand. He looks all around, searching for her. He had become separated from his mother, and his anguish broke out through tears of sorrow. Tears flowed unceasingly down his cheeks, his eyes swollen and red from crying. His cheeks were wet and tears dripped down onto his clothes.

A man saw the crying child standing on the side of a road filled with people. He went near and asked him the reason for his tears. The child said he had come to the festival with his mother. He had become separated from her and was now lost and alone. The man consoled the child saying his mother would surely come soon. But the child could not stop crying. The man bought the child an ice cream and offered him chocolates, wanting to calm and reassure the child. The man even bought him toys to play with. As the child received each gift, he would stop crying for a while and enjoy them. But soon, thoughts of his mother would overwhelm him, and he would burst out in loud wails of sorrow. The man became convinced that nothing on earth would replace the joy the child received from his mother.

The man held the child's hand as they walked forward in search of the mother. After walking for some time, the child suddenly spotted his mother and screamed out loud, "Amma." The mother turned around on hearing her child's voice and came running to him. She pulled him into her arms and tightly embraced him. The child stopped crying. His eyes shone with a joy that no earthly object could ever give him.

This is the state we are all in. We seek joy in many things. They may be objects, relationships, or power and fame. But the joy they give us will be temporary. Whatever we may try to experience in this world, nothing will give us perfect contentment.

The joy and relief the child feels when the mother comes to his side is beyond our ability to describe. What if the mother were the empress of this universe and also his mother? This is the great fortune experienced by Amma's children. We sought joy and peace in all corners of the world, away from our mother, the mother of this universe. Nothing outside us could ever give us perfect peace. But upon reaching Amma's abode, we experience a sense of security and a calmness that nothing else can ever give us.

The life experiences describing how Amma takes each child by the hand and leads them forward, how safe they remain in her embrace, and how deep the peace and security they experience are innumerable. This book contains the blissful experiences of Amma's children as they recounted them in person, in Amma's presence. Each experience of Amma they share remains unequaled. Amma gives what is needed for each one of her children. When we read each of these experiences, a lambent picture of Amma's love, affection, and protection becomes clear within our hearts.

This is the second volume of The Ocean of Grace, a collection of the life experiences of Amma's children from all around the globe. It is a colorful mélange of the uplifting experiences of Amma's children and the bonding that happens between mother and child — love which is not confined to the earthly plane.

Swāmī Jñānāmṛitānanda Puri

Turn Within

A Message from Amma

Children, many of us despair when we encounter problems in life. In truth, there is infinite power and wondrous abilities within each one of us. But more often than not, life passes us by without our knowing of these powers and abilities or doing anything to awaken them. We have heard of instances when some people demonstrated amazing abilities when faced with great danger. If we are ready to quieten the mind and look inward with self-confidence, we can find the strength to face any situation and thus achieve success.

Once, a world-renowned musician came to perform before a crowd of thousands. The program started. The musician took up his violin and started playing. But something seemed to be amiss. Nothing he played sounded right. He looked closely at the violin. He was shocked when he realized that the violin was not his! He hurriedly went backstage to look for his own violin but could not find it anywhere. One of his adversaries had replaced his violin with another. For a moment, he was filled with despair. The very next moment, he gathered all his strength and firmly told himself, "Music does not lie in the instrument. I will prove today that music is in my soul. May God bless me!"

He returned to the stage, bowed to the same violin, and started playing. The audience sat enthralled by the melodious flow of majestic music that issued forth from his violin. His performance that day proved to be among the finest in his musical career.

This incident proves that there is infinite power within us. In every person, there is music that has lain dormant for a long time. Our potential is boundless. Through effort, each one of us can discover and manifest that potential.

Similarly, everyone has the ability to control and uplift oneself. Even people who consider themselves highly impatient evince patience in front of their bosses. Even the cruelest criminal has tender feelings of love for his own child. There is patience, love, courage and compassion within everyone. The only thing is, it does not shine equally in all. If we look within and strive with awareness, we can awaken all the noble qualities.

The outer world will throw challenges at us. It will try to discourage us and make us retreat. Then, if we look inward with a meditative mind, we will find a power and a peace that far surpasses everything,

1

Opening the Eyes of Knowledge through Selfless Service

Isabel Signes – Spain

Life can be compared to a tennis match. There is always some action or reaction taking place, like when a tennis ball is hit from one side of the net to the other. When we receive an easy ball, in the form of a good event, we are happy; but when a difficult ball lands in our court, in the form of a bad event, we are challenged. In a similar way, spirituality is the art of using the situations or experiences we receive in life in the best way possible. The Guru is like the coach who trains us how to do that.

In tennis, we cannot choose the ball that comes to us. But once it is on our side, we choose what to do with it. Recently, a Spanish tennis player, Rafael Nadal, won the Australian Open and entered the record books with his twenty-one Grand Slam titles. When he was fourteen years old, after winning a local competition, a reporter asked him, "Now that you have won, what will you do?" "Keep training, keep training!", he said. That attitude of training and persistent effort, no matter what, has taken him to the top of the tennis world.

On the spiritual path, we need more of this quality of persistent effort, and also, detachment from the fruits of our actions.

Sage Patañjali explains this attitude in the *Yōga Sūtras*:

> *abhyāsa vairāgyābhyāṁ tan nirōdhaḥ*
> 'Constant practice and dispassion restrain the modifications of the mind.' (1.12)

We need to practice, to make the effort, without attachment to the results, in order to still the mind. Put simply, do whatever is needed and be ready to accept whatever comes. The situation we had to face during the Covid-19 pandemic helped me understand persistent effort and non-attachment in a deeper way.

During the lockdown Amma said, "The situation the world is facing now is not under our control. But there is one thing we can always keep in check — our mental attitude. Let us be strong and optimistic. To do this, we should focus on the eternal. We should hold on tightly to the feet of the paramātman, the Supreme Self. This steadfast faith and focus on the paramātman can lift us beyond all kinds of limitations."

And that is what my husband and I decided to do, hold tight to Amma's feet. I had time to improve my sādhanā (spiritual practices) and my yōga practice, and stay more focused and less disturbed. Although I had to face financial losses, we both focused on the opportunities that each moment presented, rather than imagining what we were missing. We are very lucky to live in the countryside, and since we had more free time, we began to cultivate the land and plant our own vegetables, like tomatoes, potatoes, cabbage, etc. We used the vegetables for ourselves and provided them to others as well.

I still remember the day I received the message from Swāmī Śhubhāmṛitānandajī informing us that we could watch Amma's webcast every day, live from Amritapuri. We were hiking on a mountain at the time, and upon hearing the news, we raced back down and ran home like crazy. Since then, I have tried not to miss a single day of Amma's program.

Let me confess, I have not always had that strong an attitude. When I met Amma, I had so many worries about my family, and about me! During my second darśhan[1] in Barcelona in

[1] Amma's divine embrace.

2004, I mentally asked Amma to help my sister, my brother, my nephews, and my parents. Amma whispered in my ear in Spanish, "No te preocupes," which means, "don't worry."

My worries did not vanish in an instant, but I could see clearly that I was the one holding on to them and not the other way around. Although it has been hard for me to let go – and I am still trying – as I spend more time in Amma's presence, little by little, darśhan by darśhan, a certain feeling of security and peace is growing in me. Amma planted that seed in me. If anything has changed in me, if anything is of any value, it's because of all the love that Amma has poured into me.

In one of her messages on Guru Pūrṇimā[2] Amma said that the Guru principle, the Guru's presence, and the Guru's grace are always present, regardless of time and space. They are everywhere, pervading everything. Just as the mother's womb expands to accommodate the developing baby, so is the master's presence around the disciple all the time.

Personal Connections and My Amma Dream

The daily webcasts have also helped me develop so much respect for the āśhram residents. I used to think that the residents are so lucky to have settled with Amma without any obstacles. But when I heard them speak about their experiences, it was an eye-opener for me to see the many obstacles some people had to overcome to reach the āśhram. In one case, parents even tried to kidnap their son when he decided to live here!

When I started traveling to Amritapuri on a regular basis, my biological mother would cry in despair. She is a very good person and helps a lot in the Catholic church, but she is very rigid in her views. Although I tried to explain to my mother about Amma, and even asked her to come to the Barcelona

[2] The full moon ('pūrṇimā') day in the Hindu month of Āṣhāḍha (June – July) in which disciples honor the Guru.

program to meet Amma, I was met with only disapproval and reproach on her part.

And yes! Amma knows the deepest corners of our soul which include all our longings. One day, I dreamed that Amma was in my village, a small town south of Valencia. Amma walked on the streets and even sat in our dining room! I woke up with a feeling of joy and contentment. But I knew that this could not have been possible since Amma doesn't come to that part of Spain.

But actually, nothing is impossible for Amma. When Amma visits Spain, she always comes to Barcelona, and Valencia is about 500 kilometers to the south. In 2017 due to the political unrest in Catalunya, Amma's program was shifted to Valencia.

It was a dream come true for me to see my mother, and my brother and his family, in Amma's arms for the first time. My mum had a beautiful darśhan and Amma showered her with all kinds of treats.

After the darśhan, my mum and I sat together on one side of the stage. After a while I asked her, "How was it?" And she said, "It's like the church, only that the ways and forms are different."

I was very happy that my mother met Amma, and since then, there has been no resistance from her about all the traveling I do to be with Amma.

The Path of Selfless Action

For me, Amma's teachings are my scriptures, and karma yōga — the path of selfless action — has been an important part of my sādhanā. I would like to mention a few projects that Amma blessed me to be a part of. These projects have helped me deepen my understanding of abhyāsa and vairāgya, constant practice and dispassion.

The projects have helped me to put in my best efforts, and at the same time be more detached from the fruits or outcomes. It has not always been easy, but the work is in progress.

The Telephone Support Line Project

In one of her satsangs at the beginning of the pandemic lockdown in 2020, Amma said, "Say words and messages that inspire enthusiasm and optimism. Everyone has a phone these days. So, send messages of reassurance and inspiration. Talk to and comfort each other. It is not what we receive, but what we are able to give that brings value to our life."

Inspired by Amma and these words, a group of Spanish devotees along with some of our Amma brothers and sisters in the UK began a new project a year ago with the guidance of Swāmī Śhubhāmṛitānandajī. The project was to provide support to people through regular telephone conversations. In Spanish we call it: Línea de Apoyo Telefónico — Telephone Support Line. It was launched during Swāmījī's visit to Barcelona in November 2021.

Loneliness harms our health, our wealth, and our happiness. It can even threaten our democracy. Never before has loneliness been so widespread; but never before have we had so many resources within our reach to do something about it.

Being available for others, and listening to them without judgement while keeping Amma's love and compassion in mind, has been our approach to expand the project.

The results have been very inspiring. People who have been helped report to us about how their lives have changed; and the volunteers tell us how much this sēvā or selfless service enriches them. Even the weekly meetings of the management team are truly inspiring as we walk this path together. We are so grateful to Amma for offering us this opportunity to serve, and for continuing to shower her grace, which makes this project so beautiful.

Prison Experience in Spain

In 2012, at a prison in Barcelona, we started an IAM 20[3] program. Weekly events were initiated in cooperation with the 'Quatre Camins Solidaris' (Four Paths of Solidarity) Association of Granollers, a city near Barcelona.

The program has been very successful with the prisoners. In addition to the introductory courses, weekly sessions including guided meditation are conducted. These regular activities have enabled many of the prisoners to participate in other humanitarian activities within the prison or during monthly visits to the Amma Center in Piera, near Barcelona.

A small group of prisoners even gets permission to attend Amma's program in Barcelona. They bring hundreds of letters to Amma, in addition to small gifts that the prisoners have made for her. The lives of so many prisoners have been changed; some even have a small Amma altar in their cell. Our group 'Amma Spain' has been recognized by the Prisons Institution of the Government of Spain and the program has spread to many other prisons in Spain as well.

Cataracts in Africa

I am an optometrist by profession and did my PhD on programs for the prevention of blindness.

In 2008 during Amma's U.S. Tour, I went to ask Amma a personal question. Afterwards she said to me, "Why don't you go to Kenya for the eye programs?" And I said, "To Kenya? To operate on cataracts, or to give eye glasses?" Amma told me to do both.

---

[3] IAM, or Integrated Amrita Meditation Technique, is a meditation practice formulated by Amma that integrates gentle relaxation stretches with an effective and easy-to-practice breathing and concentration technique. It is based on traditional methods and designed for the time constraints of modern life. IAM 20 is the 20-minute variant.

I didn't know anyone in Kenya at the time, and I had no idea how to manage a project there. But in 2011, after Amma's visit to Kenya, the first blindness prevention project associated with Amma's global network of humanitarian initiatives — 'Embracing the World' — was organized in Kenya. More than 300 people received the benefit of free assistance from that medical camp.

Since that first project, Embracing the World has done many free cataract surgery programs in Zambia, Burkina Faso, and Kenya. In Kenya alone, twelve surgery campaigns have been initiated so far. Almost 3,000 people have been operated on by the best doctors, using the best technology, completely free of charge.

There are more than 36 million blind people in the world and cataracts are the leading cause. In a country like Spain where we have a national healthcare system one can have cataract surgery for free. But in many African countries people have to pay for the surgery. Because they cannot afford it they just go blind and lose hope. I remember one of our patients saying, "Had it not been for Amma, I don't think I would ever have seen the wonders of this world again." Before we start with the surgeries, I pray to Amma to flow through our hands. If the case is complicated the prayers become very intense! Let me share a few anecdotes.

Our patient Evelyn was twenty-three years old when she came to our program in Nakuru. Her left eye was completely blind and nothing could be done. In her right eye she had only 10% vision remaining due to a cataract. Evelyn was very afraid because of her poor eyesight. When a patient gets restless it can compromise the surgery. In those moments I hold their hands, and I pray. Evelyn was very nervous and restless before and during the surgery. But just twenty-four hours later, 50% of her vision was restored. Three months later she had 100% vision in that eye and was a much calmer, happier person! Such success was due to Amma's grace.

Last October, we operated on the smallest baby of our program, a ten-month old boy born with bilateral cataracts. The surgeon had difficulties during the operation. Only the beep-beep of the monitor in the operating room could be heard... In that silence an intense prayer came to me, "Amma, with his health conditions this little boy will have to face many difficulties in life. At least give him the gift of eyesight..." and then my mantra kept flowing. Twenty-four hours after the surgery he was able to follow my hand with his eyes.

Martha had cataracts removed from both her eyes. She came for a three-month follow-up appointment and said she was so happy she could read the Bible again. The following morning she was waiting for us as we arrived at the hospital... "Does she have a problem?" I wondered. But no! She was waiting for us with a gift — a big sack of potatoes! She brought them early in the morning just to say thank you. Some of those potatoes even reached Amritapuri through devotees who brought them all the way from Africa.

Behind every eye problem there is a story to tell — a story of poverty, and sometimes a story of loneliness, or even violence. It has been Amma's love for her most disadvantaged children in Africa that brings us back there every year. And it is her grace that sustains each blindness prevention project.

In Africa, organizing things takes more time than in the West. But somehow everything falls into place. Amma's devotees in Kenya open their hearts and homes to these projects. The local authorities and health care workers are supportive and make room for us in their hospitals. AIMS hospital (Amrita Institute of Medical Sciences, Kochi) has provided assistance.

The doctors, nurses, optometrists, and volunteers, or the "white doctors," as they call us, travel from Spain.

Our team of doctors have really aligned themselves with Amma's teachings. They say, "Even if we sit idle, life will pass by. Isn't it better to wear away in service to the world than to rust away doing nothing?" These doctors want to spend all their holiday time doing free surgeries.

Their motto is: "It takes a long time to have well-trained hands, to be a good eye doctor, and to have the skills necessary to perform an excellent surgery. But there will come a day when these hands will be of no use. So now, while we have our skills and our health, let's spend all our free time in service."

I know our help is limited. We cannot change the poverty that our patients have to face every day; we cannot change the past. But we can do one thing; we can help to restore their vision, and that is what we do.

Amma tells the story of an old man walking on a beach who sees in the distance a young boy picking up something every couple of steps and throwing it into the ocean. Intrigued, the man approaches him. He then saw that the boy was actually throwing starfishes. On the entire beach lay thousands of starfish that had been washed ashore during a storm. Now they were struggling for survival as they gradually dried up in the hot rays of the sun. The old man told the boy, "What you are doing makes no difference. You'll never be able to throw them all back into the water." The young boy takes two steps forward, bends down, reaches for a starfish, and throws it back into the ocean. He turned towards the man and calmly replied, "It made a difference to that one." Amma teaches us to never miss an opportunity to help anyone in need.

In September 2020 Amma said, "The fragrance of a flower travels only in the direction of the wind. However, the fragrance of goodness travels equally in all directions. We may not be able to help everyone in this world. But if we are able to express our compassion to a few people around us, they will pass it on, and very soon it will spread like the links of a chain. "

All these projects would not have been possible without the collaboration of many people. Those who help us are each like pearls on a beautiful necklace. And Amma is the thread. Without her grace none of it would have been possible.

Amma says: "These external eyes through which we see and experience the external world will not rescue us from the darkness of ignorance. To wake up from that darkness, we have to open the eyes of knowledge. This means to see everything as one."

I pray to Amma that she helps me to open my inner eyes, to complete the journey. May my thoughts, words and actions be of benefit to the world. May I be able to transmit all the love Amma has showered upon me and may she make me an effective instrument in her hands.

2
Love is the Answer

Sugandhi – USA

Love is the answer. We've all heard this before. It's written on leaflets and banners. It's the title of books and retreats. There is even an album with Amma's bhajans or devotional songs that has this name. It sounds nice. But I never gave much importance to the phrase. I never really contemplated its deeper meaning. Love is the answer. Its simplicity hides its depth. The more I express love and am loving and kind in my speech and actions, the more I'm discovering the truth of these words.

Love really is the answer. Love is the answer for world hunger. Love is the answer for climate change. Love is the answer for that argument I had with my neighbor. Love is the answer for the temptation to turn off the alarm and keep sleeping when it's time for archana.[4] In one way or another, love is the solution for every problem in this world.

Love has been the answer to some challenging situations in my life. My only qualification to be here is that I am Amma's child. I have yet to fully understand the principles I speak about. Please accept this as my experience of how Amma has brought love and beauty into my life.

On Amma's last European tour in 2019, I went to the program stage to ask Amma a question. As I waited behind Amma's chair, a little child ran up excitedly. He told Swāmī Amṛitaswarūpānandajī that he had just seen Amma internally in his

---

[4] Chanting of the 1000 names of the Divine Mother. Here the author refers to the daily group chanting practice in Amritapuri which starts at 5 o'clock in the morning.

meditation. He wanted to ask Amma if he was enlightened. We had a good laugh at this.

A few moments later it was time for my question to be put to Amma. I sat right beside Amma's chair. Swāmījī told the child to wait a little bit, but he enthusiastically scooted up next to me. We were squished together, two children peering at Amma as she gave darśhan, wanting her guidance. Swāmījī translated my question. Before Amma answered, she looked at this little boy quizzically, as if wondering what he was doing there. When Swāmījī told Amma about his vision, Amma burst out in her beautiful laughter. We all laughed.

Then, just as suddenly as her laughter had erupted, Amma's mood shifted. Her eyes became oceans. She looked out over the crowd, as if she were seeing all of creation at once, and said that only when you can see Amma in everyone are you enlightened.

I have heard Amma say these words many times before, but this time it went deep into my heart. The innocence of the child evoked the innocence dormant within me, and the laughter we all shared helped me to relax and be more in the present moment. Because of this beautiful situation created by Amma, I became more receptive to receiving her grace and grasping the truth of her words. This shows that everything Amma does, even her laughter, is for the upliftment of her children and for the good of the world.

Since then, I regularly contemplate Amma's words and try to put them into practice. Obviously, this is not easy, but the experience gave me the enthusiasm to try. To see Amma in everyone would mean loving everyone as I love Amma, and remembering that each creature on this Earth is Amma's darling child.

Amma says, "Bhakti is love — loving God, loving your own Self, and loving all beings. The small heart should become bigger and bigger, and eventually, totally expansive. A spark can become a forest fire. So, to have only a spark is enough, for the spark is also fire. Keep blowing on it, fanning it. Sooner or later, it will burn like a forest fire, sending out long tongues of flame."

Though I have a long way to go, fanning the little spark of love within me has been truly transformative. The more I strive to be loving and kind, the more peaceful and harmonious my relationships become. The world around me appears more beautiful; I feel more peaceful and happier.

Yet the more I try, the more I realize just how challenging this practice is. Even Amma says it's very difficult to love everyone. Only Amma can love us fully, because only she is fully established in love. That divine love is our true nature. To truly love, one needs a broad heart and a pure mind. But in my case, my mind and heart are littered with negativities and false identifications. Anger, fear, grief, jealousy — these are all burdens that can cause us to close our hearts to others.

Amma says, "When you learn to love everyone equally, genuine freedom will emerge. Without love there can be no freedom, and without freedom, there can be no love. Eternal freedom can happen only when all our negativities have been uprooted."

***

Amma tells the story of a disciple who goes to his master lamenting that he cannot let go of the difficulties and pains he carries from the past. He asks his master to help him overcome this problem to find peace. The master gave various instructions, but the disciple kept having the same problem. Finally, the master gave the disciple a big sack of vegetables, instructing him to carry the sack and not put it down, even while sleeping. He must do this until the master tells him otherwise.

The disciple faithfully obeyed. When he went to sleep, he kept the sack on his chest, so as to not put it down. The sack was very uncomfortable and he couldn't sleep well. Soon the vegetables started rotting and stinking. As they decayed, a liquid started dripping from the sack, causing even more discomfort and itching. Finally, the disciple was unable to bear it. He ran to his master and asked permission to throw away the stinking burden. The master granted permission saying, "That is exactly what I have been advising you to do with the mental burden of the past that you carry. It is heavy, painful, and irritating to your mind! If only you could throw it away like that sack, you would be relieved!"

Like the disciple in this story, we all carry sacks of burdens and negativities that we struggle to put down. This has often been my state. Even after meeting Amma at a young age, I still carried around many burdens and sorrows due to a lack of spiritual understanding and surrender.

My biological mother met Amma in the late 90's after seeing a poster for Amma's program in a yōga studio. Later, my mother told my sister and me about a woman saint, a Guru from India, who hugged people. She gave us a picture of Amma and some mālās or rosary beads. I had no concept of Indian culture and didn't understand what a spiritual master was either. But looking at the photo of Amma, I knew instantly that she was my Guru. Her smile and her glowing eyes captivated me. My mother also gave me a copy of Amma's biography which I read in a couple of days. I couldn't wait to meet Amma myself.

The next year when I was thirteen, Amma came back to Dallas and we attended her program. Amma's smile was even more beautiful in person. The bhajans took me to another world. I was mesmerized by how long Amma could sit and give so much to so many people.

At the time, my parents had just gone through a very painful divorce which put a shadow over our whole family. My sister and I ended up living with our father. We would spend school holidays and weekends with our mother. My father read some books about Amma to make sure he was comfortable with this new influence in our lives, but otherwise was not interested in receiving Amma's darśhan. He had no problem with my love for Amma as long as I went to church with him every Sunday where he taught a Bible study class.

When Amma came to the U.S., we would see her with our mother a few times, if we were lucky. I didn't have a connection with any local satsang group,[5] nor did I get involved in AYUDH, Amma's official youth wing; I simply didn't know any other devotees.

After a couple of years, my father remarried and we moved to another state. My stepmother had two daughters my age. We couldn't understand each other. My father was stuck in the middle. He mostly kept quiet and was often away for weeks at a time, traveling for his job. I felt like an unwelcome outsider in my own family. There was so much tension in the house that I graduated from school a year early and moved out.

I was left with a lot of pain about my family situation and resentment towards my stepmother. I felt completely alone. I carried these negative emotions around like a sack of rotting vegetables for many years.

***

Growing up, I felt like I had to do something about the suffering and injustice I saw in the world. In my first year at university, rather than dealing with my mind and emotions, I channeled

[5] Devotees meet on a regular basis in local satsang groups to chant the divine names, listen to spiritual discourses, and do devotional singing. In general we can call satsang a meeting of people to listen to and/or discuss spiritual matters. It also means spiritual discourse.

all my energy into fighting for social justice. I'm sure we have all experienced that when we focus on the needs of others, it's easier to forget our own problems. I was striving to do this. But I wasn't able to accomplish much or gain any mental purity or peace because I lacked maturity.

One time, I skipped a week of classes and drove to the other side of the country to protest the United States' economic and military actions in Central America. Rather than white flowers of peace, I got a shower of rubber bullets and tear gas. That was an apt reflection of the state of my mind. In another incident, some classmates and I took over the chancellor's office to pressure our university to adopt fair labor practices in their business dealings. We hung pictures of young girls who were supposed to be sweatshop workers from the ceiling and chained ourselves to sewing machines that we brought.

Amma knew it was time for an intervention to protect me from either getting arrested or expelled. That summer I thought I was going to miss Amma's program, but when she came to New Mexico, through a series of miracles, I ended up at Amma's retreat at the last minute. I was eighteen. It was the first retreat I went to without my mother. It was a major turning point in my relationship with Amma. I don't remember my darśhan or any experience with Amma in particular. But I vividly recall the bliss I felt while drying dishes as the bhajans blasted over the speakers in the kitchen. It was the first time in months that I had felt peace. It was the first time I was in Amma's physical presence for Guru Pūrṇimā and one of the rare times that Amma sang the *Mahiṣhāsura Mardini Stōtram.*[6]

In the *Mahābhārata*, one of the great epics of India, Lord Kṛiṣhṇa says, "Do actions, but not with greed, not with ego, not with lust, not with envy, but with love, compassion, humility,

---

[6] Hymn in praise of the Divine Mother who slayed the buffalo demon.

and devotion." My actions at that time were full of the former qualities and missing the latter. Not being able to understand real love, I was fueled as an activist by grief and sorrow.

Amma has done more to improve the lives of suffering, poor and marginalized people than any politician, government official, or activist. Really, Amma has done more than anyone, ever, to uplift others. That is because her solutions harness the power of love and compassion. By awakening her children to spiritual principles and values, we go beyond the limitations of intellectual and political solutions. Amma has created a true revolution of love.

After that retreat, Amma really began the work to open my heart and loosen the shackles of the heavy burdens I carried within. I read all the *Awaken Children* books, started chanting my mantra more, and a few months later, I learned the IAM (Integrated Amrita Meditation) technique. I can't say my practice was very regular, but what little effort I put in was sincere, and over time, Amma's love started to seep in.

Amma says that when we take one step towards God, God will take a hundred steps towards us. My mind became calmer. I understood that the best way to do something good for the world was not to fight external battles, but to fight the inner battle of overcoming the negativities that closed the doors of my heart and agitated my mind. After I obtained my degree in 2007, Amma fulfilled my wish to go to Amritapuri.

Amma was already bringing about many changes in me, and helping me see myself more clearly. But some burdens I could not put down, especially the resentment towards my stepmother that was still rotting within me. These feelings were further aggravated in my early twenties as my relationship with my father and stepmother deteriorated further. I held strong feelings of resentment towards my stepmother whom I blamed for isolating me from my family and straining my relationship with my father. This was not just a little potato going foul or a carrot getting soggy. I was burdened with a whole sack of giant, stinking, rotting pumpkins of negativity!

In Amritapuri on the other hand, I had a lot of enthusiasm for sēvā (selfless service), especially during my first few years of spending more time in the āśhram. It was a way to channel negative thoughts and emotions that simmered beneath the surface. For a while, I would do as much sēvā as I could possibly fit in a day: gardening, cashiering in the Western Café, drying the tulasī leaves in the afternoon, and cashiering again after bhajans. At one point, when I was really struggling with my mind, I committed to chanting five archanas a day for a few months. That helped me a lot.

I was keeping my mind constantly engaged so it couldn't spiral down into mental turbulence about my family situation and other difficult experiences. Prayer, sēvā, and sādhanā were the rungs of the ladder that allowed me to climb out of self-pity, grief, and anger. I gained more inner distance from those situations and strengthened my heart. Amma says, "selfless service is the only soap that truly purifies," and I was desperate for that soap to wash away the painful rotting vegetables from my mind.

There are endless examples from Amma's life of people criticizing her or attacking the āśhram. Amma always responds with love and compassion. Amma was even able to console and share love with a relative who attempted to kill her, due to his misunderstanding of her divinity. Amma often shares the lessons she learned from Damayantī Amma, Amma's biological mother, through her strict discipline. For a spiritual aspirant, difficulties only help us grow. Amma says, "Impediments are the fertilizer that make us grow stronger spiritually. These obstacles will help our hearts to blossom fully."

Reflecting on this, I was finally able to see my family issues as great teachings. They helped me to develop humility, compassion, and self-reliance. I developed more detachment and gained a deeper understanding of the nature of the world. I recognized the limitations of taking refuge in human relationships rather than in God or Amma alone. I developed Self-reliance and moved forward. I relied on my inner Self, my inner Amma. I began expecting less from my family and it became easier for me to accept and love them as they were. I was able to forgive and be more patient.

As my inner burdens lightened, my heart began to open towards my stepmother. The more I was able to open my heart and express love towards her, the more her attitude changed towards me. She softened and became more loving. I understood how her actions had been influenced by her own difficulties, and I felt compassion for her. I could start to see her as Amma's child as well. I chose love, and then love only increased. Now those past animosities seem so small.

A few years ago, my father passed away suddenly and unexpectedly. Miraculously, my stepmother and I came together to plan his memorial and settle all his affairs. In the entire three weeks we spent together, there was not even one harsh word exchanged. We were able to offer each other love, support and patience. That was truly Amma's grace.

***

At the end of 2014, Amma gave her blessing for me to study acupuncture and traditional medicine. This has been a great gift from Amma. It is both a sēvā and a sādhanā. Working with patients is the perfect training ground to practice seeing Amma in everyone, putting others before myself, and expressing love through my actions. Often I find I have quite a way to go.

At the end of my studies, I did a final clinical practicum with an NGO in Nepal. As a new practitioner, I was happy for the opportunity to serve and I started off with great enthusiasm. I was there for four months. During the final week, I got very sick and was distracted by some personal issues. Love and enthusiasm drained away from my actions. My patient interactions and treatments became mechanical. I just wanted to finish and get back to Amma and the āśhram. The patients who had been coming regularly felt the difference; the treatments I gave that last week were not as effective.

My flight back to Kochi went through Delhi. In the airport washroom, I was greeted by a short, thin bathroom attendant with a huge glowing smile. She lovingly took me by the hand and led me to a stall. Before letting me go in, she wiped down the already sparkling clean toilet seat. When I came out, she pumped liquid soap into my hands. Then she started the sink tap for me. Finally, she gave me a fresh paper towel and I left the washroom completely dazed.

Once I was on the plane, tears of gratitude and remorse poured down my face. I felt that Amma had come in the form of that woman to show me my mistakes in Nepal. Amma was teaching me what love in action really looked like. It wasn't just what the woman did, but how she did it. She had so much love and innocence in her actions; she turned that bathroom into a temple.

Whether cleaning a bathroom, doing our sēvā, or even getting our lunch, actions done with love allow us to express the divine love that is our true nature. Then we can see the divinity in all of creation. Amma's grace flows into us and supports us. In love, there is no room for 'Me' or 'I' or ego. Love can only transform someone when it's expressed. Once expressed, love leads to the expansive vision of seeing Amma in everyone.

Amma's love has made me stronger. Amma's love is helping me overcome my weaknesses and ego and is opening my heart. Amma's entire life is a ceaseless flow of divine love. Each embrace, each smile, even her reprimanding is drenched in love, and are for our upliftment. Amma's love has been the answer to the suffering and sorrow of millions of people around the world.

Amma sings the following lines from the bhajan *Svīkarichhīṭu Mama Mānasa Pūjā*:

'A fully blossomed mind is a mind that leads to fulfillment, a mind that yearns for the welfare of others, a mind that is full of pure love, a mind which the Divine Mother uses like a garland of blossoms.'

I pray to Amma, "May this heart and mind be full of your pure love and always yearn for the welfare of others. May the doors to this heart not only open, but fall off completely, and the walls crumble under the dance of your feet. May this heart, and all of our hearts, become so full and broad with your love that they encompass all of your creation, and have no room left to expand, but to merge into you."

3

Lessons Learned in Amma's Masterclass

Kavya – Switzerland

I first met Amma thirty years ago. One year prior to meeting her, on our first trip through India, my husband Bruno and I learned about Amma in Thiruvannamalai. She was described as a saint living in Kerala. When we met her, we brought our two-year-old daughter Alena with us. I had no idea what masterclass I had enrolled in, but Amma's attraction was incredible, something I had never experienced before.

My first darśhan with Amma was a real heart opener. I couldn't hold back my tears. I cried as Amma held me lovingly in her arms. That was my first masterclass lesson: to allow myself to connect with my feelings, including the sadness of never having been accepted unconditionally. My biological mother did her best, but it wasn't until I had a child myself that I realized how much I had missed that motherly love. Over the years, Amma helped me to grow beyond that feeling of lack and into my own empowerment.

At that first darśhan, we misplaced little Alena's shoes. The search for them led me to the woman who was organizing Amma's programs in Switzerland at the time, and who also hosted monthly satsangs in her house. That's how we started helping with Amma's programs in Switzerland.

My next interaction with Amma was a year later when it was time for her program to start. A lot of people were standing outside the hall and I thought, they'd better enter quickly now so we can welcome Amma in a dignified way. So I jumped around and invited people to go into the hall... and I completely forgot that I should have been standing near the items kept ready for the pāda pūjā[7] to put a garland on Amma on her arrival. My only thought had been to create a beautiful setting for Amma's arrival.

In the middle of it all, Amma's car stopped next to me. Amma got out, looked at me, and laughed! She took me by the hand and together we entered the hall. She led me to the place for the pāda pūjā so I could still garland her.

This was the beginning of my second masterclass lesson: sēvā. Through sēvā, I felt an incredible amount of energy and an enthusiasm I had never experienced before. It just felt right to get myself totally involved.

After my first time assisting with Amma's darśhan line, Amma's darśhan attendant told me that Amma was very happy with the way I had assisted. Again, a flood of tears — that's how overwhelmed I was.

After that, things developed very quickly. The Switzerland programs grew and we had to keep looking for bigger halls to accommodate the visitors. Soon after that, Amma wanted us to offer food to the visitors — another milestone for us. It became clear that we needed more preparation. At our first tour meeting, the management responsibilities for different departments were assigned, and I, usually very quick by nature, missed all the departments I would have liked to manage. The coffee bar was my favorite option, but I didn't stand a chance.

Finally only one question remained: how to coordinate all the volunteers that will be required to make all of this work? I was the only person left who needed an assignment, so yes, I took

---

[7] Pāda pūjā is a sacred tradition that involves the ceremonial washing of the Guru's feet.

over the responsibility of sēvā coordinator. I had no idea where this task would lead me, but I started with a big sheet of paper and a simple list. Everything was good and simple.

I met a lot of people, and the scope of my sēvā grew incredibly fast from year to year. Then computers appeared, and Bruno started to learn how to use them. Through sēvā coordination, I learned all aspects of Amma's program, and grew naturally along with it.

I was initially reluctant to assign people to clean the toilets. I thought it was something unpleasant. So after the evening program was over, I would do it myself. I cleaned the toilets as best I could, but one morning the cleaning supervisor came to me, indignant about the state of the toilets. She complained that the cleaning was very badly done and asked me who was the useless person who did it.

Ashamed of the reprimand, I simply assured her that I would look for a capable person. I concealed the fact that I had been the awful culprit. That same day, another person came forward and explained how this would be just the right sēvā for her; to clean the toilets every now and then, and enjoy Amma's program in between.

At some point the desire arose in us to have a place in Switzerland where devotees could meet together for satsangs and bhajans every week. We were very fond of Amma's bhajans and we loved to sing. Bruno, a pianist, learned to play the harmonium very quickly. We used to organize Indian classical concerts before we met Amma, so the music was very familiar, especially to him.

We found a big house in the countryside with three flats and a big garden. With Amma's blessing, the first Amma house was built there. Amma asked us how far the house was from the hall at that time. It was over an hour's drive and not easily accessible. But Amma named it 'Bhavānī House' after the Divine Mother.

Well, shortly after we moved into Bhavānī House, the old hall burned to the ground and we were forced to look for a new hall. After a long search, there was only one option, and it was only a few minutes' drive from our new house. Amma agreed to stay with us and we were beside ourselves with joy.

That was the year 2001. Amma was scheduled to arrive in early October after the terrible 9/11 attack. Everything was up in the air and the first part of Amma's European tour was canceled — including Switzerland. A series of ups and downs followed. One day we were told to go ahead and the next day again everything was canceled. At some point I felt blocked and didn't know how to deal with it any more. We finally canceled everything: the hall, the kitchen equipment, etc.

A few days later, Swāmī Rāmakṛiṣhṇānanda called and asked me if Amma could come the next day! I simply said "Yes!" and the odyssey began. At that time, only a few people had computers or email. Some had a fax machine, so we started to get everything going: informing the devotees and helpers, re-ordering all the equipment, the food, etc. It was a huge chaos, and a huge blessing — we were finally preparing the house for Amma and the swāmīs.

When Amma arrived at the door, we ran breathlessly to welcome her into our house. Amma beamed at us and sat down, telling us that the prayers of her children had brought her here!

What a gift! We could hardly believe our luck. But now the really hard part of Amma's visit began, which was setting up the hall. Not to mention, my responsibilities as sēvā coordinator were barely in place. We did our best to prepare a program for the next day, but things were missing everywhere — and the helpers sometimes got very angry and complained. My mood was down, and at that point I decided to go home and at least finish my sēvā coordination responsibilities. To my surprise, as soon as I arrived home, Amma walked around the house and sat down with the swāmīs and a few devotees.

One of the devotees started to ask a question about Vēdānta. It was a philosophical question pertaining to the highest truth. At this point my inner pressure, my despair about the chaos in the program hall had increased considerably. I could no longer hold back my tension. I blurted out to Amma how bad I felt and that I was afraid we would not be ready for her program the next day. Amma looked at me sympathetically and explained that 80% of people complain about whatever happens, and only 20% of people ever support you. She repeated it and finished by saying that not even Amma can please everyone. What a relief! Up to that point, I had thought it was because of my inability alone that many things didn't work out.

That was masterclass lesson number three: we try our best, but the result is out of our hands. There are no superhero things with Amma, she is the only superhero here. We can serve Amma, become an extension of her, become her instrument. However, only years later did I realize what a chance I had been given to learn from Amma and serve her mission.

***

I was always a stubborn, impatient student; I had my own ideas about how things should be done and this created so many problems. With Amma's help, I was able to learn a lot about surrender and she gave me the chance to discover my potential as the swāmīs started calling me the main coordinator of the Switzerland program.

Only after the following incident did it dawn on me what a great honor it is to serve Amma in a position where she can mold you. Being a board member in Amma's Swiss organization was very difficult for me because I had different ideas about how things should be done. This caused many conflicts, and I came to a point where I gave up. I decided to officially resign from the role of board member after Amma's visit.

On the second day of the program, I was assisting Amma to put on her shoes before she went downstairs for the evening program. Amma looked at me, walked a few steps, turned to Swāmījī and said, "Amma is very sad that someone wants to leave the board." I first thought she meant another person who was also unhappy. Amma's statement had a profound impact on me. As the evening went on I realized Amma was talking about me.

Amma indirectly let me know that she would be very sad. Of course, I knew Amma didn't need me, but I needed her! I still need her. She had given me a chance and I rejected it. This brought about a decisive change in me. As Amma says, she doesn't make gold out of gold, but gold out of rusted iron. She was taking care of me, changing and transforming me.

She let me know that I was under her guidance and ready for her masterclass, which she imparted by having me as a member on the board. No more running away from challenges.

Many lessons followed; in some I succeeded, some I failed. Amma always made sure I did not become too comfortable in my role. Amma's every visit was met with unforeseen challenges, and I slowly became quite a formidable troubleshooter.

Just coordinating tour dates and program halls was a real challenge. In Switzerland, everything is very orderly and contracts are signed early. But since we couldn't confirm Amma's program dates until after the U.S. summer tour at the earliest, it was a difficult undertaking. I had to come up with many different arguments, put the managers off for months, and keep promising "I will confirm as soon as possible." Around Amma, we never know what she is going to do next. "As soon as possible" could mean within hours, but it could also mean many weeks later. I tried my best to get them to reserve the most popular weekend dates for us.

There is one story I would like to share with you.

A few years ago, the dates for the European tour kept changing and the whole thing was a huge puzzle. Finally, when we got the dates for Winterthur, we had no hall. The Eulachhalle, where Amma usually went because it was affordable and ideal for our needs, was completely booked. This caused me more than just a stomachache. After all, I was responsible for obtaining a hall.

So I booked a flight to Amma's Toronto retreat to talk to her about this dilemma. On my first evening there, Swāmī Rāmakṛiṣhṇānanda told me that in the past, Amma had been to different halls and locations in Switzerland. He said Amma gave us two date options. Both were in November which is the high season for fairs, and accordingly it would be very difficult to get a hall.

My personal Toronto retreat with Amma then took place almost entirely in the hotel lobby, the only place with internet. I had gone over all possible venues and it seemed hopeless. It was the last morning of the Toronto program and I was desperate. I just wanted to sit on the stage near Amma, but since I didn't have a darśhan token I waited at the stairs for Amma to pass by.

Amma came down the stairs. She took my hand, turned to an attendant and said, "Switzerland problem — no hall." Desperately, I said "Amma, we need your help." That was all. I flew back to Switzerland and called all venues once again, without success.

In my distress I also wrote an email to the Eulachhalle manager even though I knew it wasn't available. I said I knew the hall was booked but if there was a cancellation, we would be delighted to be able to host Amma there.

In the evening I saw a message from the Eulachhalle manager in my inbox. She wrote that just that afternoon, a long-time customer had canceled for the exact dates Amma had given.

I jumped for joy, I was immensely relieved and deeply grateful to Amma. That was another masterclass lesson; Amma is always with you, just rely on her. And also, you don't necessarily have to fly halfway around the world to let her know that you need her help. Because she let me know that even before I could tell her, she already knew.

***

Preparing for Amma's program is a large-scale group project. It requires teamwork. It is a miracle every time that we transform three sports halls into a program hall, a dining hall and a sleeping hall. We also set up a kitchen.

When materials are delivered at 6 a.m. the day before, there are mountains of pallets lying around, and I always wonder how we will manage.

It took time, patience and creativity to build a stable team. Preparation meetings with team members helped to strengthen and encourage them, and create a sense of belonging and togetherness.

I learned all these leadership skills from Amma. She taught me to be kind and patient, to have compassion and respect. Amma taught me to accept the devotees as they are, and to find them a place where they could feel comfortable and contribute to the success of her program.

I learned to give people space and let them do things their way. But sometimes I had to put my foot down and be a spoilsport. That was difficult for me at first because I have a need for harmony and always would prefer for everyone to be happy.

But if you remember, in lesson three of Amma's masterclass, Amma taught me that even she can never please everyone. This lesson carried me through difficult situations and helped me to be strong when I had to say no to certain ideas or suggestions in the interest of the greater whole.

***

These profound experiences with Amma have also helped me in my work as an art therapist working with mentally ill people. I have accompanied many of these patients on their journeys towards healing. Because of the light Amma shares with me, I can help them overcome the effects of violence and abuse, or lack of being accepted, which led them to deep depression and hopelessness.

When I listen to their stories of immeasurable suffering, I imagine Amma embracing them, or standing by our side, to help endure the pain and give hope. I never tell the patients about Amma directly but try to incorporate Amma's teachings wherever I can.

A patient once came to a therapy session and told me that she simply liked coming here because she liked the atmosphere of my therapy room. It reminded her of an Indian woman whom she had met who hugged people. She knew Amma! So I showed her my Amma picture.

Amma has taught me the importance of having patience with people, really listening to them, and assuring them that they too can find a way out of the depths of despair. I often use meditation and mindfulness techniques, imagination and relaxation.

One of the greatest lessons from Amma's masterclass has been the importance of self-love. Most of my patients are full of self-hatred as a result of their painful experiences. I have had patients who wanted to burn themselves and were marked by terrible scars and cuts all over their bodies; young girls who were emaciated and refused to eat because it was the only way for them to exercise control in their lives. Without Amma's presence, it would be difficult as a therapist to continually witness all this suffering. It takes tremendous strength.

***

Over the years I have been able to accompany Amma many times on tours through India, Europe, Australia, Singapore, Malaysia, Reunion Island, Mauritius, Kenya, and various cities in the USA. In the early years, when Alena was still small, we took her out of school to travel with us. In 1995 we were in Mumbai for the inauguration of Amma's Brahmasthānam[8] temple, and a hospice located outside the city.

We traveled to Mumbai on our own, and when I think back, I see how Amma guided and protected us. We traveled by train through Mumbai to the place where Amma's hospice was to be inaugurated. As soon as the train left the station, the landscape changed and the station signs were written only in the Devanagari script which we couldn't read. I wondered how we'd ever reach the right stop. At the next station, an elderly woman joined us in the compartment. She opened her bag and pulled out an issue of *Matruvani*.[9] I smiled at her and soon realized that

[8] 'Abode of Brahman.' The name of the temples Amma consecrated in various parts of India and in Mauritius. The temple shrine features a unique four-faced idol that symbolizes the unity behind the diversity of divine forms.

[9] 'Voice of the Mother.' The āśhram's flagship publication dedicated to disseminating Amma's teachings and chronicling her divine mission.

we were all going to the same place. So, we went to the hospice inauguration together.

We then traveled with Amma's group to Pune for the next program. Soon after arriving there, typhoid broke out and Alena, then five years old, fell seriously ill. She had a high fever which could not be brought down and she refused to swallow the big medicine pills. Nothing worked. Some people advised me to fly back to Switzerland but that was not an option for me. Was there a better place than with Amma? — I felt a deep trust.

Staying next to a child with a high fever day and night was very difficult. Amma's program two floors below was in full swing. The hall was densely crowded, there was no way through. But I needed Amma. So I managed to walk through the hall, with my feverish daughter in my arms. When I reached Amma, I put Alena in her arms. She looked at me and asked, "Fever?"

Lovingly, she stroked sandal paste over her hot forehead and instructed me to leave it on for as long as possible. Afterwards she asked me to sit behind her on the stage for a while. Amma turned to us again and again and covered us with her loving gaze.

The next day the fever had gone down and Alena was almost well again. We knew we were in the best hands and received the best treatment. That was also our last day. Amma traveled on to Delhi, and we would soon return home. Before leaving, Amma asked if Alena's fever was better and blessed us with her darśhan. Deeply grateful we traveled back home with a recovered child.

Many journeys followed, and small miracles happened again and again, which enabled me to travel with Amma. On these journeys, I experienced indescribable moments of heart opening, and many inspiring spiritual experiences. I also learned how to make samosas and cucumber raita in Melbourne, how to make coffee during a tour of Australia, how to manage the darśhan line in Kenya and many other places, how to clean toilets in Paris (properly this time!), how to prepare for and assist with pūjās or worship ceremonies in Europe, how to serve at the bookstalls, how to make chapatis in New York, and much, much more.

I thank Amma from the bottom of my heart for accepting me, a wayward student, into her masterclass, and for never giving up on nurturing me, and guiding me.

4

The Value of Failure and Suffering for Spiritual Growth

Vishakh - France

Amma says our experiences are the greatest Guru. In two words, the main lessons Amma has taught me through life experiences are acceptance and surrender. Amma taught me these mostly through failure and suffering. So, the main point of this talk is to understand the value of failure and suffering for spiritual growth.

I will also take this unique opportunity to tell you of my love for India and the Indian people. I feel a strong connection with India. In 2006, I came to Amritapuri for my summer vacation. It was in July during monsoon, and there were puddles everywhere. The rain had turned the red earth into mud and it looked dirty to me since I was coming from Paris. I have always liked cleanliness, so I didn't like this dirt. But five weeks later, when I boarded the plane to go back to France, I cried. I was not sad to leave the āśhram, nor to leave Amma, I was sad to leave India. During those five weeks, I had discovered something beautiful, deep, and essential behind the external dirt that had disturbed me at first. Amma says, "For thousands of years, there have been countless mahātmās (great souls) born in India, and innumerable devotees who followed the path leading to liberation. Those vibrations saturate the atmosphere even now. We can tap into them through a life of devotion and self-discipline. This is not the case outside of India."

Another time, as I was flying back to India, when I saw that the plane had crossed the sea and was flying above the coconut trees, I thought, "Now, if the plane crashes, I don't mind; I will die in India. I am safe."

India is my spiritual home and living with Indians is a constant source of inspiration for me. I am most touched by the kindness, śhānti (peace), and ahiṁsā (nonviolence) that I often see expressed by my Indian brothers and sisters. I have always had a tendency to be anxious, but I feel that living in India is healing me from this anxiety. The people and atmosphere here are so peaceful that I feel there is nothing to fear.

Before Amma's first world tour, a brahmachārī was sad about her leaving the ashram. She explained to him: "In the Western countries, many of Amma's children are also waiting for her. In the East or West, many people are engrossed in worldliness." Then Amma compared these people to hummingbirds immersed in mud puddles instead of sipping honey from the flowers and she added: "Amma must make them fly by clapping her hands." In my case, Amma had to clap her hands for ten years to make me fly to her.

I first met Amma in 1987, in Switzerland. I was twelve. My father had heard about her and wanted to ask her a question. I accompanied him. We arrived late at night. I was standing next to a pillar, watching the scene. Amma suddenly looked at me, smiling, and beckoned me to come to her. I was surprised because I had come only as a bystander, so I said, "No, no! I don't want." I didn't want a hug from a stranger. But she sweetly insisted and the people around me gently pushed me towards her. I fell softly into her lap and got her darśhan. That is all I remember from my first encounter with Amma.

After meeting her, my father became a devotee. When Amma came to France each year, he took my mother, younger brother and me with him to receive her darśhan. But after one or two years, I no longer wanted to go. I was a teenager and a bit rebellious. Yet, I still had a spiritual inclination. Since I was a child, I had wondered about God and the limits of this visible universe, and I felt a strong connection with nature and wildlife. On my fourteenth birthday, I asked my family what was the purpose of life. There was a big silence. Although they were all interested in Eastern spirituality and had read a lot of books about it, they didn't have an answer.

After meeting Amma, slowly, sorrow came to my life. As a teenager, I lacked self-confidence and felt uneasy with others. I felt lonely because I was different from others; no one around me seemed to care about the purpose of their life. They wanted to get a particular job or lifestyle, have a family... These things didn't make sense to me. The only lifestyle that attracted me was that of a hermit: living alone in nature and practicing contemplation. But I thought this way of life was not possible in this current time, so it remained in the back of my mind as an impossible dream. Looking back, I think the Divine Mother gave me suffering to turn me away from the world and to make me look for her. As time went on, I faced failures in two things that mattered a lot to me: relationships and studies.

For teenagers in the West, flirting is very important. Although I wanted a girlfriend, for some reason I could not get one. When I entered college, another mysterious thing happened: although I studied well, when I sat for the examinations, my mind went blank and I didn't know what to write, so I got poor marks.

These failures were very painful to me. I was raised with the belief that, 'If you want, you will.' I was practicing martial arts and I had developed a strong will power. But here, in spite of all my efforts, I was helpless. Helplessness is needed for surrender to happen. So, failure can be good for spiritual aspirants! What worldly people consider negative is often helpful to grow spiritually.

When I look back, I feel that all my failures, although painful, were blessings in disguise. But back then, I was simply miserable. I went to a psychotherapist for help. She also didn't understand what the problem was. Finally, she told me that, if I wished, I could consider traveling for a long time. She said traveling more than three months is therapeutic. I was delighted and took off for Asia, the part of the world where I felt most connected to. I traveled alone for seven months, through seven different countries. India was the last stop on my trip.

I wanted to go to Amritapuri because I thought I might find an answer to my essential question: What is the purpose of my life? I stayed ten days in Amritapuri and that was the turning point of my life. Although Amma was not there — she was on her U.S. tour — I met her through her teachings. Her words went straight into my heart. What she said about love and self-sacrifice touched me deeply. It was not a discovery but rather a rediscovery; I had known it intuitively when I was a child, but had forgotten it because nothing in my environment nourished it. As the Dalai Lama says — and it is applicable to India too, "In Tibet, even if you are not interested in spirituality, everything in society pushes you towards it. Whereas in the West, even if you are interested in spirituality, everything in society pulls you away from it."

***

I had finally found my goal in life: Self-realization! By Amma's grace alone, I got my bachelor's degree and returned to Amritapuri. I wanted to see if I was fit for āśhram life before committing to brahmacharya (celibacy). But once again, I failed.

I wanted to be a perfect brahmachārī, follow the āśhram routine exactly, do lots of sēvā and eat only the brahmachārī's food. I started a fight with my mind: "You, mind, shut up! I am the boss, I decide. You obey." It would take me years to realize that this is not the right way to tame the mind. One should not fight like in boxing, but rather like in judo or aikido — using flexibility. And, be patient and humble. But I was rigid and relied only on my own effort. I didn't understand the concepts of grace and surrender.

My body wasn't used to living mostly on rice. After two or three months, I was so skinny you could see the bones of my neck. I was undernourished and exhausted. I couldn't do my sēvā or wake up for the early morning archana. I had to admit defeat, rested, and bought snacks, because no matter how much rice I ate, it didn't fill me (there was no Western canteen in 1999). In my daily diary, I would write the number of bananas and the quantity of peanuts I had eaten. And while eating each banana and each mouthful of peanuts, I was feeling so guilty, "I am not a good brahmachārī! I don't have determination!" Failure makes you humble because you realize you are not in control — Amma is. I felt full of negativity, but Amma on the contrary, was showing me so much love! I remember one darśhan when she kissed my hand and looked at me with a lot of love... I felt embarrassed, "How can she kiss such a dirty person?"

It would take me a long time to accept myself as a whole, with my limitations, and learn how to be gentle with myself. Amma said that to catch a cow, you don't run behind it with a stick, it will run away. Instead, offer it a handful of grass and call it gently. We should do the same with our minds.

After one year, exhausted by constantly fighting with myself, I went back to France realizing that I had failed — once more — in what was the most important thing to me: a monastic life. I became depressed and had no desire for anything. But I didn't want to depend on my parents financially, so I had to work. It took me one year to recover and two more years to find a stable job.

I wondered why Amma had not protected me, guided me, and helped me overcome my inner obstacles. I didn't realize then that she'd done all she could. Her teachings were there, her love was there, her grace was there. But I was closed to them. As Amma says, we complain that our room is dark and that the sunlight is not coming in, but we are keeping the shutters closed. She is patiently waiting outside but only we can let her in. Īśhvara kṛipā (God's grace) and Guru kṛipā (the Guru's grace) are always there. Ātmā kṛipā (our own grace) is what is missing. I spent the following ten years in the world, and Amma continued to teach me acceptance and surrender mostly by two means: relationships and work.

When I was younger, I badly wanted a girlfriend. Amma finally fulfilled my wish, and this experience taught me the biggest lesson of my life about detachment. I fell passionately in love. It was a wonderful experience but as intense in sorrow as in joy. I plunged into this relationship with the same passion and intensity I had plunged into brahmacharya. The desire was the same: it was a desire for union, for becoming complete (pūrṇam), born of the same feeling of incompleteness (apūrṇatvam). But this time, instead of trying to become one with my Self, I wanted to become one with this woman.

She tried to leave me several times, but I would run after her and cling to her, exactly like the guru in Amma's story who clung to a thorny bush and pretended it was the bush that was clinging to him. Finally, after two years, she left me and I was so sad I cried every day for a month. I felt completely alone. I even forgot that Amma was with me.

Then the pendulum of my mind swung to the other extreme and I hated her. As Amma says, hatred is close to love; they are two sides of the same coin. 'I cannot live without you' soon becomes 'I cannot live with you anymore.' Finally, I became aware of my excessive attachment to her and I swore to myself, "Never again will I be deluded by romantic love!"

After that, I had other girlfriends and I even fell in love again, but it was never with the same intensity. I always kept some distance with my feelings instead of being identified with them. This distance helped me develop acceptance. Reacting brings pain whereas acceptance brings peace and freedom.

***

Amma also taught me detachment and surrender through work. After struggling for three years to find a job, I was offered one — without asking — in the best engineering school in France. It was my first real job and the conditions were difficult. My boss was tough; she didn't like me and wanted to get rid of me. I became so tense and anxious that, on the weekends, I was unable to see anyone; I was nervously exhausted and had to rest in my room. My parents advised me to quit the job, but I knew that the real problem was not outside but within me. I had to become more self-confident and detached to overcome my anxiety.

I remembered Amma's teaching: Instead of trying to change the paristhiti (external situation), you should change your manasthiti (mental attitude). If you try to escape from a difficult situation instead of overcoming it, the same situation will come back to you later with more strength. Amma tells the story of a man who receives a visit from his uncle, a war veteran, who always talks for hours about his military experiences. The nephew tries to escape out the backdoor but his uncle is coming by the same way and finally, the nephew has to listen to him standing in the hot sun instead of being comfortably seated at home.

Although I tried to overcome my anxiety, I felt helpless and I called Amma for help from the bottom of my heart. But she didn't respond. I was surprised because my call was sincere and one-pointed, and Amma says when that is the case, she always responds. So why was she not responding this time?

I had forgotten that months earlier, in Barcelona, I had actually asked her for suffering, "Amma, please give me suffering, because I feel that only through suffering will I remember you!" Such was my request; the same one Kunti Dēvī made to Śhrī Kṛiṣhṇa in the *Mahābhārata* epic. Amma looked at me with a lot of love and caressed my cheek with her two fingers. After a few months, she fulfilled my prayer but, by then, I had forgotten it... So when I asked her mentally to help me, she was already busy fulfilling the first prayer. It seems Amma doesn't have a cancellation policy... So be careful what you ask for!

Feeling unable to overcome the situation by myself, I once again went to a psychotherapist. It did help me, but didn't solve the problem. One day, after three years of this situation, I got angry at Amma and talked to her aloud, sitting in front of her picture: "I have been praying to you for help for so long but I'm still suffering so much! Is this the fruit of my devotion to you? Is this the fruit of my prayers?" Amma says that getting angry at the Guru or expressing other negative emotions towards her is a powerful way to connect to her. At least then we're one-pointed!

As a result of this unusual practice, the outer situation (paristhiti) didn't change but my mental attitude (manasthiti) did. I suddenly realized that even if I were fired, I could find another job. This realization removed a lot of my anxiety. The situation was still difficult and I was still tense, but I had the strength to face it. I confronted my boss, and even reported her to the Human Resources Department.

***

The scriptures say that the physical presence of the Guru is the most favorable environment for one's spiritual growth. One day I thought, "If Amma leaves her body, I would feel that I have wasted my life by not spending more time near her. I don't want to die with this regret; I have to try again to live in Amritapuri!"

So I took a year off from work and went to Amritapuri. But this time, my attitude was completely different. My failure in my previous attempt to be a brahmachārī had been a good lesson; I no longer tried to be perfect but simply did my best and tried to be happy, whether I succeeded or not. This attitude made me feel more relaxed and happier. In addition, Amma offered me some wonderful gifts to encourage me.

First, I joined Amma's North India Tour and it gave me a burning desire to serve, to forget myself in service. At that time, in 2010, a volunteer was needed to help set up an orphanage in Haiti, a small island off the coast of the U.S. near Cuba. A huge earthquake had just hit the country and there were 200,000 casualties. I asked Amma whether I could go and she approved very enthusiastically. This was the most wonderful sēvā experience I had ever had; it was a huge challenge, and I loved challenges because they make you grow. I was able to be engaged in sēvā 24/7 — my whole life had become service. I felt connected to Amma all the time. I was her only representative in that country, so I had to reflect her teachings in my attitude because the people there would judge her through me. This was very motivating. The difficulties I went through in my job proved to be very helpful; because I was used to being overwhelmed and in stressful working conditions, I was able to handle it.

The project stopped after three months because it was too difficult for various reasons. But I learned a precious lesson: I felt that in order to serve efficiently, I needed more maturity. I sincerely wanted to help those suffering people, but I was limited by my fear and lack of surrender. I felt that in order to truly help, I needed to develop humility, for instance, by cleaning the toilets of the āśhram.

Once again, Amma gave me what I needed. This was her third gift to me: she sent me to Gurupādāśhritānanda Swāmījī. "Help him," she said. Swāmījī asked for my qualifications. I said I was recently the director of an orphanage project in Haiti. Hearing that, he took me with him to make compost on a deserted island near the AIMS hospital. We were mixing food waste with cow dung, in the rain, stepping in the mud, alongside paid workers. It definitely helped reduce my pride: I was no longer the director of anything...

If you don't like physical sēvā, helping Gurupadāśhritānanda Swāmī may feel like punishment. But I loved it; so to me, it was a gift! Living with him and the brahmachārīs allowed me to become more familiar with Indian culture, and to be inspired by their beautiful qualities: kindness, humility, sharing, detachment, contentment, laughter and joy... I am still trying to practice these qualities.

With so many gifts, Amma had hooked me: I had no desire to go back to France! During the Paris program, I asked her whether I should stay at the French ashram – where they needed people – or if I could go to Amritapuri. When she told me to come to Amritapuri, it was the happiest moment of my life!

***

I finally settled down in this holy place in 2012. Through my sēvā assignments, first in the compost department, then at the sēvā desk, where I assigned sēvā to other devotees, Amma gave me occasions to practice surrender at a higher level. Living in the āśhram is, in itself, an exercise in surrender... Amma's advice to "see a frog as a frog and an elephant as an elephant," became one of my main subjects of contemplation. I understand it as: "Accept people as they are and don't have unreasonable expectations."

Practicing surrender is a lifelong exercise. The more we let Amma drive the chariot of our life, like Arjuna did with Lord Kṛiṣhṇa, the less we suffer. Amma says, "Ātmā samarpaṇam — Self surrender — is the secret to happiness." and also, "Surrender removes all fear and tension. Surrender leads one to peace and bliss."

It is only Amma's grace that has allowed me to come here and never remain away for more than a month. I know this may change at any moment, but as long as I am serving Amma, wherever it is, I feel safe and content. By putting forth effort and seeing its limits, I have finally understood that our effort is nothing compared to grace. We are helpless, like babies, and we depend on Amma like babies depend on their mothers. All we can do is give sincere effort and pray for Amma's grace, calling to her from the bottom of our hearts:

Śhakti tā Jagadambē
Bhakti tā Jagadambē
Premaṁ tā Jagadambē
Viśhvāsaṁ tannenne rakṣhikku Jagadambē

'Mother of the universe, give me strength,
give me devotion, give me pure love.
Give me faith and thus protect me!'

5

Lessons in Awareness, Acceptance, and Love

Jagati Olson - USA

Amma has the unfathomable ability to create situations for our spiritual growth. She is the one who orchestrates the symphony of the universe, and all aspects of manifestation respond to her. As Amma's children, we have all had experiences that demonstrate this power.

For me, the lessons that seem most special are those in which Amma accomplishes a transformation through experiences in which I suffer. Of course, it is I who is responsible for the suffering, and it is Amma who knows the exact formula to crack the prison walls of my own making. Obeying Amma's words, which is the direct route to transformation, is sometimes not the route I take on my own. Or due to my limitations, I am unaware of what prevents me from imbibing her instructions. In these cases Amma orchestrates a perfect situation to bring me along.

Over the years, especially while serving as a staff member on Amma's North America Tours, Amma has peeled off many layers of ignorance from within me. I had one experience I call 'The Tour of My Incompetence' that illustrates this point in detail.

The Tour of My Incompetence

At Amma's Seattle program in 2010, I was a new devotee, just a few years into doing sēvā and sometimes attending the local satsang group. I had not yet joined the tour staff, and the following transformative līlā, or divine play, unfolded over the five days of Amma's Seattle program that year.

A couple of weeks before the tour began, I was trying to wrap up a project at work. I was very exasperated with a colleague who was not following through with tasks, who was disorganized, and didn't understand what was required of her. In other words, she was incompetent.

I was full of anger and judgement. Because of this colleague, I had extra work to complete while preparing for Amma's arrival. The project should have been finished already, as I had planned. I was prepared to fire my colleague, and knew it would be easy for me to do so. I had fired so many people over the years!

I awoke early one morning and turned on Amrita TV. Amma was telling a story about a shopkeeper who had an incompetent employee! I was amazed and laughed out loud. The lesson in the story was that there were benefits this employee brought that only he could provide. My laughter melted my anger. I knew Amma was guiding me to have a different attitude toward this woman. I was able to deal with her without all the inner tension I had had before. However, my mind was so locked into its own rationale, that my personal progress consisted of planning to fire her gently, instead of dismissively.

Amma's Seattle Tour Began

Round #1: This was my first year working with invited guests, or what is sometimes called the VIP program. I made many mistakes in public, and on stage. First, I told the guests to come down from the stage after they garlanded Amma. One of Amma's senior swāmīs was very irritated with me and corrected me while encouraging the guests to stay. I felt like an idiot. After Amma's talk, I gave the guests flower bouquets. The swāmī told me that we should have arranged for a child to give the flowers. His irritation was visible. I was embarrassed. Then I forgot to give the guests the gift bags that were prepared for them. I felt completely incompetent, and that sentiment was intolerable for me!

Round #2: That evening, I had a sēvā shift assisting with Amma's darśhan line. Doing sēvā so close to Amma was a precious, magical experience for me. I had been eagerly anticipating doing this sēvā again. But this time, I was completely unable to do the job I had done so well the previous year! The darśhan assistant by Amma's side glared at me, then hollered at me, and after an exhausting thirty minutes, I escaped to my room to cry.

Right there, in front of Amma, I had been completely incompetent! As I cried, I knew I was meant to feel the emotional pain of failure, when people perceive you as incapable or worthless at a job. I knew Amma was teaching me humility and compassion.

Round #3: After I composed myself and went back to the hall, I reported to the darśhan line coordinator, who told me she was putting me back in the same position at 3 a.m. I stared at her blankly. Oh my God, I must try again... Within three minutes on that shift, I messed up twice and Amma's staff person then acted quickly and asked me to leave. I had been fired! I ran to the bathroom and cried in the stall. I said, "Okay, Amma...I get it!"

Round #4: At the end of Amma's visit, I was given the opportunity to take some senior staff people to the airport to see Amma off. I took a two-hour nap and went back to the program venue, the Bellevue Hilton hotel. There were three cars in our caravan and I was asked to lead. I'm sure the other drivers, who were from India, felt this was the best option, since I had lived in Seattle my entire life. But I'm an inner city kid. Although I'd been to the airport countless times, I had never gone there from this particular direction. I got confused, and twice while driving, I had to call another driver to confirm the route.

I knew the turnoff that led to the airport road would be coming up soon. Then, I saw it. I was in the far right lane and the entire caravan needed to exit immediately from the left lane! Quickly, I crossed four lanes of busy traffic to take the proper exit, and the other cars behind me managed to do the same. With Amma's grace, we all arrived in one piece, but I got several looks that seemed to say: "What is wrong with you?" By that point, I was numb to the stares that confirmed my stupidity.

The Gift of Awareness

I made it home, exhausted and defeated. I surrendered, at least in that moment. I collapsed on the bed in all my clothes. The minute my head hit the pillow, a powerful image, a full realization, instantly dawned in my mind.

Amma had blown off the proverbial manhole cover which held down all the suppressed emotions hidden inside me. For those who aren't familiar, a manhole cover is a heavy steel plate, commonly used in the west for covering the entry to an underground space. Beneath the surface of the asphalt streets, lies the muck of sewage, as well as electrical and gas power lines. The manhole cover veils the entry to the waste below.

Amma blew off this heavy emotional cover like a dry leaf is blown away in the wind. In a flash, I saw how for my entire life, I had always projected competence, at all times, in every situation. My persona of competence was like a suit of armor, a shield. At a young age, I had developed a coping strategy of projecting competence to cover up a pervasive feeling of worthlessness stemming from childhood circumstances. Underneath this armor were deep feelings of sadness and vulnerability.

I was filled with a wave of compassion for the young child I had been. All the intense, competitive drive for achievement was dissolved, and after Amma's gift of awareness, I was free. I softened my judgments of other people. I became more open to learning and accepting situations as they were; sometimes people carry out tasks in ways I feel are appropriate, and sometimes they don't. Sometimes I am competent, and sometimes I am not.

Most importantly, this healing process opened the flow of my energy to truly serve Amma. Was my sēvā done selflessly, out of pure desire to serve her? No, underneath there was a motivation to prove myself, to belong, to show that I was good enough. One cannot perform selfless service if there is an underlying egoic motivation. With a hidden agenda, our actions become tainted. It would be like offering sweet pudding to Amma in a dirty vessel.

After this gift of awareness, I was able to do sēvā with a pure heart, with an energy of light and flexibility. Joy flooded into my sēvā. Now I was truly able to serve Amma with love.

Lessons in Amritpuri

When I arrived in Amritapuri on the first of February 2022, I knew I did not want to pass up the rare opportunity to give a talk, sitting right next to our beloved Amma. But perhaps I jinxed myself by stating that lessons learned through suffering were my favorite lessons. Unbeknownst to me, more suffering was in store for me, right around the corner.

Quarantine

As many devotees have shared, this time of forced separation from Amma due to Covid-19 has been very hard. I was accustomed to my Amma time, twice a year, to get a big boost that would carry me for months. I allowed myself to be dependent on her to lift me out of my vāsanās (my latent tendencies), elevate my energy, and to help me lose about ten pounds. This was my lazy way out with least effort. I never really put in any proper effort to change; I knew I was acting like a child. Now it'd been two years since I'd seen her, and I needed to lose at least twenty pounds.

With the thirty-day tourist visa limit set by the Indian government, and the eight days of quarantine upon arrival, my mind was focused on a sense of limitation about how much time I would have remaining to be in Amma's presence. I was impatiently counting down the days until I could get out of quarantine. I was thankful I could be in the quarantine section of the meditation hall, for Amma's evening program, but I was also missing morning archana in the Kāḷī temple, doing sēvā in the Western Café, and of course, my 4:00 p.m. chai!

On day five of the eight day quarantine, I called the nurse. My nose had started running like a faucet, and the day before, I had sneezed twice while in the hall, sitting in the quarantine section. My Covid test came back positive and I was going to be moved to the Covid isolation building. I was devastated.

From Quarantine to Isolation

Having chosen to focus on limitations, I now had to deal with a whole new set of them. I was starting day one of a new ten-day isolation cycle. I had to watch Amma's program online, like I did at home. But now I was stuck in a hot room, unable even to walk outside. I was no longer near the ocean where I could hear the waves during meditation, as I had been in the arrivals quarantine section. Of course, worst of all, I came all this way and could not be in Amma's presence!

I let a feeling of misery pervade my mind as I packed up to move to the isolation building. I decided to sign up for the five-day Advaita (non-dual philosophy) retreat. I signed up not so much because I wanted to focus on deep teachings right now; I simply wanted to prevent myself from going crazy during isolation.

Loaded with Expectations

I came to Amritapuri this time with specific expectations and an image of what I wanted this visit to be. I was attached to the concept that 'I deserved a break.' I arrived shortly after a very intense and difficult time. I had a dear friend who passed away recently after a major stroke. Though he didn't view himself as an Amma devotee, he had a special love for Amma and was so proud that both his children live in Amritapuri. Just a week after his memorial service, I left for India.

So, I felt an uplifting, easy time with Amma was exactly what I needed. I imagined having awesome meditations in Amma's presence, and the feeling of floating that I sometimes get here in Amritapuri, like a weight has been lifted from my shoulders. And, I would enjoy the company of many friends who live in this holy, magical place. But, we all know that 'taking a break' is not in Amma's vocabulary. I imagined a *break* from my suffering, but Amma wants an *end* to our suffering.

Sitting in My Misery

For a couple of days I wallowed in misery, which I knew was the result of my resistance to the current situation. Whenever I resist what *is*, I am resisting the universe. When I resist the universe, the universe resists me. For example, I suddenly had many computer-related issues: online banking locked me out, skype wouldn't work, I couldn't even pull up the Advaita retreat recordings. Having a tantrum made it all so much worse!

Thank God, the timing of the Advaita retreat perfectly matched my isolation schedule. At first, I wasn't sure I could focus on the retreat because my mind was stuck in a dark cloud. But as the Advaita retreat went on, I was fascinated. Yet again, Amma gave me exactly what I needed.

I could never really get a handle on a lot of what Amma tells us, like: "You are not the doer." or "You are not the body-mind."

Amma says if we drop our wrong concepts, we will be free. But my mind used to be blank when trying to see the world from a perspective that does not depend on my body or mind. However, the concept of non-duality was explained to us at the retreat through the powerful text, *Dṛig-Dṛiśhya-Vivēka,*[10] which began the process of dismantling my false identifications.

"How do you know you've understood the teachings?", the swāmī leading the retreat asked. "You will have reached the end of all suffering. Haha!" He also encouraged us, "Don't let your own mind bring you down." I could clearly see my suffering; I was being tossed around by transitory names and forms. Obviously it was foolish to put so much focus on situations that would change soon enough anyway. I wanted off this roller coaster of ups and downs!

I had nothing but time to fully experience this Advaita retreat to the best of my ability. Besides, why waste a perfectly good uncomfortable situation and not get anything out of it? I found my mood lifting. The busy mind had something new to focus on that was positive. I did yōga, listened to the satsangs and had deep meditation sessions in the Advaita retreat. While going to the bathroom in the middle of the night, I listed some positive observations in my head: my roommate slept soundly, the room was clean, and there were no bugs.

The Cockroach Messenger

I then came out of the bathroom and the light from my head-lamp fell on a giant cockroach sitting in the middle of the floor! He just sat there in the spotlight, making sure I got a good look at him. I screamed and woke up my calm, accepting roommate. I stood ready to jump on her bed, whether she was in it or not. She calmly got up and tried to catch the cockroach. The effort was

[10] 'Distinction between the Seer and the Seen,' a methodology of inquiry as well as the title of a popular Advaita Vedantic text.

unsuccessful, and he scuttled off to hide somewhere. Now my whole world was reduced to my bed. I was careful not to place my feet on the floor. Could my misery get any worse?

The urge to feel sorry for myself rose up. But then I remembered what the swāmī at the retreat had said regarding the mind's tendency to ask, "why me?" First drop the why, then drop the me. Instead of feeling sorry for myself, I inquired, "What was my actual experience?"

It was strange that the cockroach appeared right at that time. What had I been doing? I had been acknowledging my preference for certain names and forms over others, believing that my preferences would make me happy. I was merely substituting one list of negative thoughts with another list containing positive ones in order to be happy..."at least there are no bugs." Nothing doing. The point was to focus on the essence, to identify with the sākṣhī, the witness consciousness, where happiness and bliss actually reside. I thanked Amma for the cockroach messenger.

***

With his son's persistent encouragement, my friend who had a stroke in Seattle, wrote some memoirs before he died. He wrote about how, as a child, when faced with dangerous and painful situations, he would retreat to his secret place. Not a physical location, but a safe place within. What was he actually doing? This young boy, not yet a teen, developed a spiritually deep coping mechanism. He withdrew from the world of names and forms to dwell in a place within that was safe and peaceful — sat-chit-ānanda, existence-consciousness-bliss. He described being unaware of his senses and surroundings. If a young boy can do that, then surely I, Amma's child, sitting in this sacred place, in the middle of an Advaita retreat, can do the same?

Amma gave me exactly what I needed, not what I wanted. I want to emphasize again that I wanted to take a *break* from my suffering. Amma wants an *end* to our suffering. I envision improvements in my way of being. Amma creates transformation in our ways of being. I am embarrassed that after all these years, I still choose such small goals, when the goddess of the universe is offering me liberation.

Examining the mind, it was pretty obvious: I was focused on a finite, limited perspective. I was bitterly thinking to myself how sixteen days of quarantine and isolation meant only twelve days with Amma. But could Amma be confined to the box of a twenty-four hour day? Of course not! Was I not able to reach her just because I was a few meters away? Ridiculous!

I know better! Don't I say that Amma is the life force that flows through my body? I can be with Amma daily in my IAM meditation. Sometimes, while guiding the IAM technique on Zoom, I know the whole group feels her all-pervading love. So what was the mind talking about? Ridiculous!

Once again, Amma gave me exactly what I needed. And it was far beyond what my small brain was expecting. Many people, out of compassion, felt sorry for me that I was stuck in isolation. But I am thankful that my visit unfolded exactly as it did.

How can I follow Amma's words if I have no idea what she is talking about? I still have no idea, but I have some tools to use, along with the blessings of the experiences Amma continues to give me. I offer my reverent salutations to Swāmī Ātmānandajī and all Amma's monastic disciples who conducted the retreats for us during this Covid time. They were so crucial during these times of physical separation from Amma.

To all those who sent me words of compassion and prayer for this extra trial, I thank you deeply. Amma's children are such an inspiration and a blessing! I am continually amazed by the beautiful people who do sēvā for Amma. In this case, during Covid-19, preparing and delivering meals, checking in on us, and answering all questions so quickly.

I know and trust that the universe unfolds perfectly, and I vow to continue to reduce my resistance to that process. I pray to Amma to lead me to have equanimity in all situations. With Amma's grace alone, I will be transformed.

6

Infinite Grace Illumines the Path

Dr. Balakrishnan Shankar - India

In 1992, I came to India for a visit and went to Aruṇāchala. Having read about Ramaṇa Mahārṣhi, I circumambulated the sacred Aruṇāchala mountain. Bhagavān Ramaṇa said that whatever you wish for when you walk around the holy mountain will come true. Therefore, don't wish for anything because in order to enjoy that wish coming true, you may have to take another birth. But I did wish for something. I prayed for a Guru and for the path of bhakti. And sure enough, Lord Aruṇāchala granted my wish — the very next month I met Amma.

A friend and classmate from the University of Texas at Austin, told me about Amma, showed me her photo, and gave me a pamphlet to read. On that pamphlet was a quote from Amma, "Different types of people come to see me: some for knowledge, some for devotion, some for worldly boons — I discard none. Aren't we all beads strung on the same string of life? Those who love me and those who hate me are the same to me."

That quote evoked a memory of similar words used by Śhrī Kṛiṣhṇa in the *Bhagavad Gītā*:

> *mayi sarvam idaṁ prōtaṁ sūtrē maṇi-gaṇā iva*
> 'Everything rests in me as beads strung on a thread.'
> (7.7)

Both Amma's quote and her photo attracted me tremendously, and we all decided to see her when she next came to Dallas. That day was June 27, 1992. I was completely blown away by my experience — Amma's divine presence, that captivating smile, the shining love-filled face, the eyes that dripped compassion, the bhajans, and finally Dēvī Bhāva. I have no words to describe that trip; my life simply changed forever. I had visited several holy places: Kāśhi, for my studies, then Dakṣhiṇēṣhwar, and even Aruṇāchala, but I finally saw God in a hotel in Dallas!

When we first meet someone, we normally get introduced by name, right? We ask, "What is your name?" But Amma never asks us our names; Amma has never asked my name, nor have I ever told her. It has been twenty-eight years now.

In 1999, my friends and I drove from Austin, Texas to San Ramon, California to see Amma at her āśhram there. We planned to follow Amma on part of her North America Tour starting in San Ramon, then Los Angeles, Santa Fe, Dallas, and finally back to Austin. We reached the San Ramon āśhram after driving for two days. During darśhan I sat at the back of the hall. Between Amma and me there were a few hundred people. Suddenly I thought, "Amma, you don't even know my name. I am traveling from city to city to see you. Do you see those people sitting next to you? I want to be there." Maybe five seconds passed when somebody tapped my shoulder. I opened my eyes and saw a friend who said, "I just had darśhan and Amma said, 'Ask Bala to come sit next to me.'" I was shocked. I asked, "Are you sure it's me? Are you sure it's not some other Bala?" She said, "Look, I don't know any other Bala. Go, Amma is calling you!" Wow! I just had the thought that Amma didn't know my name, and immediately she addressed me by my name. Not only that, I thought about wanting to sit near her and she called me! Unfortunately, my first reaction was fear. I thought, "Oh my God, she really knows my thoughts." Those who know me understand why I was afraid. My mind is full of garbage. Amma was silent and gave no sign of acknowledgement. But on her way out she put a chocolate in my hand.

Since then, there have been innumerable times when Amma has shown me that she knows pretty much everything. That includes insignificant details of my life which even I have forgotten. For example, because I first met Amma in Dallas, I returned there every year to see her. Dallas was my yearly pilgrimage starting point. On the weekends, I traveled to wherever Amma was on her tour to have her darśhan.

Once in 2003, I attended Amma's morning program in Dallas and then flew to California because of some work. I couldn't attend the Dēvī Bhāva program that evening. However, my wife Madhu was able to attend. Amma gave Madhu two chocolates and said, "Give this other chocolate to mōn (son). This is the first time in eleven years that he is missing Dēvī Bhāva in Dallas." When Madhu called and told me what Amma had said, I was amazed. Imagine the precision of that sentence! First of all, it was indeed exactly eleven years that I'd been seeing Amma in Dallas. Secondly, I always see Amma in several places on her tours. I have seen her in New Mexico, California, New York, Chicago and many other places. Amma has seen millions of people over the years. In spite of that, she knows exactly who comes to which programs, and for how many years — this is astonishing beyond belief!

More important than the amazing accuracy, it shows that we are always in Amma's mind. Whether we know it or not, whether we feel it or not, whether Amma externally acknowledges it or not, the fact remains that we are all always in Amma's mind or Amma's consciousness. That's because supreme consciousness is undivided and all-inclusive. Just as the ocean permeates all waves, Amma permeates all of us. A self-realized being is one with the supreme consciousness that is the witness behind everything — behind all our minds — and therefore nothing escapes its attention. I don't think Amma has a mind like ours.

Regardless, this divine being keeps us in her heart permanently and knows all the little details of our lives, whether we remember them or not.

***

Amma got me married in 2001. Before that, I thought I'd join the āśhram and become a brahmachārī but Amma had different plans for me. Amma blessed me with householder life and even conducted our marriage ceremony. It's a great blessing to be married to a person who is dedicated to the Guru. Amma says, "When husband and wife together worship the Lord, convert their house into an āśhram, and do spiritual practices, they need not seek liberation – it will come to them automatically." That's the training Amma has given us – to keep the mind always on her.

During an unforgettable conversation I had with Amma on June 21, 2003 in San Ramon, Amma said that marriage is like driving a bullock cart – the husband is the bullock, the wife is the cart, and children are the luggage. I asked Amma, who drives the cart? Amma said that life is the driver and its whips will make you move along your path. I said, "If Amma holds the reins, then it's easy, isn't it?" She replied, "Yes that's right, but nobody is giving me the reins." So I asked, "Then how will that surrender come?" She replied, "If you are hungry you will eat, right?" Surrender will come automatically.

Then Amma spoke about sādhanā, meditation and spirituality. She said that it's very easy to talk about Vēdānta, but practicing it is a totally different matter. At first, a spiritual aspirant starts with pūjā, archana and japa. Only when the mind is completely absorbed can self-enquiry begin. Amma quoted the words of Ramaṇa Mahārṣhi from his book Upadēśha Sāram effortlessly. Amma continued, "In the case of Ramaṇa Mahārṣhi, mostly serious spiritual aspirants and intellectual people came to see him, so he could talk Vēdānta to them; he could give them the highest truth. "But for me, all sorts of people come — some bring photos of four girls and ask, 'Which one should I marry? Should I get a job?' Thieves come, prostitutes come. How can I talk Vēdānta to them?" Then Amma said, "If you want to compare me with someone, compare me with Śhrī Kṛiṣhṇa. He was also like this."

At that time a friend of mine jumped in and asked Amma if there was any difference between God-realization and Self-realization. Amma replied that they are the same. She also added, "You can have a vision of God but not realize God, like Nāmdēv." Nāmdēv was a great saint. He had visions of Kṛiṣhṇa but was not enlightened. Only after he met his Guru did he attain enlightenment. At that point I asked, "Amma, we see you right now. What is the difference between this and having a vision of God?" The audience fell silent and Amma replied, "That depends on your mental attitude. At first, Arjuna thought Kṛiṣhṇa was just his friend. Only later did he realize who Kṛiṣhṇa was." Suddenly, we all understood who was speaking. I persisted, "Amma, how do we develop the mental attitude to see you as God?" Amma said, "I am not interested in anyone seeing me as God. I see all of you as God and worship you all."

Later, when Amma told me to get married, she asked me, "So, you are going to drive the bullock cart?" I said, "No Amma, I am not going to drive. Amma will drive it! You told us to get married, it's your responsibility!" Amma laughed. And it's been perfectly true. She has protected us through all ups and downs. Amma got me married to Madhu and we both wanted to live in the āśhram. Amma called us here to Amritapuri in 2005.

Amma has saved Madhu's life on several occasions. Madhu is severely allergic to all nuts — peanuts, cashews, almonds, etc. In fact, I am the only nut she is not allergic to! If she even happens to touch a nut, she will get an allergic reaction. She can't even transfer nuts from one jar to another, just the smell can trigger a reaction.

Once, Amma distributed prasad. That day, the prasad happened to be nuts. Amma looked at Madhu, held a bunch of nuts prayerfully to her own forehead, and then said, 'kazhi mōle.' Amma gave the nuts to Madhu, who ate them and nothing happened. This is the standing miracle; if Madhu touches a nut even by mistake, she gets a severe reaction. But if Amma gives her nuts to eat, nothing happens.

I remember my dad offering Amma some peanut chikki, a popular sweet. Amma gave it out as prasad. She broke off big chunks and put it into our mouths. Madhu didn't even realize it was peanuts and ate the whole thing, all the while talking to Amma about something else. I watched silently thinking, "A great miracle is happening right in front of our eyes and nobody notices." I told this story to my doctor friend who is an allergist in Chicago. The doctor said, "Bala, this is possible only for Amma. A person with Madhu's type of allergies cannot possibly take this many peanuts without a reaction."

A self-realized being is one with the substratum of the universe, the all-pervading consciousness. That consciousness enables their saṅkalpa to flow through the elements; it spontaneously flows in acts of divine grace. This is how such miraculous incidents unfold in Amma's presence.

Like Śhrī Kṛiṣhṇa, Amma discards no one. Śhrī Kṛiṣhṇa talked about the dharma or duty of a teacher, a soldier, a husband. He went down to everyone's level and covered all aspects of life, just as Amma does now. At Amrita University, for example, Amma directs all the projects: construction, research, administration and accreditation, solar installation, etc. At the same time, she directs other āśhram activities like housing, organic gardening, and waste management. She gives satsangs, sings bhajans, meditates with everyone, and gives darśhan. I haven't found another āśhram where you can sit in one place and see these actions conducted simultaneously. This is why we should compare Amma to no one less than Śhrī Kṛiṣhṇa.

***

In 2003, I was about to lose my job in the semiconductor industry which has many ups and downs. My manager warned me that I'd probably lose my job. I decided to tell Amma. She was in Europe at the time, so I phoned one of the swāmīs there. I said, "Swāmījī, I may lose my job. Would you please tell Amma?" He agreed. I returned to my manager who then told me, "Bala, it's confirmed. We will definitely be shutting down." In my mind I called out, "Amma!" and placed a second call to the swāmī to tell him I had already lost my job. When he answered the phone, he was laughing. I asked why he was laughing. He said "Bala, I went to Amma to tell her about your call. Before I could say anything, Amma herself asked me if you had called. Surprised, I said yes. Amma said, 'Tell Bala not to worry. We will help him get another job.'" So Swāmījī never explained anything, yet Amma gave the answer. You can imagine the tour scenes: thousands of people waiting for darśhan, hundreds of calls coming in... How did Amma know I had called? The reason is that the moment I called out from my heart, it registered in Amma immediately, because that's where she is — in our hearts.

A devotee asked, "Amma, you have devotees all over the world. How do you know what happens to each person?" Amma replied, "You have thousands of hairs all over your body. When one hair is pulled, you know which hair it is. Likewise, you are all a part of me." This is reminiscent of a verse from the *Mundaka Upaniṣhad*, which says:

> *yathōrṇanābhiḥ sṛijatē gṛihṇatēcha yathā*
> *pṛithivyāmōṣhadhayaḥ saṃbhavanti*
> *yathā sataḥ puruṣhāt kēśhalōmāni tathā'kṣharāt*
> *saṁbhavatīha viśhvam*
> 'As the spider creates and absorbs its web, as plants grow on the Earth, as hairs grow on a living person, so does everything in the universe arise from the imperishable.' (1.1.7)

We are all part of Amma. We are never separate from her. Whether we know it or not, whether we are a devotee or not, we are all part of the supreme reality that is Amma.

One time, Amma spoke about death and how the soul leaves the body. According to karma, the soul either goes up or down, and then it's reborn. Then she turned to me and said, "But Amma is like a balloon with a stone tied to it. I go up and I come down. For the sake of dharma I will come again and again." For the second time, I felt that Śhrī Kṛiṣhṇa was speaking, because in the *Bhagavad Gītā*, chapter 4, verse 8, he said:

> *paritrāṇāya sādhūnāṁ vināśhāya cha duṣhkṛitām*
> *dharma-samsthāpanārthāya sambhavāmi yugē yugē*
> 'I manifest time and again to protect the righteous, to destroy the evil-doers, and to reinstate righteousness.'

***

Amma asked, "Why should an āśhram start a university? In India, many students go abroad to study and work. They lose our culture, and India loses their brains. But if we had a place where they could learn both values and high-end technology, then they would gain, and India would also gain." So that's why Amma founded the university. That's also why I feel that the students who emerge from Amrita University are going to be great change factors in India's future. They will make this world a better place.

One of the greatest blessings I ever received was the opportunity to serve at Amrita University. Over the course of only eighteen years, Amrita became India's No. 1 private university with more than 2,000 faculty members, over Rs. 5 billion in funding, and over 12,000 research papers![11] Twenty years ago, Amma said that on the other side of the backwaters there would be a big university. Thousands of students would come to a great place of international learning. That's exactly what we see now. In the Times Higher Education Millennial Universities ranking, Amrita University has consistently ranked in the top 50 young universities in the world that have started since 2000. All of this is only because of Amma's vision, her divine saṅkalpa.

These are amazing achievements for any university. Every professor and industry executive I meet asks me this question: "What is the secret behind Amrita University's amazing growth?" The secret is simply this: Sākṣhāt Saraswatī Dēvī, the goddess of learning herself, is our chancellor! What else can happen with a university founded by the Divine Mother?

The aim of Amrita University is to find cost-effective solutions to everyday problems. All the research done here is for the sake of the poor and suffering. Students, staff, and faculty work together to find solutions in nanotechnology, cybersecurity, robotics, and medicine. Amma directs every project for

[11] According to the Times Higher Education, QS, and NIRF (National Institutional Ranking Framework) university rankings of 2020. As of 2023, the university has been listed in the NIRF "Top 10 Universities in India" for the seventh consecutive year.

the benefit of society. That's why Amrita University is such a fantastic institution.

Working with students has been the most appealing part of this sēvā for me. Many students didn't know anything about Amma or the āśhram, so I spoke to them. Thus began my primary sēvā. My main agenda remains very clear: somehow the students should come to Amma. Once they understand who Amma is, at least to a small extent, their whole lives will change. I have wonderful students who have published in the world's best journals, worked for top companies, and completed PhDs at the best universities. But more than anything else, the proudest moments for me are when students come to Amma and say, "Amma, I want to come back to Amrita University to serve." Then I feel I've really done something good. The students bring back tremendous knowledge in service to Amma, to the university, and in turn to the whole nation. India will become great again.

I'll conclude with a story of how Amma guided a particular university project. We wanted to install wind turbines on top of an āśhram building to harness energy. We consulted with a civil engineer who proposed a design. But first we had to inform Amma. I told a student of mine to talk to her. My student told me the weight of the turbines was 500 kg. We also discussed the dynamic loading due to blade rotation and the vibration set up in the frame due to this loading. I wondered how I would translate the concepts of dynamic loading and vibration to Amma in Malayāḷam? Deep down, I doubted if Amma would understand it. So I told the student, "Just tell her that it weighs 500 kg. Don't talk about dynamic loading or vibrations."

We both approached Amma who was about to execute my ego very beautifully. Amma asked my student, "How much load is in the turbine?" The student said, "The weight is 500 kg."

Amma asked again and he gave the same reply. Amma turned to me, "How much is the load?" I said, "500 kg." Then she said, "That's just the weight, but when it rotates, the load increases and you have to calculate that." I was shocked. Exactly what I thought I could not translate to Amma, she repeated back to me, thus explaining dynamic load. Amma continued, "There will be vibrations in the pipe. There will be sound." There would indeed be vibrations set up in the column, and some of them would be in the acoustic range. So what Amma was saying about vibrations and sound was spot on. Whatever concepts I learned from English books that I thought I couldn't explain, Amma explained them all to me in Malayāḷam with perfect clarity. Then she took three bananas from her side table and arranged them like a prism and said, "You should have a central pipe and three wires like this." I was in awe because that's exactly what we mechanical engineers call a truss. So, she explained the design and the column placement. She continued, "You have to fit the blades at different heights and check at what height you get the maximum current. You should optimize the position like that." Amma was amazing! Finally, to completely execute my ego, she said, "For all this you need a good engineer. Go get one." After that, I told my student, "Don't come to me for any other doubts about anything. Go straight to Amma." She is the fountain of knowledge in any field of work.

Among the thousand names of the Divine Mother, my favorite is:

> *ōm avyāja karuṇā mūrtayē namaḥ*
> 'I bow down to Dēvī who is unconditional compassion.'
> (*Lalitā Sahasranāma*, 992)

Dēvī is unconditional in her compassion and mercy. Regardless of our past, regardless of our character flaws, we are still her children and she accepts us. And that is exactly why I am here. I pray to serve Amma till my last breath, and merge in her holy feet.

> *yā dēvī sarvabhutēṣhu mātṛu rūpeṇa samsthita*
> *namastasyai namastasyai namastasyai namō namaḥ*
> 'To that Dēvī, who has taken the form of a mother, I bow again and again and again.'
>
> (*Śhrī Dēvī Māhātmyam*)

7

Offering the Flower of My Heart

Marleny – USA

I met Amma in 1990 and started really following her in 1996. I wanted to get to know more about Amma. Mind you, to this day I know nothing of who she is, but I wanted to know more than just watching her give hugs. So in 2001, I decided to join Amma's North India Tour along with a few other tours. I wanted to travel with Amma while she and I were still young. Who knew what the future held? It turned out to be one of the best decisions of my life. It was a life-changing, amazing time that gave me memories I will cherish and hold close to my heart until I depart.

A friend who had been at the āśhram gave me some sound advice. He said not to lose my temper or get into a fight. That became my secondary mantra. I had been to India in the late 80's visiting some mahātmās, so I knew what to expect in many respects. I knew it would be a difficult trip, as I have a very sensitive stomach, and I'm allergic to chilies among other things. We departed for the North India Tour and it didn't take long for my stomach to go into high gear, even when I avoided all chilies.

The tour bus had to stop two additional times so I could go to the bathroom in the fields. At the final stop, the bus monitor told me it would be the last stop they were making for me. I was advised to get off the bus, go somewhere else, and rejoin the group when I got better. I felt a bit terrified of being left alone, sick, not knowing the language, and being expected to get myself to the next stop without knowing where it was. I thought about it and gave him a firm response, "The only way I'm getting off the bus is if Amma herself asks me to leave."

Our chai stop happened soon afterwards. The bus monitor went straight to Amma to tell her why our bus was late. Amma was sitting on top of the hill, and several of us, myself included, were about one hundred feet or thirty meters below. I paid close attention from afar as Amma spoke to some individuals. At one point, she stood up, put her hands on her hips and started to walk toward me. I noticed an immediate commotion as people got up to leave. The devotee who had spoken to Amma walked down the hill instead of following her.

My biological mother was a fierce tiger. You knew to run when she was mad, or at least try your best to hide. If you did not, the consequences would be serious. Therefore, I assessed how Amma looked and thought she seemed a little upset due to her serious expression. I wasn't afraid, but thought, "I may have to get off the bus. Let's see how this plays out."

Amma walked right up to me and stood a few inches away. She firmly and loudly asked, "How many times bathroom?" I thought about the times the bus stopped plus the one additional standard stop and said, "Three." She responded, "Seven. If go again, take." She handed me a small white pill and walked away.

When I turned around, no one was nearby, and the bus monitor just stared at me from afar. As I walked back to the bus, I thought maybe Amma meant to ask how many times I had gone to the bathroom since I woke up. I counted, and sure enough, it had been seven times. As for the white pill, I eventually stored it in a plastic bag and had it with me for many years until it started to change color and disintegrate. I experienced 'the mother who removes all diseases and sorrows.' (*Lalitā Sahasranāma*, 551)

At another chai stop, Amma spoke of how slow the men were at unloading the luggage secured to the tops of the buses, and how the women should do the unloading at the next stop in the city of Pune. She asked for strong Western women. I quickly raised my hand. Being asked to climb buses and not get yelled at — wow, I felt so excited!

When the buses arrived, I rushed to one of them to climb the ladder to the roof. Swāminī Kṛiṣhṇāmṛita Prāṇā stopped me and seemed very concerned. She didn't want me to get hurt. I laughed and said, "I climb all the time. I'll be fine." One thing I loved as a kid was climbing trees. It got me into tons of trouble. Yet, even as an adult I still climbed trees at any opportunity I had, usually to prune them.

Taking the luggage down from the buses was fantastic. I had the best time ever with the other Indian and Western women devotees. We must have done it in record time. There is a saying: "God says, 'If you take one step toward me, I will take a hundred steps toward you.'" Such was the case with our beloved Guru, the goddess of the universe herself.

I woke up later and felt like part of me had cracked open. Every painful emotion I could imagine came up to the surface. My biological mother had expressed her dislike toward me throughout my life. As a child and as a teenager, I don't recall ever being hugged by her. I was raised and cared for by maids. The feelings of rejection, isolation and deep pain were right on the surface.

The program venue was small, as it was daytime. The large venue, which would hold thousands of people, was scheduled for the evening program. I was sitting on the stage crying my eyes out. Amma requested those who were sad to come up for darśhan. I thought, "I'm not sad, I'm devastated... she can't mean me." Others went up for darśhan. Once again, the call came for Westerners who wanted a hug to come up.

I don't recall the exact reason, but again I thought those words weren't meant for me. The third time, Amma was very specific, calling for "the women who unloaded the buses." Now I got up for darśhan.

I recall falling into her arms, losing all control. A dam broke. I cried on her shoulder for a very long time. She then put my head on her lap and continued giving darśhan to the local people. After a while, she finally pulled me up and hugged me some more. I sat back on stage still crying, but a powerful shift had occurred. I was no longer the same. I experienced 'the all-knowing mother' and 'the personification of compassion' — my true mother. (*L.S.* 196 and 581)

We did a few river swims on that tour. The spontaneity felt wonderful. One swim stands out in particular. Amma said we could only go in the river if we knew how to swim. Three of us went in with her. The current was nice, and you could easily go downstream. I made sure I gave Amma plenty of space to swim and enjoy herself. Each time I felt she was close, I would swim away and observe her from about fifteen feet or five meters so as to not intrude in her space. At one point, Amma stood up in the water, and I immediately did the same. She was walking toward me, smiling. It was the most beautiful smile and form I had ever seen. I felt so transfixed by her smile that I couldn't keep my balance and fell down in the water staring at her. I experienced 'the mother who is captivating in her beauty.' (*L.S.* 868)

Amma's Crowd Control

A few months later, we were on Réunion Island where the program venue was quite small. The hall could fit two or three hundred people, tightly packed. The local volunteers were few, but they had done an amazing job announcing her arrival on television. The response was that around five-thousand people came to see Amma. Some of us tried to put up ropes for people to form lines and make the process more organized.

I was helping with crowd control. Then it started to rain. The crowd forgot the lines and ran to pack themselves into the hall. I held hands with a few devotees to create a chain to prevent these individuals from storming Amma. I looked at the crowd and thought, "Four or five of us are going to stop this mob!?" As we held hands creating a human chain, I let go and turned to Amma who was giving darśhan. She was laughing as she looked over the shoulder of the individual she was hugging, watching the scene unfold. I looked straight at her and mentally said, "Amma, you are the only one who can stop these people."

The mob broke through the doors and ran toward us. I was holding on. Part of me was laughing, part of me was upset; Amma was playing and we were sweating this out. Then a wall of energy went up when the crowd was about ten inches away from us. I could see part of the energy wall, I could feel it. The people stopped in a perfect line when their bodies hit this energy wall. The devotee next to me looked and asked, "Did you see that?" I said, "Yes, she's put up an energy wall." I walked away as I needed time to reflect on this.

I was living in a limited three-dimensional reality. There was a whole universe, a multi-dimensional world filled with possibilities, and I felt like a pawn in a chess game I didn't want to be in. I was mad for having gotten myself onto this karmic wheel of action and reaction, and felt determined to get off it no matter what — easier said than done, of course. And all this, what seemed to be such a big deal for me, was just a play for Amma. I had observed 'the all-playful mother.' (*L.S.* 340)

The Pandemic

Most people were under tremendous stress and went through very hard times during these past two years of the pandemic.

When I spoke to them, I kept silent, as I felt it was one of the best times for me. Let me explain.

I felt so taken care of. Everything was provided for me as long as I put in a little effort. When the pandemic hit and the country went under total lockdown, everyone was encouraged to go out only to purchase food. I was participating in all the daily online satsangs. I was listening to Swāmī Dayāmṛitānanda Puri's classes on Tuesdays and Brahmachārī Rāmānandāmṛita Chaitanya's classes on Fridays, as well as a private scripture class on Sundays. In terms of spirituality, I felt complete except for not seeing Amma personally. I realized if I was going to survive and not get depressed, I had to have a plan.

My plan was simple — I decided that in order not to get depressed, I would try my best to live in the now. That way, I would not think about tomorrow. Secondly, I was going to have fun. I could go hiking, kayaking, or go to the community garden, since no one was around. Finally, I would keep my mind occupied by thinking about Amma as much as possible if I wasn't repeating my mantra.

I decided to accomplish two goals: first, finish writing my organic gardening book, which was close to completion; second, finish building the tiny house on wheels, as most of the interior needed to be completed.

Building a Tiny House with Amma

Since I had no one to talk to, I started talking to Amma even more than usual while working on the tiny house. My internal dialog was like this: "What should we work on today, Mā? Amma, what do you think, should I do wallpaper or paint? It's time for our hot chocolate with oat milk and a bit of espresso. We got a lot done today, Amma. Let's take a break and have lunch. I hope you like this almond butter sandwich. It's good for you, and the bread is good for diabetics because it's multigrain and organic.

We'll have it with kombucha which is good for digestion." And so, the days passed.

A few times, I thought I got answers to some of my questions but I told myself, "Oh please, your imagination is going wild." Then one day, I felt stuck. I didn't know how to do what needed to be done. In my usual inner conversation, I said, "Well Amma, you need to talk to that celestial architect who built the palaces for the Pāṇdavas. Tell him you have an annoying devotee who is bothering you for help. I'm sure he will be glad to help the goddess of the universe. I can't figure out how to do this."

The next day, when I sat down for meditation and closed my eyes, the first thing I saw in my mind's eye was a fully detailed drawing of how to do what I needed to do. It was very nicely laid out into step one, step two, and step three, with perfect explanations. I reviewed it twice and thought, "Wow. Amma was listening to me and gave me the answer. So I'm not going crazy when I think I'm hearing her."

It happened again where I didn't know how to do something, except this time, she knew I was more receptive to her answers. I asked, and almost immediately, the solution was shown in my mind's eye. I started talking to Amma about every detail of my day and life. I became a child doing everything with my favorite playmate.

Another time, a friend was supposed to arrive to help me by holding a post while I installed a railing for the sleeping loft. She didn't come. I got a bit upset and started pacing the house while talking to Amma. "Amma, you are going to have to figure this out. I know you and Kṛiṣhṇa have four arms, so this would be easy for you; but I have only two arms. Without help, I can't proceed."

The phone rang. It was my friend Mark. He said, "I was wondering if you could use my help for about twenty minutes. I said, "Yes, Mark! I have the perfect project that will take exactly that long." I thanked Amma many times.

***

There were some sad moments during these past two years of Covid-19, especially at the end of May, when I knew I should be flying to California to be with Amma, as her North America Tour always began on the West Coast. Yes, I knew she was with me and keeping me company, but like most of us, I was very attached to her physical form, the insurmountable śhakti (spiritual energy), and, of course, her hugs.

I found myself crying for hours at night, thinking about how much I missed her. Suddenly, I felt someone sitting on my bed and starting to run their fingers through my hair to calm me down, just as a mother calms her child who is distressed.

This past fall, I was very upset because I knew I would not be seeing Amma at Thanksgiving time again. I cried myself to sleep that night. Amma came to me in my dreams and told me not to worry and that we would see each other soon. I started checking the internet for India's travel policy. A week later, it was announced that India would be opening up for travel.

Blissful Moments in Amma's Garden

Upon finally returning to Amritapuri, I did sēvā in the garden. I watered the plants and helped haul cow manure among other things to improve the soil. I never knew hauling fresh cow manure could be so much fun. I built mini compost rows with the manure and sometimes somewhat rotting vegetables. I would wash my arms and come to get lunch at 12:30 p.m.

At the beginning, I noticed the person in front of me took one long step forward, and the person behind me took one step back. I then realized my t-shirt was covered in sweat, and patches here and there had manure or some rotting smear of compost materials. I then thought, "Oh boy, I definitely don't smell like Amma's rose right now." But I felt very happy and grateful. I felt I had helped in some small way and my gratitude had no bounds.

I'm grateful to sister Priyanka who welcomed me in the Spiral Garden and told me that it didn't matter how I smelled or looked. Amma loves the sweat of sēvā; to her it's like roses. I would continue to have lunch there every day among the sound of birds and nature.

Taking Inventory

Yes, I had hard times like everyone else. The company I used to self-publish my organic gardening book lost most of a shipment of books during delivery. They refused to pay me for the lost books. Then an old client decided not to pay me for a month and a half of work. It was upsetting, as those were major financial setbacks.

The more I thought about those issues, the more I had to put things in perspective. In the grand scheme of things, much had happened in the past two years. What started as a way to keep my mind occupied and free of fear, ended in monumental amounts of grace that transformed me.

1. My mind was now quieter.
2. I was more peaceful and content with life.
3. I felt good about myself.
4. I realized I was happier than I had ever been.
5. I had amazing support and got closer, in my heart, to my beloved Guru.
6. I felt tremendous gratitude, and at times I even felt spoiled.

I knew these changes were priceless and everlasting, by Amma's grace. These were the things that really mattered. I took my losses as karma, for what must have been some previous bad actions on my part. Therefore, how could these years have been anything but the best?

For Mother

Mother,
I have nothing to offer you as everything is already yours.
Though I want to offer something, what's there to offer?
My longing has burned my desires
into embers burning in my heart,
anguished and craving for your grace has caused the seeds of desire to explode.
Let these ashes be the fertilizer that feeds the flower of my heart.
May it bloom, and become the offering that you pluck and make it yours.
I offer this my beloved.

8

Science and Spirituality

Chandra - USA

For the last two plus years, life has been a little difficult for everybody all over the world. Amma's children have been especially sad because they cannot meet Amma in person as usual. Every year since 1987, they have looked forward to Amma's visits to the United States. Each year has been a festival. My wife Latha, who works in the bookstore during Amma's tours, starts packing for the following year as soon as the winter tour is over — every year.

Amma teaches us that life situations can change. We should be prepared to handle any situation with an attitude of acceptance. It may not be that easy for most of us, but Amma's children are handling the current pandemic situation better than most people. Amma mentioned the other day that some people in the āśhram didn't even realize that two years have passed!

My interest in science landed me in Los Alamos, New Mexico, the birthplace of the atomic age. It is located about forty miles north of Santa Fe, the capital of New Mexico. Amma has an āśhram in Santa Fe. My wife and I met Amma in the summer of 1988 for the first time there. I hadn't seen or heard about Amma before that at all, even though I lived and worked in Kollam, a city near Amritapuri, for ten years.

I remember very well the day I first met Amma with my wife and daughter. Amma's first visit to the U.S. was in 1987. Amma stayed with an American family in Santa Fe. After Amma left that year, the woman who hosted Amma was looking for someone who spoke Malayāḷam (the language of Kerala) near Santa Fe. She and her husband heard about Latha and me and came to Los Alamos. They talked to us about Amma and invited us to come and meet her the following year. I was a little skeptical in the beginning. I thought, "these Gurus are all fakes, they're trying to lure people into their traps." Then I thought, "Well, she is from Kerala, and near my hometown. Why not?" I decided to go. I was not an atheist, but a temple bhakta (devotee), with very little knowledge of the scriptures. I used to listen to stories from the *Mahābhārata* and *Rāmāyaṇa*, the two great epics of India, from my father who was a Kathakaḷi dancer. Kathakaḷi is a classical dance form of Kerala where stories from these epics are often reenacted. My father told me to study well, because you can't make a living with Kathakaḷi dance.

When I got serious in science, I started doubting the truth of the Mahābhārata and Rāmāyaṇa. I thought they were good stories, but that was it. I didn't trust anything that couldn't be explained by science. I needed proof to believe, like an equation or a graph. I thought that science will eventually be able to explain everything in nature, no need for anything else. Still, I used to wonder about the meaning and purpose of everything; why is there something rather than nothing?

We were standing near the entrance to the large tent where the program was being held when Amma arrived. When Amma walked near us, I asked Amma in Malayāḷam, "How are you, Amma?" She turned around in surprise and asked me where I was from. I said I was from Kollam. Amma might never have expected a Malayāḷi, a native of Kerala, to be in that part of the world. That is what I thought at that time. Now I know that Amma knew exactly who I was and where I came from. She gestured to us to walk along with her into the tent. We sat very close in front of Amma. While giving darśhan, Amma was looking at us over the shoulders of each person she was hugging. Her smile, her look, her expressions all mesmerized me, but especially her eyes. There is something mysterious in Amma's eyes that I have never seen in anybody else's eyes.

After some time, Amma called me for darśhan. Amma hugged me tight with my head on her shoulder. At the same instant something strange happened. I felt like I had been hit by a million-volt lightning bolt. "What is happening to me, I wondered?" I felt like a heavy weight had been lifted off my head. Amma asked me to sit by her side. After a few seconds, I started to cry; tears were rolling down my cheeks with no end in sight. My wife, and especially my daughter, were wondering what was happening. I was not sad at all. I was in a different world. After about thirty minutes or so, Amma asked whether I had to go to work the next day, and whether I would come again. I couldn't say anything and I left for Los Alamos. I was completely unaware of my surroundings while driving. It was Amma's grace that I didn't have an accident on the way. I could not sleep that night.

The next day I went to work but could not concentrate. I told my wife that I had to go back to Santa Fe. I had to see Amma. When I reached the program place, Amma looked at me and smiled, a smile so mesmerizing. Because there were not many Malayāḷis at the program, we had many opportunities to talk to Amma. She asked about our families, my job, folks back home in India, etc. When Amma left Santa Fe that year, I wanted to go with her very badly.

We moved to Santa Fe in 1998, after the āśhram was built. Amma visited our home and even stayed overnight a few times. I like gardening, and Amma walked around the rose bushes in our garden at night. Latha cooked typical spicy Kerala food. We sat on the floor, ate, and talked. Amma's simplicity, her down-to-earth character, compassion, innocence and above all her physical beauty, all attracted me to the core. I didn't, and still don't, have any inhibitions about talking to Amma about anything. We cracked jokes, told stories, and laughed. Amma used to call me "Joker" in those days. In fact, my wife says that Amma is the only person I talk to like that. I felt like I had known Amma for eons.

I can never ever put into words the blessings and experiences Amma showered on me and my family. Seeing Amma's photo or listening to my favorite bhajan brings tears to my eyes. Her presence in the world gives meaning to everything. My attitude towards scientific research took a 180-degree turn after meeting Amma. The creation is not an accident with no purpose or meaning as some scientists think. It exists for a reason and has a meaning which every human is destined to seek and realize. Amma's message that the creation and the Creator are one contains the entire essence of the *Vēdas,* the most ancient, revered scriptures of India.

Yet Amma gives the utmost importance to scientific inquiry. Amma's educational institutions are proof of that. She taught me something that no science could ever teach. I don't claim I know even an iota of Amma's greatness and wisdom. The more I try to understand her, the further away I find her wisdom to be.

I had a few simple sēvā assignments during Amma's U.S. Tour. I worked in the snack shop, did shuttle driving sēvā, translated devotee's questions, and of course, I used every opportunity to stand near Amma and talk about everything under the sun. My wife travels all over the world with Amma. I sometimes feel jealous. But Amma promised that in our next lifetime, she will make me the wife and Latha the husband!

***

What we are trying to achieve with scientific research, is to understand and explain what we see and experience in nature. Science believes that physical laws, time, and chance (probability) created the universe. Then the question arises where did the physical laws come from? What gives the laws the power to create? I believe that without proper wisdom and guidance, understanding the true nature of reality will be impossible.

The modern scientific journey to understand reality has been moving exclusively in one direction, the outward direction. This outward journey has provided lots of material gadgets for man's physical comforts. But Amma warns us about the danger of becoming a slave to these gadgets. Unfortunately, this so-called progress hasn't made man any happier or more content. In fact, it is the other way around. Life for modern man has become miserable, with no peace of mind, no happiness. Man is losing the human touch; he has little compassion for his fellow beings, animals, and nature. In fact, he is destroying them. Amma says that people commit suicide in air-conditioned mansions these days.

Long before modern man's outward journey, the great ṛiṣhis (seers) of our past took the journey in the other direction, and made it an inward journey. They knew that man could only go so far by taking the outward journey; the answers were never to be found by going in an outward direction alone. Amma says that man needs both the inward and outward journeys. The journeys will have to meet eventually, because the Truth is the same for both.

It is only a great personality like Amma, who has a clear vision of both journeys, who can lead us out of the dilemma which we ourselves have created. All of Amma's actions in the world today are meant to help man progress both in the inward and outward journeys. It is up to us to listen and follow Amma's teachings. I dream of Amma's educational institutions becoming the world centers for both man's inward and outward journeys.

Some people will say that the findings of our ancient seers have no scientific merit and cannot be proven. In fact, their discoveries about the physical world are on a par with, or even better than those of modern science. According to the late American astrophysicist Carl Sagan, the Hindu religion is the only religion that has a clear understanding of the nature of creation. The knowledge acquired in ancient India in subjects such as astronomy, medicine, mathematics, etc., is amazing. For example, the velocity of light mentioned in the scriptures is 189,000 miles per second, very close to the modern measurement of 186,000 miles per second. That is not an easy experiment to do. The scriptures mention the existence of ananta koṭi (billions and billions) of galaxies in the cosmos. Every time we launch a new instrument to study the cosmos, we are discovering new galaxies, with no apparent end. Remember, at the dawn of modern science, we thought Earth was the center of the universe and our Milky Way was the whole cosmos.

The age of the present universe calculated from the Vēdas is about 15 billion years. That's not far from the Big Bang estimate of 14.7 billion years! The scriptures say that the time measured in different lōkas (reference frames, realms of existence) is different. One year in Dēva Lōka, the heavenly realm of the gods, is not equivalent to 365 days for us. Time and space are relative (Einstein's theory). They are determined by the total energy content at a location. Time slows down in the presence of greater energy. Might it be due to differences between physical and subtle planes? How much time do you experience when you sit the whole night near Amma? Not enough time!

Amma says very often that you have to be a zero to become a hero. It is not that easy to become a zero. You have to strip off everything; your attachments, mental delusions, and ego to become a zero. Scientifically, it also has great significance. All the scientific theories break down when you approach zero; it is called a singularity. A similar situation arises when you go in the other direction, to infinity. Math and science, the way they are understood now, can't handle zero or infinity. They can't handle nothingness. They use tricks like quantum fluctuations, the uncertainty principle, zero-point energy, re-normalization, etc., to handle the problem.

On a physical level, it is proven that matter is created and annihilated continuously in a vacuum. Richard Feynman, American physicist and Nobel Laureate, estimated that the energy contained in one cubic meter of vacuum can boil off the entire ocean on Earth. Many physicists believe that the vacuum (nothingness) holds the key to a full understanding of nature.

But our great seers had an entirely different perception of nothingness, a notch above that of modern science. They perceived nothingness as the substratum of creation. It pervades everywhere. Everything originates from it and will dissolve back into it. They called it pure awareness, pure consciousness, it is Śhiva — the auspicious, the ultimate truth, the inner Self! Only Amma, who has traveled to the beginning of creation and knows the Truth can make such a statement; be a zero to become a hero.

The scriptures compare knowledge to light. When you attain pure knowledge, everything is transparent to you. There are no space-time limitations. I'll share an example from the theory of relativity. Light from a faraway galaxy may take 15 billion years to reach Earth when you measure it from Earth. But as far as the light is concerned, it reaches Earth the same instant it leaves that faraway galaxy. So, if you travel with the light, or can be in that state of awareness (knowledge), there are no space or time limitations. You are instantly everywhere at the same time! So be aware. Every time you cook up a sneaky plan in your head, Amma knows it instantly!

Numerous scientists are starting to wonder whether we are reaching the limit of our physical ability to understand reality. How far and how long can we travel outwardly? We have been dividing matter into smaller and smaller particles with no end in sight. We have turned our telescopes deep into space, and still haven't seen the edge. One thing is certain for science, the whole cosmos is like a web, it is interconnected. For now, science has different theories and descriptions to explain the web: It is described as the strong field, the weak field, the electromagnetic field, the gravitational field, the Higgs field, etc. However, science also believes that these are all different manifestations of one field, one energy. Science is searching for that one thing: the theory of everything.

Amma mentions in her talks that when a butterfly flutters its wings, the vibration travels through the entire cosmos. We measured a similar effect recently, in 2015, when two large celestial bodies collided in space. We will be able to listen to butterflies flutter, eventually, by using an instrument. But Amma, who is in the pure state of knowledge (light), doesn't need an instrument to hear butterflies flutter.

***

Science has become a technological enterprise dominated by master craftsmen. They can make better gadgets, TV's, smart phones, airplanes, rockets, etc. Of course, these may be the necessities of the time. We can enjoy them and use them in order to live in this world. But use discernment and don't get entangled in them, Amma warns; because there is only one thing beyond all of them which is permanent.

Real science is an inquiry, a thirst, a search for truth. The gadgets are its byproducts. What we need in science now are deep thinkers, like Einstein, Bohr, Schrödinger, Oppenheimer, etc. They were seers, like our ṛiṣhis. They went inward more than outward for answers. They all had an intuition, a glimpse of that supreme knowledge behind their discoveries, which made them humbler. Some of them even openly admitted it. For example, Oppenheimer quoted verses from the *Bhagavad Gītā*[12] while he observed the first atomic bomb exploding in the dry desert of New Mexico.

Many prominent scientists realize that perhaps the most fundamental truth about creation is simply beyond the capacity of the human intellect to understand; humans will not attain knowledge of that ultimate truth with logic and language alone, according to Steven Weinberg, American physicist and Nobel Laureate. There are many examples in modern scientific theories, where man's intellect hits a brick wall. Yet amazingly, scientists often discover these examples by themselves.

In physics, there is a principle called 'Heisenberg's Uncertainty Principle.' This principle comes out of the quantum nature of certain particles. According to quantum theory, a subatomic particle can manifest in different forms, at different locations, at the same time! What this really means is that such a particle doesn't have an existence the way we think it does. This has a deeper philosophical or spiritual meaning. It means that we can never know the true nature of reality from our physical perceptions.

It is like māyā — the cosmic delusion, illusion, or appearance. What is māyā? It is our inability to see reality in the true sense.

---

[12] 'Song of the Lord,' one of the most sacred texts of India. It is a practical guide to overcoming crises in one's personal or social life and is the essence of Vēdic wisdom.

Our perceptions and understanding of the world are intimately entangled with prakṛiti, the primordial nature of creation. Thus, we never know for sure the absolute nature of reality. Then who can know it? Lord Kṛiṣhṇa says to Arjuna, "I am in all of creation, but none of the creation is in me." Only a person who is completely detached, and not affected by the world at all, can know the absolute truth. We are sitting in front of such a person right now. Amma reminds us to be like butter floating on water.

Here is another example. Austrian mathematician Kurt Gödel's Incompleteness Theorem, proved that truth is beyond provability using any logical system like mathematics or language. In reality, he proved the existence of an ultimate reality, God, beyond what we perceive and infer from within the system of logic and language. He also inferred that matter becomes divine when the correct theory of physics is discovered. It means that matter is not the substratum of creation, but something beyond. Consciousness perhaps, he wondered.

Modern science is at a crossroads right now. There is an awakening in the attitudes of even some great scientists, that we should look at science with new insight. Many great scientific discoveries happen when the mental state of the scientist is like that of a person in meditation. The secrets of creation will only appear when the mind is devoid of all stains, veils, and obscurations. I believe that the scientific inquiry is very similar to that of a spiritual inquiry. Both are attempts to pierce into the secrets of creation.

Amma teaches us to prepare our minds for any kind of inquiry through persistent effort, lifestyle choices, and spiritual practices. It is time for science and spirituality to work together; both can benefit from each other. It is here that the guidance and direction of great masters like Amma become even more important. Just watch as Amma talks to a scientist or to a sannyāsin. Amma goes to each one's level to communicate. She knows each person's perspective and where they are coming from.

I have a photo of Murray Gell-Mann, American physicist and Nobel Laureate, meeting Amma. He proposed the Quark Theory in physics. Ironically, he compared his theory to the Eightfold Path in Buddhism. True science should be open to all possibilities. Leaving out some options makes our search incomplete.

May Amma bless us all to have the right perspective towards science and life. May she continue to guide us on this journey.

9

Discovering Faith and Surrender

Arpana - France

I have had many great learning experiences over the last few decades as the main organizer of Amma's public programs in the south of France, as well as coordinating the Lou Paradou āśhram. Learning how to stay peaceful even while dealing with stressful situations, how to be loving and patient, how to accept people and situations as they are... the lessons go on and on. That is the greatest blessing of having a master like Amma. She gives us hands-on practical training which makes it easy for learning to happen in a deeper way.

Amma says that following dharma[13] is like swimming against the current. I can assure you, I did a lot of swimming and my inner muscles got strengthened over these last few years. I was so happy to have Amma as a guide beside me during this time of Covid-19. She was my life raft. When everything was uncertain, she was my certainty. Considering the āśhram as the Guru's body, we continued to do our practices and take care of the āśhram on a daily basis. At the same time, we tried to offer light for those who were suffering. We were few, but all went well with Amma's grace.

I met Amma physically in 1992, but I first discovered her in 1991 when I saw a picture of Amma at a friend's house in London. Looking at the picture, I said to myself, "I really have to meet

[13] 'That which upholds (creation).' Dharma generally refers to the harmony of the universe, a righteous code of conduct, sacred duty or the eternal law. Here, the author means to do what is right or in harmony with the universal law in any given situation.

this woman." But at that time, I was in London, and Amma was in France. When I went back to France, Amma went to London. We just missed each other!

The next year, I had a partner who had already met Amma. So we went to see Amma together in the southwest of France, near Bordeaux, in the summer of 1992. The program took place under a large circus tent at a beautiful site. We were waiting on the grass lining up for hours as there was no token system at that time. Since there were just a few people, Amma took a long time for each person's darśhan.

My first meeting with Amma felt like an instant recognition. It was as if I had been waiting a long time for this feeling of being at home. Still, it took me a few years to get involved with Amma's organization. I did sēvā slowly in the beginning, when Amma was there for her yearly program. Gradually, over the years, I was longing for Amma more and more, so I started going to a few satsang meetings with other devotees. Then in 1998 a miracle happened.

I had already been thinking of moving to the southwest of France when it was announced she was coming to the southeast of France for the first time. I jumped into the opportunity to prepare for Amma's program with so much joy. Even at night, I was awakened with a bhajan in mind. At last, Amma was taking the right position in my life.

We welcomed Amma during the summer in a charming outdoor venue. Before Amma's arrival we had to clean the place many times. Each time we cleaned the area, a new party or wedding occurred there, and we had to clean it again — it takes so much determination and perseverance to organize Amma's programs.

That year I discovered the deeper meaning of sēvā. I was far from unselfish, but I began to offer my willingness to learn and grow. I was confronted with different ways of working, and realized that I could hurt someone by pushing my points of view, even if they were valid. I realized that my attention and care for other people had to increase as well – and not only for the task at hand. Let me share some of the things I learned through Amma: faith, surrender, and how to be an instrument of God.

***

In 1999 I learned what it means to have faith in Amma. That year, Amma's Europe Tour was canceled, so part of the French team decided to join Amma's U.S. Tour. I was supposed to go only to San Ramon and Los Angeles, but after those two programs I felt I could not go back home. I had to follow Amma. We traveled from one place to another with no idea of how to get to each destination, or even where to sleep. Things were not organized as they are nowadays with a tour staff and tour buses; this was a big adventure. It was only Amma's grace that made following her possible.

Amma was showing me how to continue the journey with faith, and the experience was magical. I received so many gifts on that tour. I always found a way to go by car, or by plane, and I was offered accommodations, etc.

I would like to share more about two of these gifts. One morning I was talking to a lady who was a member of the kitchen crew, telling her that I was looking for a way to get to Chicago. Right away, she offered me a plane ticket. She had an extra one because she had decided to be on the same flight as Amma. And do you know what? That very day was my birthday! The second big gift was getting accommodation in the same house where Amma was staying! It was unbelievable. I was amazed to get such a gift! I felt so touched that Amma finally brought me so close to her.

At the house Amma led a meditation in the dining room which had a huge bay window with a view of the forest. It was idyllic to see Amma shining in oneness with the beauty of nature. I remember tears falling down my cheeks. I couldn't have dreamed of something so beautiful and loving. It was like the very air was full of love. During that stay, Amma also inaugurated a pūjā room in the house to be used for worship and meditation. That memory still gives me goosebumps.

The tour went on. Since the previous year, I had been trying to get a spiritual name from Amma without success. After a few attempts, my turn had finally come and I knelt at her feet. Swāmījī proposed different names from the archana. But Amma kept saying, "No." Suddenly Amma said, "Arpaṇā!" As soon as Swāmījī told me it meant "the dedicated one," I burst into tears. I felt so recognized and seen from a place deep inside myself. At that point, I realized Amma was my whole life.

During that tour, I got into the question line with the resolve of surrendering at Amma's feet, telling her that I would do whatever she liked, that I wanted to serve her. I was ready to go wherever she said. I had thought well about this commitment. She could have told me to go to the moon and I would have prepared my luggage for it!

To my surprise, Amma told me that she would be going to the south of France in October and I should coordinate the preparations! I was torn between immense joy and fear; but the joy in my heart prevailed. Since I had done all kinds of sēvā during the U.S. tour, and had learned so many new things, I felt ready to share these experiences with a new team in France. Amma knows what needs to be done to prepare us. She is the best organizer.

On the last Dēvī Bhāva of this eventful U.S. Tour, when Amma whispered the mantra in my ear, it was like an explosion happened inside me, reinvigorating my spiritual practice. It was with all that love and the new mantra packed into my inner luggage that I went back to France. As soon as I arrived, I received a phone call with the news that if we wanted Amma to come, we had to find a program hall within five days! Five days, including a weekend in between — imagine the challenge! But with all our faith, we contacted the devotees from Avignon to Nice to get information on possible halls.

A proposal for a venue in Toulon appeared and I went straight away to meet the venue managers. They were very welcoming and even accepted that we would pay the fees only at the end of the program, as we had no money beforehand. We were able to find all kinds of solutions for the various needs, even cooking the food on a terrace! All this was incredible! Amma's grace was flowing through everyone. When we do actions with prayers, Amma will be following us like a trail of stars.

Amma says, "The lamp of faith is within you, you just need to light it."

I had a new reason to light it. The program was getting bigger and suddenly we had to find another hall! To organize a big concert hall like the huge Zenith Hall in Toulon was far beyond my desires or capabilities. I was scared I wouldn't be taken seriously. In order to rent this hall, I 'took my courage in both hands,' as we say in French, and with Amma's love went for an appointment to see if it was possible.

We rented only the bottom floor the first year to make it more affordable. We never thought it would grow so much and attract so many people, that ten years later, we wouldn't be able to hold programs there on weekends, because even the entire place was too small.

As in all of Amma's programs throughout the world, we arrived and transformed every corner of the space. The first task was to clean. The director of the venue and his team were always amazed by how we cleaned with joy. It was actually considered the cleaning of the year! We even found personal belongings that had been lost nine months earlier. Once, the assistant director of the venue told me that seeing us always working with smiles on our faces was Amma's hallmark. She was so impressed by the joy. She also said that the hall itself benefited from Amma's visit. It was as if the hall kept shining long after the program was over.

We learn tremendous lessons by organizing Amma's program. How do you put such different people together? How do you respect their individual ways while keeping up the good work? How do you maintain an overview and also keep an eye on the details? How do you step in if there is a problem? How can you be prepared to be ready to change absolutely everything if needed? And how do you let go of your likes and dislikes? We learn how to be more flexible, how to have inner fluidity.

Another lesson was about the notion of doership. One night I was facing so many different problems that I had the feeling my head was literally going to explode. The pressure had built up because I thought I was the doer. On introspection, I discovered that if I depended only on my little power and my little knowledge, I wouldn't go far. I had to let go of my doership notion and try to let the Guru work through me instead. Everything is in God's hands. I was learning to accept Amma's guidance and to be her instrument. Everything is so huge around Amma that all we can do is surrender to God to make it all fall into place.

This is difficult to do on a daily basis, but I have experienced that if we try, we will find that we are never alone in action. I try to remember this fact when my shoulders are tense, and then I think, "Oh, the 'I', the doer, is back again..."

While taking care of the Lou Paradou āśhram, too, there are so many ways to practice Amma's teachings. I was leading a five-day retreat at the end of 2021 for participants to look back on the year. It was an opportunity to 'empty the vessels', so to speak, and to be able to receive a brand new year. I was sick for the first day of the retreat and was not able to eat anything. There was no other option, but for me to lead the program in that state. There was no one to replace me for chanting the archana. I wondered how it would be possible, because each time I opened my mouth I thought I would vomit.

So, I prayed to Amma, "You have to do it through me. I am too weak physically." The experience of chanting that day was as if flying in the sky. I felt so much love while chanting. Afterwards, other people also shared with me how blissful they felt during the archana. This was a great experience for me, learning how much grace takes over if we manage to surrender. I need to remember this truth in all my actions. My wish is to become a clear flute in which Amma can play nice music.

***

Let me share how this āśhram was born, so as to describe Amma's grace in action. Our activities were growing in the south of France but we had no fixed place to prepare for Amma's yearly visit. So in 2009, I went to Amma to ask for help. She answered, "Look for a place." I was shocked and happy at the same time! We were even more surprised, as France already had a center in the northwest near Paris. At the beginning we thought it would be just a hall where we could meet together, but when asked for more details about it, Amma added that people had to be able to sleep there as well — the project was getting bigger!

Amma was so kind, guiding us step by step to bring this idea to life. We looked for many months without finding anything suitable, and at one point we even gave up and stopped looking. That year I went to India in August for a visit, and again brought up the topic with Amma. Seeing Amma's enthusiasm and her clear vision for such a place, I got the strength to keep searching. While still in India, I called the devotee who was helping me look for places in France. She had just come across a property. In fact, the very first place we looked at was what would, in the end, become our center. But it was a long journey to reach that point.

The owner didn't want to let us visit the property with the real estate agent without proof that we had the money. Since we actually had no money at the time, we just let it go. Then in October, just before the program in Toulon, feeling ashamed for still not having found a property for Amma, I told the devotee in charge of looking for places to try to see that first place again.The real estate agent suggested the devotee contact him directly. When she did, he told her he had just been looking for her number to offer her a visit to the property. All along, I felt Amma was silently following the case.

We took all the necessary information to present to Amma. She said, "Such a price for all these old stones!" Finally she said, "Yes, go for it." and suggested a reasonable amount for us to make an offer. I went out of the hall and called the agent. He accepted. Yes! Now, how do we do it? We still had no money, and no administrative structure in place to make the purchase. But we had faith in Amma and her assurance helped us to move forward. I waited throughout the night of Dēvī Bhāva until I was called to sit near Amma to explain the deal that had been struck. Amma smiled beautifully and then began to talk to me at length.

I was trying to imbibe each of Amma's words, while not understanding anything! I told myself that all the cells of my body will get the energy of what she is saying. Finally, I got the full translation of Amma's words from Swami Shubhāmṛitānandajī and all the details that Amma had laid out for us to move ahead.

It took six months to set up the administrative structure and to finally close the deal. Three days after signing the papers, we opened our doors to a welcome with three hundred people, and since then we have never stopped except during the lockdown. June this year will mark the tenth anniversary of the Lou Paradou āśhram. With Amma, nothing is impossible if we put in the right action with faith. All this is just her grace.

***

As I reflect on thirty years with Amma, each action I did in Amma's name: helping people after floods, teaching IAM, the Integrated Amrita Meditation technique, talking to groups, organizing Amma's programs, taking care of the āśhram; it has all been a gift for me. It is said that flowers in the Divine Mother's hair are just getting more fragrance from her, not the contrary. Similarly, each action offered to Amma gets the special fragrance of compassion, openness, joy, and transformation...

Like Amma says, we should be like a bird with one wing called bhakti or devotion, the other called karma yōga or selfless action, and jñāna or knowledge as the tail. I started my life with Amma through devotion and sēvā, and for a few years now, I've started to grow a tail. I hope this bird will fly high, improving its flight in all circumstances.

To summarize, I'll compare myself to a seed. This seed couldn't sprout in any soil other than Amma's soil. This little seed was drying up by soaking in what the world had to offer. It was trying to flourish, but nothing held its roots in place so that this seed could grow into a flower, and bloom to serve others. What would my life have been like had I not met Amma? I don't dare think of it. Through Amma's teachings, I have become a much better person. I care more for others, feeling the link between us all. I have better discernment and more courage. Serving has become my life, and I pray I will be able to do it for a long time to come.

10

Meeting Amma with My Inner Eyes

Apoorva - Canada

My first birthday into this physical form took place in September 1968, in the Netherlands. My second birth, my spiritual rebirth, took place in July 2002, at a retreat in New Hampshire, United States, when I met Amma. By God's grace, I now have the opportunity, in this precious life, to prepare for the real birth — the experience of oneness, of knowing all beings as the Self. It will be a birth into blissful union with God; a birth into freedom from the bondage of desire and attachments; a birth into the realm of spiritual heights as a soaring bird in the sky of the Divine; a birth as a refined instrument in the hands of God.

In 2007, during a program on Amma's North America Tour in Boston, I asked Amma's darśhan attendant if she could please tell Amma that it had been five years since I met her. She did so, and Amma called me in front of her. She treated it as a birthday darśhan. She fed me chocolate, gave me an apple, showered me with flower petals, and was absolutely loving toward me. She told everyone seated around her that I was five years old that day! I burst into tears.

I left Amma's chair and sat to the side, weeping with intense emotion. Amma had expressed it perfectly. It was truly a rebirth, the start of a new life, with new meaning, in the true home I had been searching for — Amma. As I wept, I considered what she had said, that I was five years old. Those words gave me such relief. I could relax and accept myself despite my multitude of faults and weaknesses. It was the most moving darśhan of my life. Even now, I often feel as if I am five years old. I have been with Amma for nineteen years now; I should be more mature. And yet, I feel the truest connection with Amma when I am in the innocent place of a five year old, communing with my mother, who is my deepest source of love.

Amma says we can be like a baby calf that drinks milk from the udder, or like a mosquito that lands on the udder and simply sucks blood, missing the true nourishment of the udder. Sometimes I feel like a mosquito. Seeing her outer form and actions, I adore Amma. And yet, besides the precious moments when Amma has intentionally looked at me and communicated with me, the depth of Amma's love, compassion, and the awareness of her divine nature has not always sunk deeply into my heart.

Each experience of Amma needs to be relished internally. Savoring impressions, memories, and experiences with Amma in solitude, helps to make Amma my very own, deep within. That is how this little calf is nourished by Amma's milk of divine love.

When I first asked Amma if I could come to the āśhram or help in one of her humanitarian activities, it had been only four days since I met her. From the start, I had no doubt that Amma was a Satguru, a true master, and a divine incarnation. Since my primary longings in life were spiritual, I didn't waste a moment. However, responding to my question, Amma gave an anecdote about a disciple who, looking at a burning candle, kept asking the teacher, "What is it?" The disciple kept asking this same thing until the candle burned out. Though watching the candle carefully, the disciple was unable to really see the light, or get the meaning of what was being shown, by directly looking at it. Likewise, Amma showed me that staring into the light, which is Amma, and plunging directly into āśhram life, was not the best way for me to receive and imbibe Amma's divinity and love, at least not initially.

And so, I did not come to the āśhram for another nine months, and this turned out to be a blessing. Amma gave me a gentler way to get to know her. She first helped me to experience her divine love in circumstances untainted by my ego. Amma richly blessed me during this period with constant synchronicities and events that reminded me of her presence, and huge amounts of grace in meditation that filled me with bliss and the sweetness of her love.

Before coming to the āśhram, this was my morning routine: Get up comfortably at 6 a.m., take a bath, have a good coffee, and sit for archana. I closed my eyes, and imagined Amma before me. Each day I had such sweet meditations on her form. When finished, I would feel blissful, happy, and excited like a child with her mother, or like a lover with her beloved. It was completely satisfying. Amma blessed me with the experience of her love.

***

With Amma's permission, I went to Amritapuri nine months later, hoping to become a renunciate and make the āśhram my home. Then I discovered why Amma hadn't let me come immediately. I didn't know what I was getting into. I really had no understanding of the spiritual path, and what challenges would arise. I had been on a blissful inner honeymoon with Amma before arriving.

I tried to adopt a renunciate lifestyle immediately. My life underwent many changes. My nightly sleep time dropped from eight hours to six hours. Gone was my morning coffee. I managed about two weeks on a diet of only Indian food before I broke down one night and bought a pizza.

To the best of my ability, I followed the āśhram schedule. My new routine was like this: Wake up at 4 a.m. for morning archana — I tried everything to become alert. I showered, did haṭha yōga (physical exercises, āsanas), all to no avail. Despite hearing the divine names, this archana was really turning out to be a challenge for me! Why do these chants sound so much like a lullaby? Even after just the introductory mantras, deep lethargy set in... I couldn't keep my body upright. I would always make sure I was on the balcony so I could stand up and pace. If I stood still, my knees would buckle. Even walking, I might run into a post.

Finally, after the concluding mantras, sometimes in a terrible and desperate mood, I would rush out for chai. My mood was sometimes so bitter at that point that I dared look only at the ground lest my bad mood show! And really, why was it that chai was served only *after* the archana?

Thus, upon arrival at the āśhram, the cobra hood of my likes, dislikes, and self-judgments was quickly raised. Along with the sudden changes in habits and culture, my own shortcomings glared at me. As a result I felt separate from Amma. I remember vividly walking on the temple balcony feeling self-conscious and ashamed as Amma gave darśhan. I projected onto Amma all the negative feelings I had toward myself, imagining that Amma also saw only those negative characteristics. I was blind to her love.

During that time, we went to Kochi for Amma's fiftieth birthday celebration. We were staying in one of Amma's schools. One night, I sat alone behind the building in an area full of trees, grass and rocks. I cried deeply to Amma, "Oh Amma, do you even love me?" At that moment, I saw the most enchanting sight: Two large snakes were dancing together, vertically entwined, and in the background, from the Brahmasthānam temple, I heard the chanting of the ārchana. I felt Amma was showing me in this profoundly creative way, that the deepest love is the union of the jīva, the individual soul, and the paramātman, the supreme soul, and that of course she loved me.

Despite struggling in my first month at the āśhram, I asked Amma, "May I please become a renunciate?" Amma said to me, "If you *like* it, you can stay." Actually, at that moment I didn't like it. I had been trying to force myself to like it, like forcing a flower bud to open. Her words were the reset my mind sorely needed. Soon thereafter, ever so naturally, many aspects of my āśhram experience and my unique relationship with Amma started to blossom. For example, Amma gave me sēvā in the sweets department. Literally! I was asked to do the baking in the Western kitchen. Through the sweetness of this sēvā, I experience Amma's sweetness, and it has given me much happiness.

***

Now, onto the topic of this satsang which is meditation. You now know my issues with alertness, so you might find this choice amusing! I offer these words proclaiming that there is hope for all humanity, as even I, who have strong obstacles to success, have something to share on this topic. I chose the subject of meditation as a motivator to overcome my tamas, my lethargy, and lack of focus. I also wanted to share how, as a practice, meditation has fundamentally deepened my bond with Amma and my surrender to her.

Years ago, I went to Amma and asked if I should discontinue the practice of the IAM technique as I could not visualize anything and I was getting nowhere with it. Amma's response at that time was, "It's like flying in an airplane; you may not feel as if you are moving forward, but in fact you are." May these words give hope to all spiritual aspirants who struggle with visualization and concentration.

Amma says many different things about the purpose of meditation. She says it is to purify the mind and to dwell in love with God. She also says it is to attain one-pointedness and concentration by finding the source of happiness within oneself instead of relying on external sources.

In June 2020, during the pandemic, I asked Amma for help with visualization, as her guided group meditations include detailed visualizations. Amma supports many of us who need such help by having the images to be visualized projected on a screen. The images on the screen help in two ways: when losing alertness, we can refocus our attention by opening our eyes and immediately referring to the images on the screen, and then with eyes closed, the memory of the images on the screen can become the very tools we need for continued visualization.

Regarding the struggle with tamas, Amma continuously helps us all remain vigilant. Initially during the Covid-19 lockdown, Amma would throw small pebbles at us if we dozed during meditation, like in the olden days, and more recently, she strikes a gong periodically to refocus our attention.

I remember one experience as if it were yesterday. I had a great seat up front for meditation. It was very hot and there was no fan above me. My mask felt suffocatingly hot. I had just finished kitchen sēvā, so it was nice to sit down and relax. My meditation seemed to be going ok. I heard a little clattering of pebbles around me, now and again, and thought, "I wonder who those pebbles are intended for?..." After the meditation, I opened my eyes, and Amma was looking at me with amazement and expressed with dramatic hand gestures my very lost-in-space state of sleep samādhi, my version of the transcendental meditative state. She seemed genuinely astonished that anyone could be so unaware. I felt foolish and wanted to disappear into my chair. Clearly the pebbles were meant for me. That should have had the intended impact — it was a very big wakeup call. And yet, the impact still didn't go deep enough. Why was that? Fundamentally, the biggest obstacles in sādhanā are the lack of longing and love for the goal, as well as the level of attachment one has to external supports.

As Amma says, you need to have intense longing for the goal, like a drowning person desperate to breathe air; like a fish on the seashore flailing to get back into the water. Or, like a mother who lost her child at a fair. She has such one-pointed focus on retrieving her child, that no outer circumstances or even physical pain can distract her from the desperate search for her child. That kind of intensity is needed.

If Amma's recent words were to be reviewed, perhaps her instruction to not waste time would appear as one of her most frequent expressions. It has become my second mantra. Amma says, "We should understand that we are wasting our lives if we succumb to sleep and waste the time of meditation."

If urgency for the goal is deep within me, if I can truly be aware that every moment wasted is a moment lost, then such awareness in itself can create great vigilance and attention. So then, how does one overcome tamas? What seems to work best for me, is to cry out to God deeply and intensely. That is a good way to gain śhakti or spiritual energy, and it also uncovers and intensifies the longing for God within, which can easily be dissipated through constant engagement with the material world.

Amma has emphasized that devotion is the easiest spiritual path. And in terms of meditation, Amma says, mānasa pūjā is a method to keep the wayward mind fixed on God. She also says that every action can be turned into meditation. We should have present moment awareness, and imagine our beloved deity in each of our daily actions. How? How do I imagine my beloved deity beside me in all my activities? Basically, I like to be alone.

But when Amma is giving darśhan, or at the evening programs, there are hundreds of people around her. That presents a challenge for me.

Therefore, I like to use my imagination to pretend Amma is with me all day long. For example, it's time for my morning shower...I think, "Oh Amma, my bathroom is very narrow. Will we both fit in there? Can you please pass the soap? Amma, be very careful that you don't scratch your delicate skin on the tap or on the laundry stone! Oh Dēvī, this water is ice cold! Do you like cold water? I cannot just leisurely pour it over your head!"

Then in my imagination, I go to the kitchen where I do my sēvā in the bakery. Amma arrives, and there's a huge crowd around her! I think, "Everyone else must go. No entry! This is a private session!" Ok, now I'm alone with Amma. What is it like? I imagine her shining, laughing eyes. She is lightly and playfully engaged in the sēvā of scooping the cookie dough as she thinks of the children, she will soon lovingly feed. Next I think, "Amma please, don't go to the compost! Amma, I had to work fast. I was under time constraints. I didn't mean to discard those sesame seeds. It is difficult not to waste those tiny little things. I'll really try to have more śhraddhā (attentiveness) next time, Amma." Like this, in all our unique and personal ways, imagining Amma with us in each moment provides yet another way to make Amma our very own, bringing her deep within ourselves.

***

From my experience, there has been no greater way to purify the mind than through simple innocent prayer, and through mānasa pūjā — both of which are easily and perfectly blended. Amma again and again emphasizes the need for childlike innocence. What is this innocence? It is complete trust, a fully open heart, and total surrender of the ego. This happens with full present moment awareness. Calling out to God intensely is the easiest way to attain concentration quickly. Why? Because it touches us to the core. It touches the basic human longing to be loved, to love, and to commune at the deepest level with the eternal source of love. Anyone can cry out sincerely; it requires no skill at visualization. But as love grows, then spontaneously, visualization also grows.

The mānasa pūjā practice is a great purifier of negative emotions and obstacles such as hurt feelings, anger, jealousy, guilt, and lack of confidence. These inner obstacles and unresolved emotions cannot escape revelation if any real communion with God is to take place. Those emotions become healed through offering them to the Divine. In order to reach the place of true innocence, these emotions must be surrendered, and as the longing for deep concentration and communion with the divine intensifies in the meditation, this happens spontaneously.

If I am unable to access the essence of true innocence, then through introspection, the source of my problem will reveal itself. Once revealed, it can be worked on and released. For me, this longing for innocent communion with God is the greatest healer. I am so grateful to have found this great purifier.

Despite the beauty of mānasa pūjā and spiritual practices in general, Amma has repeatedly said that the greatest pāda pūjā is service to the poor and needy. Spiritual practices must be reflected in our actions. So at any moment, we should be able to drop meditation, if selfless service is the need of the hour. Self-sacrifice is paramount on the spiritual path. Amma says, "You will recognize someone who meditates by his or her character. The meditator will be humble and will have the attitude 'I am nothing.' Only if we develop an attitude that 'I am the servant of everyone,' is God's vision possible."

***

Recently, I struggled with a lack of confidence, feeling completely uninspired and unqualified to write a satsang. Even so, Amma's grace did bless me after a small act of self-sacrifice.

By the end of October 2021, all Westerners holding tourist visas had to leave the country due to Covid-19. This included many people who were assisting one of Amma's wheelchair-bound devotees with her daily needs. Therefore, many new time slots needed to be filled to assist this devotee. As soon as one time slot was filled, another vacant slot would appear. The devotee had to have faith that help would always come at the right time. In her divinely creative way, Amma gave beautiful opportunities for this devotee's spiritual growth and for the growth of each person who assisted her.

Initially, when I saw a list of the times when help was needed, I thought with some relief, "Oh well, none of these time slots correspond with my availability," so I went on my way. Then the devotee herself approached me about it, and together we saw that the schedule could be adjusted so that I could help. This meant sacrificing my precious sādhanā time in the morning. Ouch. But, ok. I remembered Amma saying that service to another being in need is the greatest offering to the Guru. So I readily agreed, and felt Amma's grace in it.

Soon after I started this sēvā, the devotee gave me a little booklet titled *108 Quotes on Meditation*. Initially, I thought, "Apparently she hasn't observed me struggling to stay awake in the hall during meditation time!" But shortly thereafter, I felt inspired to choose meditation as my satsang subject. Who is the giver of inspiration? God, of course. I felt that Amma blessed my tiny action with the huge gift of inspiration to write this satsang.

I am eternally grateful to Amma, as she has patiently, and for the most part, quietly, guided me by these various means and techniques to make me more receptive to the experience of her deep and abiding presence within my own heart.

On that note, I will end this satsang with a song from my childhood that has always evoked feelings of devotional love in me:

You are fairer to me, than the fairest summer's morning.
You shine brighter to me than all the stars.
You're a refuge to me, in the storm of life, a shelter.
You're my spring of life, my well of joy, my God.
You're the light to my path, giving hope and bringing meaning,
To what otherwise would be the darkest night.
You are all in all to me, for without you I have nothing.
You're my spring of life, my well of joy, my God.

11

Choosing the Magical Life

Vilasitha – USA

Amma is our Guru in a million unique ways. I will start by sharing two experiences where Amma brought me self-awareness. A relative called me on the phone. He vented his anger for more than forty-five minutes about how everyone else was more dharmic than me. Usually, getting a long scolding doesn't bother me, so I remained calm and later said, "Thank you, good night."

After the conversation I felt uneasy. Somehow his accusation seemed correct, though I hadn't done anything bad in particular. For hours my mind proffered arguments in my favor. However I still wasn't at peace. During bhajans with Amma the next day, I remembered a basic principle of Indian astrology (jyōtiṣh). "Ah! My horoscope indicates that I am dharmic. Yes, he is a person of karma (action). He works hard, but because my horoscope is more about dharma than his, I can forget his words."

This thought made me very happy, but my good mood lasted only for ten or fifteen seconds. Though I was at the far end of the crowd, Amma turned her head suddenly, and instead of starting the next song, looked directly at me and said, "Can a person be called dharmic if they have likes and dislikes?" Instantly I understood why I had the suspicion that I was not quite all that dharmic. I'd been self-indulgent for months, without serious spiritual discipline, living on the whims of my mind. Amma had corrected my assumption right away, without even calling out my name in public.

The next experience happened in the San Ramon āśhram. Another family member called me and said something very unfair. I was practicing stillness in those days and closely watching my mind. I had no reaction to her words. After some time, I was driving down the steep āśhram hill. I have driven up and down the same hill thousands of times before, casually without particular focus. Suddenly, a single thought shot up to the surface of my mind, "How dare she say that?" At that exact moment, instead of turning the wheel one inch, my hands turned the wheel an extra inch around a sharp turn and the car literally flew off the road.

Only by Amma's grace did some small bushes catch the left front wheel on the driver's side. The other three wheels were in the air, and the car was hanging off the edge of the hill! I got out carefully, hoping the car would not overturn onto me, or roll down the hill while half of me was inside. Amma's protection is over all her āśhrams. Both the car and I escaped without a scratch, but I had learned two major lessons: first, even one angry thought can cause serious danger. Second, I had overestimated my equanimity. Even though my mind was mostly still at the surface level, sharp thoughts could still pop up from below the surface prompting me to react.

My Love for Reading

I grew up in India and later studied in the United States. From the age of five to fifteen, I read a new book every day after school. On weekends, I would read from morning till midnight without a break. My happiest memories are huge volumes of Russian folk tales and books on the opium trade in China or on emperors and farmers in Europe from centuries ago. My parents believed I would surpass other kids in the race of life by reading extensively. My father used to save every penny to buy real estate, but he enthusiastically also spent a fortune on my books. In the 1980s and 90s most of my friends' parents wouldn't do that.

A Dharma Lesson in Hindsight

I've never faced any injustice in my life, except for one situation in childhood — or so I thought. Every evening my mother would supervise our homework. Immediately after the books were opened, my younger brother would start his comedy routine. He could imitate any person or animal. Once I started laughing, I couldn't stop. I would laugh with tears rolling down my face and suddenly my mom would give me a sharp tap on top of my head with her knuckles, and say, "Stop laughing, because of you he is behaving like a monkey." A hard knuckle tap on the head is very painful. Even more painful was being insulted in front of a boy who was secretly celebrating my misfortune. I would argue, "His monkey behavior is not my fault, why don't you spank him?" My mother would give me another painful tap for talking back.

As a child, my brother was frail. If he got a whack, he would collapse, and if he got an angry look, he would forget that 2 x 2 = 4 in his exam. The teachers were threatening to make him repeat another year in the same grade. My mom scolded me, so that my brother would become a bit scared, just enough to focus a little. I felt my mother was the best mother in the world, but somehow this seemed unjust. Only after observing Amma and learning about the higher perspective of dharma did I realize that my mother had actually been right. Every look, word, or gesture by Amma only ever serves to encourage people towards their greatest good. We should behave similarly and never act in any way that might encourage another person's downfall.

Teenage Sadhana

In my teens, I thought I needed some special blessings to be more successful than my classmates. It seemed like too much effort to learn pūjā, or yōga, or meditation. When I discovered japa (repetition of a mantra), it seemed like the simplest thing to do, so I started repeating God's name all day.

In the *Bhagavad Gītā,* Lord Kṛiṣhṇa says one should depend entirely on God and fix one's concentration on him. At that time, my understanding was that as long as I wished all beings well inside my heart, it was okay for me to pursue anything I wanted, in a dharmic manner. I started to ask God for every little thing from morning till night, from having egg fried rice, to getting the best grade on an exam, or making sure that if I arrived late to class my teacher would also arrive late.

I had thousands of practical experiences where God helped me when I did my japa. My classmates were always worried about little things; their emotions fluctuated up and down. I was fixed in my faith and never felt stressed. During those two years of doing japa, I didn't feel the need for a guru and also didn't believe that Gurus who were knowers of the Truth existed in today's world. When I heard about Amma, I thought, "Well, just in case Amma turns out to be a jñāni (a knower of the Truth), this could be a huge upgrade from a one-way to a two-way relationship with God. So far, I've been asking God for whatever I want. Now God can reply verbally and tell me if there's something better."

Meeting Amma

My first darśhan with Amma was on July 4, 2001 in Chicago. It was both Independence Day and Guru Pūrṇimā. Only years later I realized the significance of this date: Independence Day pointed towards Amma freeing me from identification with my limited self, while Guru Pūrṇimā symbolized the meeting of the student and the teacher.

When I got my first hug, Amma gave me the most magical and innocent smile I had ever seen. I was blown away. Then my logic piped in, "A smile alone is not sufficient to indicate a jñāni. Maybe Amma had this innocence because she was not spoiled by formal education. Maybe other villagers in Kerala also had such innocent smiles." I left after one hour... Twenty-one years later, I know for certain, there is no one in the world who can smile like Amma.

After that first darśhan I returned to my classes, assignments, lunch with my study group, etc. Everything was completely normal for four days. On the fifth day, I felt a huge weight all over me. I could not understand this heaviness. After some time, I realized that my mind had returned. For four days after meeting Amma, I had no background thoughts at all. Suddenly, the background thinking was back. This great heaviness had in fact accompanied me all my life.

I was completely shocked. I thought I was advanced compared to all the other college students who had so many fluctuations due to their immature vanity. I wondered, how much heaviness had I been carrying since my childhood? Every book I read, I entered with all my emotions. Every feeling my parents had, I also felt. I thought I was very privileged. But now, after meeting Amma, I felt that spiritually I was at zero.

For ten years after meeting Amma, I wanted to unlearn all the wrong concepts that had accumulated in my mind. And the only way to do that was to absorb the palpable silence around Amma which felt like the truth. I listened happily to anyone who narrated their experiences with Amma. The few words Amma said to somebody felt like the only real, living scripture. I bought the *Awaken Children* books and read them with a mixture of awe and tears. I was moved by a deeper understanding of life.

My Journey to Acceptance

Amma can give us anything, but we must ask with a whole heart. After a few years, I began to struggle badly with this. I could no longer ask Amma for anything with an undivided mind. By definition, a satguru represents the Truth. How could I give any suggestions or express my preferences? That would be dishonest.

When you meet someone as magnanimous as Amma, it is natural for the question to arise: "Should I surrender my will to Amma? The self-will I have carefully nurtured all my life?" It was the only important thing I owned, or at least I thought I owned it. But Amma was always gentle with me. Whenever I asked Amma a material question, she suggested the most prosperous option. Amma never asked me to do anything particularly heroic. I had read that anything a mahātmā says is for our own benefit. Even then, it was not always easy.

At the age of twenty-five, I had the most depressing year of my life when the inner struggle reached its peak. On the outside, my life in Boston was totally charming. Yet, it was devoid of any deeper meaning and I felt hollow. I could no longer ask Amma to grant me any wish, because my conscience knew that surrender to a real Guru was the highest path. Gone were those days when I asked God for every tiny thing because I now had a real teacher.

Finally, exhausted, I decided to surrender fully to Amma. With great focus, I practiced having no thoughts or opinions other than the minimum required for my job. I resolved to do anything Amma said. Amma smiled often at me, approving my sincere efforts. Anger and sorrow often arise when we lack control over a situation. Surrender makes us powerful because we learn to be happy even when things are not in our control.

This surrender practice lasted for two years and was extremely helpful for regaining all the energy I had lost during that one year I spent worrying about whether to surrender.

Just when I was secure in my surrender, Amma mysteriously created a situation and I realized that I wasn't even fit to consider surrendering. When the moment came to obey Amma's suggestion, old conditioning surfaced from below my "still" mind. I understood that no one can surrender through mere willpower or good intention. Developing full surrender can be a long journey... When I worried about my inability to obey, Amma smiled reassuringly at me, indicating not to worry — she would love me the same even if I could not follow her guidance. Amma has often said that life should not be forced. We are all like buds that must blossom naturally to give fragrance. Over the years around Amma, many of my preferences have dropped off spontaneously, and my life has become more fluid, simple and graceful.

The IAM (Integrated Amrita Meditation Technique) helped me to stop overthinking all the time and I became decisive. In everyday situations I would make a reasonable decision and then not look back. This saved me lots of precious spiritual energy. After failing all the spiritual tests of obedience, I took a new approach so I could move forward. I would do what I wanted and fully accept the good and bad results without complaint. I would only ask Amma questions where I could obey Amma's answer joyfully. Thus I wouldn't incur the demerit of disrespecting the Guru. I had no more doubts. I went on all the international tours for the next ten years as a volunteer and I focused on having a good day each day. There were many wonderful times where I was immersed in the nectar of Amma's presence.

A Taste of Fearlessness

In June 2012, I left Amma's summer tour briefly for a few days after the San Ramon program to attend a family event in Ladakh. While entering a shaky little helicopter to travel from Delhi to Leh I received a message from a friend. Amma had remembered me on the very first morning of the Los Angeles program and asked, "When is she coming back?" Despite thousands of people in the program, Amma had noticed my absence. I was happy to see the message, though the compassion of the Guru hadn't sunk in yet.

The scenery at the India-China border was breathtaking. On the next leg of the journey we had an experienced driver. Yet it was obvious at every moment that one tiny skid, one small swerve from a vehicle opposite us, and our jeep would fall thousands of feet into a bottomless valley. My family was half admiring the views, and half praying to God frantically. I was the only one who really absorbed the view of the awe-inspiring mountains. After some time, my father stopped acting brave. He exclaimed that this was a foolish trip, it was like staring at death, and no one could be sure of returning home. I spoke up comfortably, "I don't know about all of you, but I will return alive, because Amma asked when I'll be back." Even to enjoy the beauty of nature on vacation, we need the Guru's blessings.

Extraordinary Beauty

If someone asked me about Amma in the early years, I would speak for ten minutes about how Amma is exactly the jñāni described in the *Bhagavad Gītā*. People would listen respectfully, and never ask me another question. My ego was forced to accept that no one comes to Amma unless they have the destiny for it. Out of several hundred classmates, friends, coworkers, and acquaintances, only three or four people came for darśhan in twenty years, and those few never returned for a second darśhan. My old pals are very successful. They have no expectations from God, no interest in scriptures, they're emotionally balanced and follow basic dharma, and they are humble in their behavior so they don't have to endure major ego lessons. Almost all of them have excellent personal and professional lives. Even during the pandemic in 2020, they seemed to be thriving.

I pondered why such people should even go to see Amma when they have neither interest in meeting a Self-realized master nor any worldly problems? Then an answer dawned in my heart. Every human seeks an experience of beauty. We get a job and go to work hoping for a beautiful experience. We eat garnished pancakes to relish a beautiful breakfast, some people watch sunsets, others go to Hawaii. But those are ordinary beauties. Then there is extraordinary beauty, such as Amma taking part in our lives. There's a beautiful vibration the moment we enter Amma's hall. Not even the smartest people, nor the cutest babies, have eyes like the twinkling diamonds that are Amma's eyes.

A Magical Life

When Amma went to the Vatican, an Israeli friend and I walked all around Rome. We saw statues of ancient emperors and philosophers in impossibly commanding postures. I thought these postures were very unrealistic, probably just expressions of art. Later, during my first India tour with Amma in 2017, the stage was much higher than the audience, and I saw Amma from a different angle. Suddenly it struck me that the Roman statues were very similar to Amma, even in the way the robes flowed.

When it comes to nature, I can only compare Amma's form to the pristine Himalayas against dark thunder clouds... To miss Amma's beauty is a huge loss, even for those who follow dharma and are satisfied with their lives. People outside may enjoy ordinary happiness, but Amma's children have something else. They have a magical spark in their eyes. Coming to Amma means choosing to have a magical life.

Amma's living presence is strongly felt in the San Ramon, Chicago, and Washington, D.C. āśhrams. In 2009 I asked Amma if I should live in the āśhram instead of my own apartment in California, and she gave me a huge smile. After some months, I understood that Amma was happy with my question because she knew I would be happy being in the āśhram. I stayed at the San Ramon āśhram for ten years in between tours.

Sometimes I'd visit friends or relatives for dinner. At times they asked me to sleep in the guest bedroom afterwards because it was already late at night, but I almost always drove back to San Ramon. On the rare occasion when I stayed at someone's home, I felt very ordinary when I woke up in the morning. It didn't matter how beautiful the house was or how happy the people were. At the āśhram, I always had a magical feeling when I woke up, every single day.

I used to feel that Amma was lucky to have such wonderful devotees who had a bright glow and sparkling eyes. Much later I realized their beautiful sparkling glow was entirely borrowed from the Guru.

In the beginning of my spiritual journey, I had the faith that God would help me become successful in everything I did. Today my joy is in the journey, and I have become more accepting and open to life. The biggest lesson I have learned from Amma is that Amma is happy with me when I am happy. No one is happier for me than Amma when my heart breaks into a smile. Finally, I have understood that the only thing Amma truly approves of is the stillness of my heart when my mind is silent.

12

Self-Effort and Grace

Akhilesh – Finland

I'm indeed very happy to be reunited with my brothers and sisters after such a long time, and I'm immensely happy to be reunited with my Amma. It's been almost three years since I've been in Amritapuri, and two and a half years since I last saw Amma. It goes without saying that I was super excited to come here, although my visit was only going to be a very brief three weeks due to my work, but once I booked my trip, I thought, "It's better than nothing." Just a week before our arrival at the āśhram, the quarantine protocols were removed. My wife Priya and I were overjoyed that we would be able to spend the whole time in the āśhram without any quarantines. When we arrived, I felt as if I were a lost child who had been violently pulled out of his mothers lap, and just found his way back again. Seeing Amma in front of me again, seeing her smiling and talking directly to me during our first darśhan, was the ultimate "I'm home" feeling.

On the third day, during beach meditation and bhajans, I started to feel slightly feverish with some soreness in my throat. After bhajans, I went to my room and took a Covid-19 test and sure enough, it was positive. I was moved to quarantine for eleven days. I calculated in my head, "So, eleven out of the twenty days of my visit will be spent in quarantine." Just as I had sighed in relief at seeing Amma again, I was pulled away from her once more. Once I closed the door of my quarantine room and started unpacking, I realized what had just happened. I couldn't hold back my tears. I was in total disbelief. And then of course, as you would expect, a couple of days later I was reunited again, not with Amma, but with my wife Priya, in the quarantine room. She also got Covid symptoms and tested positive two days later. What a great trip!?!

For some reason, with Amma, every "negative" incident is turned into a positive one in a matter of hours. On the second day of my quarantine, I felt better already. I slept a lot, paced back and forth in the room for miles on end, contemplated my satsang, and talked to pigeons who came to say hi every now and then. The highlight of the quarantine was getting a phone call from Amma, and also all the messages and help we received from all our āśhram brothers and sisters during that time; we are forever grateful.

Covid Garden

When Covid-19 hit the world in early 2020, we were living in Santa Cruz, California. We were taking care of a thirteen acre property in the middle of the redwood trees. We were lucky, and Amma's invisible hand seemed to protect us during the worst of the pandemic. Maybe a little eleven-day quarantine in India was not that bad, considering the suffering that so many people in the world had to go through because of the pandemic.

Amma's way is always to accept the situation, no matter what comes in life, and once the acceptance comes, we start to find solutions to make the circumstances around us better. Amma is the walking, breathing example of the saying, "When life gives you lemons, you make lemonade." When the first Covid-19 lockdown happened, we had two options: We could be angry at the world and the circumstances, or we could make lemonade. We tried to follow the second option to the best of our abilities. So, we decided to start a Covid garden.

At our property, we had waste pallets and stacks of waste wood from which we built raised beds. The ground was full of great, beautiful, dark and healthy soil. Our neighbor had horses, so we could get horse manure for fertilizing. Everything was already there. We just needed to build it and plant the seeds. We grew vegetables, planted fruit trees, started flower beds, fed the birds and started beekeeping as well.

Since we missed Amritapuri so much, we decided to call this garden the Amritapuri Garden. We even named all the flower and vegetable beds with the names of the buildings here: Bhakti (devotion), Kaivalya (liberation), Mā-Ōm (mantras used in Amma's guided meditation) and our beehive was called Madhu Bhavan (honey house). Even though there were many critters and deer who came and ate our vegetables, we had so much food we couldn't eat it all ourselves, so we also shared it with neighbors, friends and family.

Although physically away from Amma, she was in our hearts. The lockdown time forced us to try to find Amma inside ourselves. The webcast programs and online satsangs were a lifeline keeping us connected to Amma. But nothing compares to being in Amritapuri. Living out in the world is like going through the charcoal factory that Amma talks about. You'll always get some stains, no matter how careful you are. We missed Amma's divine presence and Amritapuri greatly during this time.

To me, there is no greater miracle than Amma's divine presence. Or to be more accurate, the transformation that happens to people when they experience Amma's divine presence. All the satsangs and stories we've heard from people of different backgrounds, highlight how fortunate we are to be in that divine presence in these current times. The personal stories that people have shared on this stage, are a testament to Amma's infinite glory and greatness. My story is just one of them. I don't know what made me the most fortunate person in the world to be here with her, but having Amma in my life has given a direction and sense of contentment in my life that nothing else can give.

"Swimmer Boy"

Amma calls me the "swimmer boy." I swam twice in the Olympics. My whole life was dedicated to my sport. During my career, I practiced two or three hours in the morning, and again, two or three hours in the evening, six days a week. On average, I swam five kilometers per practice session, so about ten kilometers per day. I've been swimming since I was six years old, and professionally, I swam for eight years. I calculated that in my career, I swam over forty-thousand kilometers. That equals once around the globe. One day, I realized I literally must have had to swim around the world to reach Amma's holy feet, because everything I had done up to that point led me to her.

I met Amma in Finland in 2009. I had just finished my swimming career and was very unhappy with my life. Everything I ever achieved in sports felt useless and empty. Whenever I won something, my mind would always want more. My swimming career was a perfect example of how anything we achieve externally can never bring us eternal happiness. Outer achievements just lead to sorrow, disappointment and craving for more. My deep hunger to find true contentment was what led me to Amma. While watching Amma after my first darśhan, a thought came to my mind, "Everything I have ever wanted in my life, whether it's success in my career, my family, or in any other field, has been a craving and yearning for one thing only — Love. Motherly love."

Time in India

I consider India to be my home. India's spiritual tradition is truly the most precious gift to humanity. Sanātana Dharma[14]

[14] The 'Eternal Way of Life,' the original and traditional name of Hinduism.

and Amma as its embodiment, never rejects anyone. In that tradition, nobody is a sinner, and even if you have committed mistakes in your life, God never forsakes you. The doors are open for anyone who wants to enter. You can be an atheist and still walk on this path. You can even hate God and attain the realization of God, like Kaṁsa. Or, you can be a robber and become a saint, like Vālmīki. In God's eyes, everyone is perfect. In this tradition, every single being, as Swāmī Vivēkānanda says, is "potentially divine."

After meeting Amma I wanted to come and visit India. The first time I arrived here, I didn't want to leave. Āśhram life was a perfect match for me, and it was not very difficult for a former athlete to slide right into the āśhram routines and disciplines. Initially, one thing that was pretty tough was my appointed sēvā: composting. Working with food waste, cow dung, and other biodegradable materials was not my idea of an āśhram life. But of course, Amma knew better. My restless mind needed some physical sēvā to settle down a little bit. After the initial shock, I really started to enjoy it, and every day at the composting department was like a celebration.

My life in the āśhram was full of joy in general. It was the best time of my life up to that point. I really and truly had found my spiritual home. Every single day I woke up with the excitement of a little boy. I ended up spending a little over five years here. During that time, I had one doubt that would creep up every now and then from the back of my mind. That doubt was about escapism. I was brought up in a fairly traditional way in Western culture. My family asked, "Why aren't you settling down? Why don't you get your life together and stop running around the world like a little hippie?"

I wrote a long letter to Amma, basically saying that some people come to spiritual life to run away from their duties in the world, and I want to make sure I don't do that. In the middle of the translation, Amma interrupted and said, "Do you think spiritual aspirants are idiots?" She proceeded to tell this story, "A man was walking through the desert with his donkey and he had a long way ahead of him. After some time, there was a passerby who came along and asked, "Why are you walking with the donkey? Why don't you just ride it?" The man thought that was a great idea, jumped on the donkey's back and started riding it. Then again after some time another passerby came along and asked, "What are you doing? You're in the middle of this hot desert. That poor donkey is suffering! Spare that donkey! Jump off its back and continue your trip on foot." The man thought maybe he was right and jumped off the donkey's back. This continued back and forth — he was jumping on and off the donkey's back because he couldn't make up his mind. Finally, the man ended up carrying the donkey on his own back." Amma continued, "You need to have a vision in your life. If you want to get married, you need to get a job." I had a desire to get married, so lessons were learned then and there.

I knew my time in the āśhram was over. Of course, I was sad, but at the same time, I knew the direction I needed to go, and what my path was from then onwards. Although it was painful in the beginning, I knew it was the right thing to do. In the West, many people ask me what I learned in the āśhram. The time in Amritapuri gave me the foundation for my life. Life without spiritual values feels hollow. Those values were missing from my life, and are missing from many people's lives in general. The time here gave me strength to face the world and never lose sight of the most important factor in life, God.

Amma also once told me as I was driving her to the airport after the Finland program, "Your time in the āśhram was training for your married life." I couldn't agree more. Marriage based on spiritual values gives meaning to married life. A couple can work together towards their spiritual goals and at the same time help to uplift society.

Out in the World

In the world of sports, where human bodies are brought to extremes with intense training, athletes can bear quite a bit of physical pain. The career of an athlete is focused solely on self-effort. It's very good in many ways, because you learn that nothing is given to you. You learn to be disciplined, and have resilience. Very quickly you learn the value of self-effort. It is the only thing that matters in sports. In our training sessions there was no talk about God's grace being a factor in success, or having the attitude that, "You have to be a zero to become a hero," as Amma says. It was more like, "If you are not a hero, then you are a zero."

Athletes generally have pretty big egos, and a lot of confidence in themselves and their physical abilities. I felt I could do anything, lift anything, win any competition, and be unbreakable, at least physically. As I said, in many ways it was really good, since it gave me mental toughness. Athletes generally are not afraid of a challenge, especially if it's a physical one. The downside is that this kind of a superhero ego needs bigger blows to learn a lesson. I'm a prime example of this kind of superhero ego. Nothing tickles me and my inner superman more than to think, "I'm the only one who can solve the problem and save the day," no matter what the situation.

Amma's Program Coordinator

I have a feeling that Amma has given me certain responsibilities just so I'll understand that my efforts alone are not enough. God's grace is the essential part. One of the greatest blessings I've ever received from Amma, was the time she asked me to help with coordinating her program in Finland. The previous main coordinator was stepping down and Amma asked me to step in and help. As I said, nothing tickles my inner superman more than knowing that I'm going to be the one to make things better. But as always, Amma knew there was a lesson waiting for me.

Coordinating an Amma program is a difficult job. This was especially so during my first year doing it in 2017. We had so many challenges even finding a suitable venue for Amma, since the hall she used to come to was not available. Just two months before the actual program date, we found a hall that was not at all what we had hoped for. It was basically a sports hall on the lowest floor of a building, almost like a basement, and it didn't have many of the essential things for the program. First of all, it was too small. Second, the tour staff accommodation was terrible. Next, it was very expensive for what it was, the plumbing was non-existent, there was not enough electricity for the sound system, and many other such issues. Fortunately, these issues were solved and we were able to make it happen. It was definitely not ideal, but we thought it was better to have Amma come to Finland, even though the hall was suboptimal, rather than cancel the whole program.

As the program dates were approaching my personal stress levels were shooting up. I swam in many major events during my career including the Olympics, the World and European Championships — all in front of television cameras and millions of people — but I have never, ever been as stressed as I was during Amma's program days, and the days leading up to them. I was, of course, not able to sleep before or during the program days, and I was nearing a breaking point.

During the program, the fire department came twice and the police department came once. There was an oil leak in the kitchen, a fire alarm in the staff room, the staff were not happy with the accommodations, and many other incidents happened that sent me to the edge. I felt sad that I was not able to offer Amma what I wanted to offer her. Swāmī Śhubhāmṛitānandajī came to me at one point during the program and said, "You guys did an amazing job considering the circumstances you were given." I couldn't hold it together anymore and burst into tears.

In retrospect, I felt I needed that breaking point to learn the value of God's grace in my life. When we do break down, we truly become humble. When we become humble, we go nearer to God. And being able to arrange the program has made my bond so much closer to Amma; so indeed, it is a great blessing.

Arranging the next program in 2019, my approach was completely different. I prayed more, had maybe a little less superhero attitude in me, and I was humbled by the lessons learned from the previous program. This program went smoothly. We had a great hall, a record number of visitors, and even the staff seemed to be happy. The only issue was that the Finnish crowd didn't outwardly laugh at Amma's jokes; but that's nothing new, since Finnish people are not known for being very expressive with their emotions.

As I said, it's always a challenge to arrange Amma's programs, but it's the greatest way for a stubborn mind like mine to learn how, and with what kind of attitude, to approach the responsibilities given to us. Self-effort and grace have always been the topics that have intrigued my mind. Amma says that self-effort brings us to a state of effortlessness. It is my firm belief that with every action, every step we take towards God, we slowly start to understand that it's through God's power only, that we are able to do anything.

Swimming Lessons

Currently, we are living in the United States. I work with kids coaching a swim team. Teaching was also something that Amma inspired me to do. She had me teach the brahmachārīs and the āśhram residents how to swim in India. Teaching is a way I can give back to the world and use my abilities for the benefit of others.

I have three groups of kids on my swim team. Around sixty to seventy kids in total: little ones, pre-teens and teenagers. Being a teacher requires the ability to understand the kids, to go to their level. Some of them have ADHD (attention deficit hyperactivity disorder) and they cannot stay still. I have to give them a task, otherwise they become bullies or create havoc during practice. Others are just lazy; I have to give them a challenge to get them moving. Some kids are forced by their parents to be there. I still have to make sure they leave the practice with a smile on their faces. Some kids are really good, able to focus, they work hard and give it their all. I have to be able to work with all of them individually.

There are multiple lessons to be learned from dealing with children. Amma's teachings fill my mind when trying to overcome or solve a teenager's broken heart issue, or trying to get the ADHD child to work harder and stay focused. Or, trying to discipline the team in a way that keeps them inspired and working out of love, rather than out of fear of their coach. Sometimes I'm successful and sometimes I'm not.

Learning the ins and outs of spiritual life is almost like learning how to swim. The basic idea of swimming is very simple. You have a floating device in your body, which is your set of lungs. If you have some extra fat, even better, it's impossible for you to drown. Swimming is nothing other than trusting that you will always float to the surface of the water when your floating device is full of air. So, learning to swim is nothing other than internalizing that idea and moving in water. The key is to relax. Many times, the reason people drown is the fact that they start fighting with the water; they don't understand and trust that they have the ability to float and swim already within them.

Even in a raging ocean, where the waves are going back and forth, we tend to react to the water. But if we learn to read, listen and understand the rhythm of the water, and then move along with it, even the stormy ocean becomes a joyful playground. Then, as Amma says, "We can enjoy the waves of the ocean like an expert swimmer."

In spiritual life, we have to be able to adjust to any circumstances that may come our way. Life is our ocean, Amma is our floating device. If we just understand that she is always with us, we can enjoy swimming in the waves and storms of the ocean and stay afloat.

13
The Gift of Devotion

Deepa Lele – USA

When I was in college, I was feeling hopeless and depressed. I would try to picture my future, but I would only see nothingness. A blank. It was very unsettling. I met a friend in a public health program, before meeting Amma, and I remember telling her that I was scared because I couldn't see a future for myself. Only after meeting Amma did I feel like my life had any purpose and direction.

I met Amma in the summer of 1999 at her two-day Dallas program. On the second day, I received a mantra during Dēvī Bhāva. I felt that I had met a lot of nice people and that I'd love to see Amma again the following year. But just one day after Amma left, I saw an airport shuttle with a sign that read 'Chicago $69!' I burst into tears because Amma was in Chicago and I wasn't.

A few months later, some members of the Dallas satsang helped me to attend Amma's autumn program at the San Ramon āśhram. Every day was a different wave of emotion — feeling so happy, so sad, so worthless and so accepted. By the time it ended, I knew Amma was in my heart permanently, and my goal in life was to feel her with me, always.

In February 2000, Amma blessed me with deep longing for her. I had never heard of crying for God. I hadn't read that crying for God is purifying, that it even purifies the atmosphere. Amma says, "Children, pray and shed tears as you think of God. That is the greatest sādhanā. No other sādhanā will give you the bliss of divine love as effectively as sincere prayer." Everywhere I went, I desperately wanted Amma to be right there with me.

That was my sincere prayer. I listened to the bhajan *Sṛiṣhṭiyum Nīyē*:

> *sṛiṣhṭiyum nīyē sṛiṣhṭāvum nīyē*
> *śhaktiyum nīyē satyavum nīyē*
>
> *paramāṇu chaitanya porulum nīyē*
> *pañcha bhūtangaḷum nīyē*
> *Dēvī... Dēvī... Dēvī...*
> 'You are the creation, you are the creator.
> You are both energy and truth.
>
> You are the essence of the individual soul,
> And you are the five elements as well.
> O Dēvī! O Dēvī! O Divine Mother!'

I thought deeply about the meaning of these words, "Isn't God in everything?" I looked for Amma in everything, even in the five elements around me: earth, water, fire, air and space. I cried, "Let me see you Amma! Why can't I see you? Where are you?" I especially cried for Amma whenever I was alone in my car or at home. I had a long commute to work and that's when the tears would flow. It is only because of Amma's grace that I was never in any accidents. This went on for about two weeks. Then, in my total ignorance, I prayed for the tears to stop.

One day, I was at my altar crying for Amma, and also praying that the tears would stop. I didn't think I could take it anymore. And then something splashed onto my face and surprised me. Real water drops were falling from the top of the window ledge, hitting the window sill below and splashing onto my face. I was so surprised that I stopped crying... and the drops stopped. I thought I would have to check if we had a leak. But there was no leak and it wasn't raining. After a while, I started crying again and the drops started again! I realized then that Amma was crying with me! Amma's tears were falling in front of me! And again I was so shocked that I stopped crying and the drops stopped again. I was stunned by what happened. I couldn't cry anymore. Amma was with me. I had witnessed a miracle! Amma proved to me that she heard me, all the way from Dallas, and she was with me, while she was in India!

For weeks afterwards, I would spontaneously feel so much joy, just overwhelming peace and joy. I felt Amma could hear me, see me, was with me, and I wasn't alone. I wrote a little song then. Here is part of it:

The full moon pales in your radiance!
It would take a lifetime of tears of joy
To express my gratitude for you!
The full moon pales in your radiance!

When I heard Amma speak about our longing for God, I realized what a blessing I had been given by having those tears. And I remembered how those tears seemed to flow upward from my heart, like a rising tide and then overflow from my eyes. I have hardly ever shared this part of my life with anyone because I am ashamed that I didn't have the courage to hold on to that longing.

Later on, I asked Amma how to increase my longing again. I sat by the chair while the interpreter explained my question to Amma. She turned to me and said, "If you thought about God as much as you think about food, you wouldn't have to ask about longing!" Amma, I'm sorry that I could not hold on to that level of longing for you. With your grace, it is a goal I can strive for.

Crying also led me to being on tour staff, except this crying was more like a child's tantrum. While visiting Amma's programs in various other cities in 2000, I learned that there was a limited number of people who would commit to taking on sēvā responsibilities for the entire tour and that this was known as 'tour staff.' How desperately I wanted to be a part of the staff for next year! But despite my best efforts, they already had enough staff for the tour next year. I was devastated! After my last attempt had failed, I ran out of the venue in Rhode Island and cried on the grass like a little child. When I cleaned myself up and came back to the hall, Amma glanced at me and just slightly nodded her head towards me. I thought that meant that she was aware of my crying, which was really comforting and made me feel better instantly. What I didn't know at the time was that Amma's slight nod meant that she was rearranging the stars and planets with her saṅkalpa (divine resolve) so that this pretty useless daughter would be invited to join the kitchen staff!

Here is how the miracle happened. Leading up to the 2001 tour, I answered an email from a devotee who was asking for volunteers to help build part of the San Ramon āśhram dining hall that had been destroyed during a fire the previous year. Although I knew nothing about construction I was accepted to join this sēvā. I helped in whatever way I could. What I didn't realize at the time was that I was meeting a lot of people from the kitchen staff. I ended up going up to Seattle with them. While we were helping to set up the kitchen tent, one of the kitchen supervisors called me over. She told me there was a cancellation and asked if I would like to be on staff. I was so happy, I immediately said yes! With Amma's grace, I have been on Amma's North America Tour staff since then, except for one year, until the Covid-19 pandemic started.

Years later, I would remember Amma's slight nod in Rhode Island and realize what a huge blessing she had given me at that moment. I realized that getting to be on staff was Amma's divine will. When anyone asks me how to attain the things they long for, I just say, " Pray! Pray to Amma! Turn it over to her! She will hear you and if she wishes, she will make things happen and find solutions in ways that you could never have imagined!" And in my mind, I would also usually think, "Cry! Cry to Amma like a two-year old! She will hear you!"

***

In Toronto in 2017, I asked Amma a question about the new MA Center in Dallas and Amma spontaneously said that I could stay there if no one else was in residence. I was a little hesitant to agree to Amma's request before asking my dad. I tried to ask about him, but Amma lifted her hands and said, "It's just a suggestion!" Umm, Wait. Was I actually arguing with the Mother of the Universe? I mumbled something, "Ok, Amma, thank you Amma, yes Amma," and ran from the stage.

About a month later, I was helping the Dallas āśhram facilities coordinator by mowing the grass as my sēvā. On August 21, 2017, we had made a plan to meet at the āśhram to mow. There was a total solar eclipse that day, going right over Texas. We had both heard Amma's warnings about not being outside during the eclipse, but anytime before and after was fine. So I decided to come in the morning, and the facilities coordinator would come in the afternoon.

After my sēvā, I entered the main house and I heard the smoke alarm. I didn't see or smell any smoke, so I thought it must be a low battery alarm. I followed the sound and you can imagine my horror when I looked up and saw water dripping from the smoke alarm. Then I saw that the ceiling had fallen down in the laundry room.

We only have one bathroom upstairs so I ran up there. Sure enough, a small connection piece had broken underneath the toilet tank, and water was gushing out fast. I tried to shut it off but couldn't, and had to race outside to turn off the main water supply to the āśhram. I thought, "It's too bad no one was here to turn the water off sooner...oh wait. Amma told me to stay here!"

It could not have been a coincidence that I was the first one there. This event happened on a Monday. There had been a satsang program on the previous Saturday evening. So the water could have been running after that, and all day and night on Sunday because no one was there to turn it off. No wonder Amma wanted someone at the āśhram!

After I shut off the water, I went back upstairs. I grabbed a towel and went to the bedroom and started mopping up the water. It was still raining in the office below. There were probably hundreds of gallons of water flowing through the house and I was getting maybe a few ounces in my bucket. That was how one of our neighbors found me. She looked at me and said, "Oh, honey. You're not going to fix this problem with that towel!" We called a restoration company, and they came quickly.

This was again Amma's grace, because if this leak had happened one month later, we would not have had any help because Hurricane Harvey came ashore and hit Houston. All the local restoration companies went there to help in the recovery after that hurricane. I hope I get credit for fasting that day, because with all the commotion of the restoration company arriving, and still being in shock, I didn't even drink water until the evening.

The office area near Amma's bedroom was completely destroyed by the flood, but somehow, Amma's bedroom was almost untouched. Our satsang area and the kitchen were fine, so we were able to have satsangs in the main house, and later at the cottage, until the repair work was finished. Because the office area had to be completely rebuilt, we were able to renovate the spaces of three separate rooms and greatly expand the size of our satsang area. Before the flood, the satsang area could hold about twenty people. After the renovation, we could fit one hundred people! These amazing changes that happened to the Dallas āśhram were all because of Amma's grace!

I took it as a reminder to follow Amma's instructions to the letter, because we usually have no idea what the reasons are for Amma's words or actions. But, if we do make mistakes or have a lack of śhraddhā, attentiveness or faith, Amma is there to help pick up the pieces and turn it into something beautiful and full of her grace. If we put our worries and troubles in Amma's hands, only good will come out of any mistake or difficulty.

***

I am very grateful to Amma for the examples set for me by my parents. When I was a child, we would chant evening prayers. My mom loved the *Hanumān Chālīsā*,[15] so it became part of our evening chants for many years. Not long before she passed away in 2007, my mother told me she felt Hanumān in her heart, and Lord Rama in Hanumān's heart.

My father was born in Vārāṇasī, India, and went to the Saṅkaṭ Mōchan Hanumān temple for many years. If you have seen an image of Hanumān dressed all in orange, it comes from that temple. My father wrote a detailed explanation of the *Rāmacharitamānasa*, which is a poem based on the *Rāmāyaṇa*, the epic scripture describing the life of Lord Rāma. Still today, at 80 years old, he participates in Rāmāyaṇa chanting online and in temples around Dallas, while also serving as a pūjāri (temple priest). I love Hanumān too. Every morning I wear a shirt with his picture on it as I do my morning sādhanā.

Lately during the meditation time in Amritapuri, Amma sometimes comes to sit in front of the Kāḷī temple. After

[15] A devotional hymn on Lord Hanumān by Gōswāmī Tulsīdās comprising 40 verses. 'Prayer of 40 verses' = chālīsā.

meditation, sometimes one or two āśhram kids give a talk or sing for Amma. Two days after getting out of quarantine, I was sitting in the special 'visitors' section, right in front of Amma. One of the children started to sing the *Hanumān Chālīsā*. It was unbelievably special for me to hear that hymn and watch Amma's enjoyment of it! She smiled so beautifully and tapped her feet. It brought back memories of my mom and dad from back home. Thank you, Amma!

There are so many more experiences. To be able to give satsangs about how Amma has touched our lives, and to share those experiences and memories, which are like precious gems held in our hearts, is a miracle in and of itself.

***

When the Covid-19 pandemic began, my massage jobs were put on hold. I started to babysit my niece. Both my sister and her husband needed to work from home without distractions. I had the time to help. It was such a blessing from Amma. My brother-in-law's company started to give a stipend to anyone taking care of their employees' children. Suddenly, I had a full time job, and later I was able to give massages on the weekends.

Amma says, "Spending some time with children is a sādhanā. A child has all the signs of one who has reached perfection. The innocence of children will reflect in us also. Forgetting everything, we will sit looking at them. Vāsanās[16] are only in a seed form in them and have not yet manifested. Children have the eyes of one who has attained perfection."

Amma also says, "It is good for you to spend some time with children. They will teach you to believe, to love and to play. Children will help you smile from your heart and to have that

[16] Latent tendencies or subtle desires that manifests as thought, motive and action. Also, subconscious impressions gained from experience.

look of wonderment in your eyes." That is so true. My niece and I would dance to bhajans in the afternoons and that is something I never used to do before spending time with her.

Amma helps us in so many ways. I noticed about a month before coming here, that I was reading a lot of fiction — mysteries, action, romance — but while I was getting ready to come to Amritapuri, my interest in those things started to fade. Now, being here, I have had no desire to read those books and it amazes me! With the extra time on my hands, I started writing my mantra in a notebook. I pray to Amma for help in dropping that fiction vāsanā even when I go back to the U.S.

Amma's grace works in our lives in such a variety of ways. Everything from seeing our job as Amma's sēvā, to helping us get through tough situations, or looking back and understanding how Amma found a solution to something when we felt stuck.

Amma looks for that little gap of space we offer her to come into our lives to bring peace, joy and happiness. We just have to make a little room in our minds for her grace to flow — like the Gaṅgā or the Yamunā (sacred rivers in India) — or like the river of water flowing through an office ceiling!

14

Transformation through Amma's Compassion

Sree Devi Osorio – Colombia

A friend of mine asked me, "Why have you decided to live with Amma?" Thinking about it, I came to the conclusion that it was not me who decided, it was Amma herself. I will narrate how she found me, and brought the desire for change into my life. The experiences of transformation are greatly due to her grace.

In the first volume of *Awaken Children*, Amma asks a devotee, "Son, where are you coming from?" Devotee: "Do you know me, Mother? You speak to me so sweetly; as if speaking to your own son after a long absence." Mother: "Do you think you would come here if we had not been acquainted in the past? Many people are very familiar to me. Between lifetimes the memory sits dormant, then finally, some people are able to remember."

We meet Amma for the first time, but she assures us that we have already been together in many other lives. We have forgotten them, but she remembers each and every one. It is said that it is not the disciple who finds the Guru, but the Guru who finds the disciple, and that the Guru decides the place and time of the meeting. Amma says, "God takes a body not for the knowers of the Self. God's incarnation is to bring the ignorant to the correct path." Looking back, before meeting her, we may realize Amma has been present in our lives for a long time, preparing us, guiding us towards the blossoming desire to know God.

I was born and raised in Colombia. In 2001, my family moved to Spain. I was an introverted person which made the transition into a new culture difficult for me. Later, I was going through hard times due to insomnia and back pain, and after visiting a few doctors without any results, a friend suggested I try yōga. There just so happened to be a yōga center near my house. I became very fond of yōga, and people there introduced me to a Buddhist center to practice meditation. It was there that I met an Amma devotee who became my friend. She brought me to Amma.

We dedicate our lives to the search for happiness which we believe lies in objects and relationships. We are ignorant of the fact that the source of true happiness lies within. We turn our energy outwards to satisfy desires and sense pleasures which only provide temporary gratification. Then we find the search to be aimless and often painful. That was my condition before I met Amma.

However, even in the midst of that foolishness, I still had a need to believe in something. I wanted to find peace and meaning in my life, to end the continuous dissatisfaction. The loneliness and emptiness I felt was so painful. What little relief I could find in objects and people was fleeting. I knew very well that I did not want a conventional family life with a husband and children, but at the same time, I didn't know how or where to search. Once, filled with sorrow, I cried out to the heavens, "God, life cannot be just this. There has to be something more!" In that moment of despair, without knowing it, I opened my heart to Amma, placing myself in her hands. Today, I know Amma was that 'something more' missing in my life, and that she immediately took me into her care. That was the turning point when Amma adjusted the reins of my destiny, directing me towards that path that would bring me closer to her. In

Awaken Children, Volume 6, Amma says, "Although God may not be visible to you now, He is always there, guiding and controlling you, holding the reins of your life. As you advance through life He draws you to Him. You may resist at first, but you will soon realize that you have no choice than surrender to his pull. It is at this point that you will start your way back to God, the source of your existence."

***

I met Amma in November 2009 during her visit to Barcelona, Spain. I remember just a few things from that program. However, information about her humanitarian projects under Embracing the World caught my attention since I was involved with an NGO in my early teens. I thought Amma was a nice person wanting to help people. What I remember most was my friend taking me from one place to another, so as not to miss anything, and finally to see Amma.

My friend reserved two chairs near the stage to watch the Ātmā Pūjā (worship of the Inner Self). I held the cup of holy water in my hands and thought, "Now what do I do with this?" I remember people running to Amma at the end of the Dēvī Bhāva, calling out her name, crying inconsolably. My friend dragged me towards the crowd. I felt uncomfortable and became irritable. Why were they crying and calling out like that? I didn't understand.

When the mind does not welcome what is unfamiliar, the heart closes. Blinded by my closed mind and heart, I didn't realize these were expressions of love, devotion, and gratitude. It was only after experiencing Amma's compassion that I could relate to their feelings. It takes a change of perspective, a willingness to expand the limits that we impose on ourselves, to open ourselves to love. Love changes everything. It gives us a new vision with which to appreciate the world.

I feel like I have just started this spiritual journey. Currently, I am in spiritual kindergarten. Everything is new to me. As I take these first steps, my bond with Amma is that of a child to her mother. I am her dear daughter, her little one who needs to hold onto her sāri[17] so as not to fall. Amma once said in Amritapuri, "Here, there is no Guru-disciple relationship, but only that of a mother and her children. And, if Amma showed her true Guru Bhāva (attitude of the Guru), there would be no one left in the āśhram." For most people without any spiritual foundation, it's not easy to adhere to strict rules, discipline and austerities without the mind rebelling and seeking an escape. To help us, Amma personifies all the maternal qualities that make us fall in love with her, and with which she guides us on the spiritual path.

I am amazed by Amma's loving kindness. She has traveled the world multiple times in search of her children. I offer my eternal gratitude to Amma for having come to my rescue, and for giving me the opportunity to grow under her guidance to become a stronger, better person.

When I was about thirteen, I remember saying, "Either I'll marry a millionaire and travel the world, or I'll become a Buddhist nun!" Wait, what? Buddhist nun? Where did that come from? How could I have known it was a hint into my future? In any case, I became disappointed with the idea of renouncing the world. I wanted to enjoy my friends and travel. The thought of becoming a nun would wait for many years.

***

[17] Traditional outer garment worn by Indian women.

I don't recall feeling anything special at my first darśhan, perhaps because my mind was too busy waiting for something extraordinary to happen during the hug. Many people cry after Amma's hug, overwhelmed by the emotions that her healing contact awakens in them. In my case, the balm she applied to me produced a nervous laugh. Amma gives us just what we need. At that moment in my life, what I needed most was to smile. Amma cracked the mask of stiffness I wore, and took away a lot of my tension.

My friend had warned me that hundreds of people would attend Amma's program. That was my main concern. How would I be able to handle the anxiety of being in such a crowded place, not just for a few hours, but for a couple of days? It was a great challenge, and I would not be able to overcome it by myself. But Amma already knew very well what I needed because I was not a stranger to her.

At some point, I sat in the audience and observed the pavilion full of people — the vibrant activity, the constant noise, people standing, sitting, talking. Everywhere I looked I saw people! Good grief!

Typically, such a situation would have filled me with tension and irritability and I would have run away. But then, the opposite happened. As I watched all this movement, I realized everything was calm inside me, and I felt a deep peace. I was nothing more than a witness, an observer of what was happening, not affected by anything. I truly enjoyed experiencing the peace and neutrality of observing without judging. That was totally new for me. Amma was preparing me for her āśhram and for her tours: lots of noise and great crowds flowing into the immense sea of love that is Amma. She trains us to be calm and balanced internally despite any external chaos.

It helps me to see people as my own reflection, and to think they have come here because we share the desire to be with Amma. A few may come out of curiosity, or like me, at the insistence of a friend. Some come to see what they can receive, or to resolve an issue, but all of them are in search of that 'something more.' They are going through a transformation process, just like I did. This attitude helps me not to feel overwhelmed on days when the āśhram has many visitors. Above all, it makes me think that, to improve the world, more people need to come into contact with mahātmās who are capable of awakening consciousness and the desire to change.

***

My story with Amma is not one of love at first sight. It is nothing like the experiences of some who say they felt a strong urge to meet her after seeing her photo, or those who upon hearing her sing, burst into tears of devotion for God. No, not even close. My story begins with curiosity. Our relationship took time to build. I was not receptive. Amma was knocking on my door, waiting patiently, but I, immersed in the illusion of the world, turned a deaf ear to her. Every year as Amma's Europe Tour approached, my friend invited me to go to the program again, but I refused. I didn't want any constraints on my freedom. So, every year I found an excuse to decline her invitation.

I bitterly regret having wasted those years. I thought the decision not to attend the program was entirely in my hands. I didn't know then that God governs the course of our lives. My heart and my mind were overwhelmed by negativity and sadness; there was no space for a ray of true light. Also, I still had experiences to go through that would enhance my inner emptiness and disenchantment with the world. In God's plan, everything has its own time and meaning, although we do not know it.

In 2012, I started participating in a satsang group. At every satsang I attended, the devotees shared joyful experiences of being with Amma and visiting her āśhram. Their faces lit up and their eyes twinkled, immersed in sweet memories. One day, as I listened, I felt an intense excitement within me, like butterflies in my stomach. Well, those butterflies wanted to burst into the open sky! I thought, "Maybe I should go to India and see for myself what is so fascinating." There was no going back. That was December. In January I bought my plane ticket and quit my job. In February 2013, I reached Amritapuri.

When I first saw Amma there, she had already sown a seed in me, a seed that until then had not found the right conditions to germinate. For an expert farmer like Amma, there are no barren lands. Every tree bears fruit in its season. In my case, the water that made my seed sprout was the satsang group that had awakened my curiosity to know more about Amma and her āśhram.

I have always felt that my arrival in Amritapuri was planned by an external force. I was like a chess piece moving from one square to another without any opposition. The interesting thing is that I never had a desire to visit India. Without knowing it, I had just taken the biggest step towards a new life. This transformation has been possible thanks to Amma's compassion which gave me the desire to change, and allows me to live in an environment conducive to my awakening consciousness. My old beliefs about myself were nothing more than obstacles to reaching the fullness of this existence.

My first stay in the āśhram was painful. I felt so exposed and vulnerable when Amma showed me my shortcomings. My fake image of a strong, confident woman broke apart. My negativities like anger, impatience, arrogance, and sadness were crystal clear. I knew of their existence before, but I saw them as necessities for moving forward in life. Amma showed me the unpleasant reality. She comforted me while leading me to transcend my limitations.

***

In the āśhram, it can be risky to walk under the peepal tree near the Kāḷī temple in the early hours of the morning, when all the birds living there wake up. One morning, as I passed under the tree, I saw someone, and a very negative thought about that person crossed my mind. Just then, I felt the warm, wet, stinky impact of a bird's deposit on my head. Days later, the same scene was repeated! I saw someone, had a negative thought, and got the well-deserved reward. Action–reaction in its purest form — Dṛiṣhṭa phala, the visible result of action, courtesy of the birds.

At first, I felt humiliated. I looked up and snapped, "Oh come on! Again?" But then I thought, it couldn't be a coincidence since the two occasions were practically identical. I realized my error and felt sad when I recognized my feelings of negativity and animosity towards others. I clearly saw Amma's loving hands behind the play, pointing out my mistake in a way that I could easily relate to. After that I paid attention to the quality of my thoughts, especially when I walked under the peepal tree. I didn't want to repeat the stinky experience, not just because of the smell, but rather because of the pain it caused me when I recognized that I harbored those thoughts in my mind, fed them, and let them flourish. My first strategy was simple; I walked while looking at the ground, mentally repeating, "Don't think badly, don't think badly. Don't look at anyone, think positively, don't look at anyone!" The next step was not to look at anyone while repeating my mantra as quickly as possible, leaving no room for other thoughts. The experiment was working well. I was more alert to the contents of my mind, and the birds confirmed it by no longer pooping on me!

Over time, I felt more confident and was able to keep my eyes up and repeat my mantra without tension. I felt great relief as I noticed fewer negative thoughts. With Amma's invaluable guidance, and through self-observation, I am becoming a better person for the benefit of others, and I am experiencing more peace. Today, I am calmer, more positive, and much more patient. I can still lose my temper if the situation catches me off guard, but I can understand and surpass, to a great extent, the unhealthy attachment to sorrow and anger that I felt for many years. Amma tells us, we need a mind that sees God in everything and everyone. We have to try to love everyone, but if we are unable to do so, we should at least try not to get angry at anyone.

Amma has said that her children have come here for different reasons. Some decided to come because they experience a total detachment towards the objects of this world, others imitate this group and come out of an initial fervor or impulse. Even if some come out of an initial fervor, if they try to understand the teachings, assimilate them, and put them into practice, they can really change. Thus, Amma blesses those who don't have an inherent predisposition towards spirituality, by opening the doors of her abode so we may enjoy her divine presence and teachings and put them into practice. However, Amma makes it clear; just the atmosphere of the āśhram and Amma's physical presence are not enough. We must open our hearts and have the desire for knowledge. Only when a bud is ready to bloom can it benefit from the sunlight.

At first I imagined that the āśhram would be a place of continuous peace, love, and smiles. How could it be otherwise if we all have the goal of experiencing true bliss? Well, I soon realized it was not the paradise I had imagined. I am not saying it is not a joyous paradise, it is. But, it's different from what I imagined. We all come here carrying a burden of negativities. We are deeply attached to our egos, our likes and dislikes and are just beginning to understand how to let go of these burdens.

In the āśhram, Amma has created the perfect setting to test our progress day-to-day. Aśhram life is Amma's polishing machine. She says we are like stones with sharp edges. She puts us all together in a drum and spins it until our edges are worn, polished, and we are transformed into precious gems. Amma says the only way to determine our spiritual progress is by seeing how we respond to different situations. We cannot see progress if everything goes well, without any obstacles. Or, if we avoid life and isolate ourselves from the world, locked in a cave. We can only gauge our progress by how we interact with others, in our daily transactions such as sēvā, queuing at the juice stall, interacting with a roommate, etc. Under these circumstances, Amma gives us a pop quiz to see if we have done our homework and she measures our progress.

Amma makes herself available and gives us all the necessary tools to battle our ego. It is certainly painful, but every time we fall down, Amma comes to our side, lifts us up, wipes our tears, and encourages us to continue fighting until we can completely surrender our ego at her lotus feet.

One year, I joined the queue to pass through security to enter the venue for Amma's birthday celebration. It was packed, the queue was barely moving. The pāda pūjā was about to begin. Getting impatient I thought, "I'm going to miss it anyway, I'd better get out of here." I looked for the exit and realized it was impossible to move. There was no way I could cut through the mass of people gathered there. I panicked! I imagined myself screaming, pushing my way through the crowd! When I was about to lose control, Amma gave me the thought of chanting my mantra, which I did, frantically. With each repetition, the tension began to dissolve. I calmed down and gradually regained my composure. Amma had come to my rescue. Had I tried to get out of there by force, I could have harmed other people.

I have learned that by chanting her name, I find calmness, confidence, support and solace. Still, at the end of the day, I'm sometimes surprised to find that I have chanted my mantra very little. I have not been able to maintain my connection to Amma. I have not put in the right effort. I pray to Amma to never let go of my hand, to help me overcome negativities like laziness, anger, impatience, and arrogance which stand like a wall between my heart and her lotus feet.

Thank you, Mother, for your love, patience, and dedication towards your naughty children. Without you the world is empty. You are the light that shines in our hearts. May we never forget to thank you. Let me end with a prayer: 'Beloved Mother, please let me remember you constantly throughout the day. Let my every thought, word and deed bring me closer to you. Please let me not hurt anyone in thought, word or deed. Be with me at every moment.'

15

Amma is Always with Us

Santhi – USA

I was born into a family with many problems. Both of my parents were alcoholics, and there were other problems as well. Consequently, my sisters and I were abused and neglected. When I was eleven, my maternal grandmother committed suicide, which further plunged the family into darkness. Around that time, when I was wondering if life was really worth living, I remember having a sudden resolve, "Something is better than this, somewhere, and I am going to find it." I didn't know where this thought came from at the time. Now I feel it came from Amma.

One saving grace of my childhood was that I went to Catholic school, which gave me some knowledge of spirituality. I loved to listen to stories of Jesus, and even tried to get my family interested in a daily practice together, which we managed to do only once. I remember seeing pictures of Jesus with children on his lap and wished that he would come back before I was too big to fit on his lap. Fortunately, no one is too big to fit on our Amma's divine lap.

After my tumultuous childhood, as I grew into a young adult, I felt strongly that spirituality was the answer to the pain I felt inside. Though I went to college, I wasn't interested in having a worldly career. I changed my major several times and finally stopped going to college altogether, without having obtained a degree. I even resisted working full-time because I didn't want to waste my life by working for money to buy a lot of stuff, because I knew happiness wasn't in the stuff. But where was it?

One life-changing event happened when I was part of a cultural exchange program and I lived in France for two years. I was an au-pair in a small village in the south of France. When I had some free time, I would walk by the river in the town and ask myself, “Qui suis-je? Où vais je?” meaning, “Who am I? Where am I going?” My life felt like a boat in a storm, constantly buffeted by winds in all directions. Was there a divine being guiding the whole process? I felt that there was, so I continued searching.

I arrived back in the Bay Area in 1987, the year of Amma’s first tour, but I didn’t meet Amma until 1998. During those years, Amma was preparing me to meet her. I tried many spiritual paths, but nothing satisfied the longing I had inside for something that embraced absolutely everyone.

Finally, on June 8, 1998, near midnight, I walked into the temple of the San Ramon āśhram for the first time. The sights and sounds that greeted me made me feel like I’d just entered a foreign country. As though she were waiting for me, a woman immediately said to me, “You haven’t met the Holy Mother before, have you?” I was speechless. All I could do was shake my head, no. Then she guided me to a short line off to the side of the hall for Amma’s darśhan. There was no token system in those days.

Just before Amma hugged me, I thought, “I don’t know if I’m ready for this.” Suddenly, I was in her arms with my nose buried in the carnation garland Amma was wearing. “I can’t breathe,” I remember thinking. “Oh, yes you can,” Amma’s reply was in my mind immediately. I checked again, and Amma was right; I was breathing just fine. In that first meeting, I learned that Amma knew my thoughts and communicated with me beyond words. Six days later at my first Dēvī Bhāva darśhan, I received a mantra from Amma, and I knew the direction of my life had changed.

One time, Amma showed me that she was with me, protecting me, and even anticipating my needs. It was the summer of 1999, in San Ramon. At the final program there, I was debating when to go for darśhan. "Get in line," I heard the command very clearly in my head. Again, I knew Amma was talking to me. I hesitated to get in line because I didn't have a darśhan offering for Amma. I felt very empty-handed as I advanced in the darśhan line. Then, just as Amma was taking me into her embrace, I thought, "Amma, what I have to give you tonight is my heart." Immediately, Amma cupped my face in her hands, looked at me joyfully and said, "Mā?" I interpreted that as, "Really, do you mean that?" I responded with a very affirmative "Mā!" by which I meant, "Yes, I do mean that." Amma then called me her daughter for the very first time. Afterwards, I was so moved, I cried and cried. I knew my search was over. The Divine Mother herself had called me her daughter. Amma again reinforced that she knew the correct timing for everything, and she would take care of me. This was a very important reassurance, having grown up in the uncertain circumstances of my childhood.

***

The significance of Amma's gesture of cupping my face in her hands became apparent a few days later. I was working in a summer camp as a one-on-one aid for a child with autism. One day, as the child and I walked around a nearby lake, I noticed some poison hemlock growing nearby. Since this girl was at risk of grabbing some and eating it, I decided to hold her hands when we passed that way again.

Two young boys soon approached me. They asked me if I had change for ten dollars. I said I had no money. They pointed to the small purse I was wearing around my neck and said, "Don't you have any money in that purse?" That should have been a warning to me, but I was so focused on the child that I didn't read the cues properly. Seeing the child's behavior, they could tell she was not a typical child. I explained to them about autism.

Suddenly, I did not feel safe in the situation. The child was sitting on the ground, making hand gestures typical of children with autism. I decided it was time to go back to camp immediately. In the background, I heard one of the boys say, "Come on!" I was helping the child to stand up when the first punch hit my jaw. No one else was nearby. Feeling concerned they might try to harm the child, I instinctively put her in front of me, and we quickly walked towards the camp. The boys followed, and again one of them hit me in the jaw. The child winced when I was hit, and one of the boys accused me of hurting her! I looked at him and very clearly said, "No, you are hurting me, I am not hurting her." As we walked, I prayed to Amma under my breath saying, "Amma, I really need your help right now." After I was hit in the jaw a third time, the boys grabbed my purse, broke its thin strap, and ran away with it. Finally finding my voice, I yelled, "Amma!" as loud as I could. The voice seemed much deeper, louder, and stronger than my own voice. Hearing me yell, the boys looked in the purse, threw it in the air, and ran away. I retrieved my purse and rushed to the camp.

Later, when I was calmer, I realized that not only had Amma rescued us from those boys, but incredibly, there was no pain in my jaw, just a feeling of pressure, like something was holding my jaw. This feeling was in the exact place that Amma had held her hands on my face during that last darśhan. Amma knew what lay ahead, and she protected me by cupping my face.

Miraculously, I never felt any anger toward those boys. I was sad that they would try to hurt someone over something as trivial as money. I had recently read Amma's biography. I remembered that Amma received a lot of abuse in her youth, but she returned only love to her abusers. It made me wonder if I could remain free of anger toward someone who tried to harm me. This situation was Amma's answer. Of course, I still have to grow to maintain that state, but Amma showed me that it is possible.

I moved into the San Ramon āśhram on December 31, 1999. I started learning Malayāḷam, and I'd often try to say something simple to Amma during darśhan. The first time I tried, I was behind Amma's chair. Amma asked someone else if they spoke Malayāḷam. Several Malayālis enthusiastically said, "Amma, Santhi (pronounced 'Śhānti') speaks Malayāḷam. Santhi, say something for Amma." I squeaked out, "Ñān Malayāḷam paḍikkunnu" (I'm learning Malayāḷam), feeling like a small child who has just said her first word.

The next day was my third anniversary of meeting Amma. I learned how to say that in Malayāḷam. I rehearsed it in the darśhan line, but when I reached Amma, I forgot half of it. All I said was, "Amma, innu mūnnu varṣhamāyi..." Amma knew what I was trying to say and finished it for me, "Ammayē kandiṭṭu." Then Amma spoke through an interpreter and said, "You are saying it has been only three years, but Amma says it has been many, many, many more years that Amma knows you."

Amma says in her *Awaken Children* books that all the children who are with Amma now have been with her before. I thought I was not included because I didn't know Amma when those books were written. By her statement, Amma was also letting me know she had been with me even before I met her in this life. She let me know that it was she who and had lovingly cared for and protected me, even in the most difficult times. Amma says that she is aware of our experiences and knows when each one of us is in pain. Just as we would feel it if one of our hairs was pulled, even though we have so many hairs on our body.

***

During Amma's summer tour of 2002, I was asked to take some items that would be needed for the first program in New York as my carry-on luggage. We were at the Chicago airport, and the tour staff wanted to get some lunch. Our flight was departing in four hours, so there was plenty of time. However, I felt awkward taking these items into a restaurant. I asked some friends to bring me some pizza while I waited at the gate. Waiting alone at the gate, I decided to chant an archana. When I was nearly halfway through the archana, my pizza arrived. With the smell wafting under my nose, inviting me to eat, it was all I could do to keep chanting. It helped me then to remember Amma's saying that, "not even our next breath is in our control."

I finished the archana and noticed one of Amma's devotees who is a nurse by profession had just arrived. I started to eat my pizza. On the third bite, the pizza stuck my throat and I was suddenly choking. I didn't know what to do! I remembered from a first aid course that I could thrust my upper abdomen over the hard-edged back of a chair to give myself the Heimlich maneuver and thus dislodge the pizza, but the chairs were all occupied by sleeping people. I stood helplessly with very little air going past the pizza, not knowing how long I had until my windpipe would be completely blocked. Suddenly from behind, the nurse devotee reached around me and did the Heimlich maneuver. The piece of pizza came flying out, and fortunately, nothing else did.

Afterwards, when people who hadn't been there asked me what had happened, I burst into tears. Several people told me to tell Amma about the incident. And so, on the first day of the New York program, I went for darśhan. I had someone write in Malayāḷam what had happened to me, and planned to read it to Amma. However, when Amma saw the paper in my hand, she grabbed it and read it. It said that I'd gotten a piece of pizza stuck in my throat and I was scared because I couldn't breathe. Amma's reaction totally surprised me. Amma laughed like it was the funniest thing she'd ever read.

I remember thinking, "This is interesting, not at all how I thought Amma would react, but whatever, Amma knows best." Then I heard a darśhan attendant telling Amma what had happened in detail. I wanted to make sure Amma knew that at least I had finished that archana before eating the pizza. I reminded the attendant to tell Amma that part. Amma's response was, "Yes, but were you thinking of the pizza or the archana?" I had to admit I was thinking of the pizza! Amma then said, "Don't worry, you won't die like that." This showed me that Amma knows my whole life, and she is in charge! No need to worry. Unfortunately, I am very good at worrying.

After the darśhan, I was still a bit puzzled by Amma's reaction. I wondered why Amma had laughed when what happened was so serious. However, over the next few hours, I noticed a change in me. I no longer burst into tears when I talked about the incident. By her laughter, Amma had taken the trauma away completely. The Guru's responses are always what the situation demands, whether they are what we expect or not.

***

Sometimes Amma works with us by having us do something we think we don't want to do. Just before meeting Amma, I finished college and got into a teaching credential program. However, after completing the program, I didn't take a full-time job. I continued substitute teaching instead. I was concerned that a full-time teaching job would make it impossible for me to go on Amma's North America Tour, since the tour often started before my school year finished. But I noticed that Amma kept saying, "it is better to wear away than to rust away" in her satsangs. By only substitute teaching, I realized I wasn't using this teaching credential to its fullest.

When Swāmī Dayāmṛitānandajī was going to Australia one spring, I asked him to ask Amma if I should take a full-time teaching job, hoping she would say it wasn't necessary. When he returned from Australia about one month later, Swāmījī said, "Amma said you should." By this time, I had forgotten the question, so I said, "I should what?" "Take a full-time job," came his reply. Oh, no! That was not what I expected, but now I knew that come what may, I needed to follow Amma's instructions.

I'll admit, I did put in some effort towards getting a full-time job, but I didn't try too hard. I secretly hoped there was some way out of it. In the spring and summer of 2005, I spent six months in Amritapuri. Once I returned to San Ramon and started substitute teaching again, I began working in a Special Education classroom with another teacher, named Ruth. At the end of three weeks together, Ruth asked me why I didn't have a full-time job. She felt that I worked well with children who had special needs, so at the end of our time together, she gave me a glowing letter of recommendation, an application, and a list of job openings. I gave these papers a quick glance and put them away, thinking, "Maybe someday."

Two months later, Ruth suddenly called and said she had spoken about me to the administrators in the Special Education department. They were interested in hiring me if I'd obtain a Special Education credential. I started looking into it. Another two months passed. Ruth called me unexpectedly and said the Special Education department wanted to be notified as soon as I put in my application. The very next day, I applied.

Long story short — I got the job. Somehow Amma arranged it so I could go on every summer tour, and every November tour as well. I was even able to go to many other places with Amma including Tokyo, Australia, Singapore, Malaysia, Mauritius, Reunion Island, Dublin, Munich, and Paris. In addition, I was able to come to Amritapuri once a year as well.

I retired from that teaching position in June, 2021. The job was difficult at times, but I tried to do my work as service to Amma. Amma taught me the value of making my contribution to the world (not rusting away), and she gave me many opportunities to hold on to her lotus feet as she helped me navigate some very difficult situations.

There have been many instances, both big and small, where Amma has shown me that she is right here with me, all the time, and she will give me what I need at the right time. I will end with one last story, which again shows Amma's ability to know and respond to my thoughts. The year I met Amma, my biological mother was diagnosed with terminal lung cancer. At the time, I was the only family member available to assist her, so my sisters flew me to Phoenix, Arizona, where my mother was in the hospital.

Having just met Amma, I didn't have any devotional music, so a friend gave me a cassette that included several types of bhajans, some in English, and some more traditional Indian bhajans. The one bhajan that really called to me was *'Dē Darśhan Mā Dēvī Mā'* ('Let us see you, Divine Mother'). This bhajan became linked in my mind with my mother and her passing. At the time, I did not know the meaning of the words, but something really drew me to it. Later, I learned that the lyrics were about the impermanence of worldly relationships.

In the summer of 2018, I reached the age my mother was when she passed. I wanted to think about my mother, especially on that particular day. I was in Amritapuri at the time, and life here can be quite busy, so I soon forgot about my intention. It was a Friday night and Amma came for bhajans. For the final bhajan, Amma sang *Dē Darśhan Mā Dēvī Mā*. At first, I didn't get it. Then, about halfway through, I realized that Amma was singing this bhajan for me, to remind me to think about my mother! I cried for the rest of the bhajan! Amma was again showing me she knew my innermost thoughts and would help me to do the right thing, even if I forgot what I was going to do.

As if that wasn't enough, the next year, on the bhajan night closest to the anniversary of my mother passing, Amma sang this bhajan again! I remember wondering if Amma would sing it that night, as the program was drawing to a close. At first, the words to another bhajan were displayed on the screen, but then suddenly, Amma changed it to *Dē Darśhan Mā Dēvī Mā!*

Amma says that all our thoughts pass through her first. Amma knew that it would mean a lot to me, and it did, especially since it was my last bhajan night in Amritapuri before having to be away for two and a half years due to the pandemic.

I have had so many experiences of Amma showing me time and time again that she is there, not only for me, but for everyone. She is the one who is orchestrating our lives, giving us exactly what we need at the right time, though my mind often likes to worry about how things will turn out. Like the story Amma tells about the child who is not afraid while swimming because she knows that her mother is right there and will rescue her if she starts to drown, in the same way, we can have full confidence that our mother, our Amma, is even more capable of rescuing us should we start drowning in the ocean of saṁsāra, the cycle of birth and death.

We just have to trust Amma and hold on to her holy lotus feet. I am so grateful to Amma for all the experiences she has given me over the last twenty-four years, and for making herself so accessible to all of us. Even during the pandemic while being so physically distant, she has kept all of us close to her through her daily webcasts. Thank you, Amma.

16

Amma's Grace in Operation

Kalyana Sundaram - USA

It is customary to offer something when meeting a Satguru. Since everything belongs to her, I offer the one thing that is truly mine, my ego. May Amma bless me to convey whatever needs to be conveyed through this satsang. Meeting Amma was the most auspicious event of my life. Since then, every day for me is an 'auspicious day,' as that is one meaning of my name, Kalyāna.

I learned meditation for the first time when I was sixteen. I started practicing it and within a few months, I met Amma in 1991 in Nagercoil, Tamil Nadu. Someone informed my father that there was a saint by the name of Mata Amritanandamayi Devi coming to town. Whenever a jñāni, or wise person, comes to town, it is customary to get their blessings, so my entire family and I went to meet Amma and have her darśhan. Later, due to my father's work, we moved away from Nagercoil. I then shifted to the U.S. for work in 1998. Busy with work and life, I didn't see Amma again for twenty years. Talk about prārabdha![18] Then finally, it was Amma who pulled me back.

In 2011, I saw a photo of Amma at a local Indian grocery store in Cincinnati, Ohio. I thought, "I will see Amma again." The thought flashed and vanished immediately. I didn't take any action. A few months passed. I went to a yōga, studio and on the table was a photo of Amma where she has both of her arms outstretched. When I saw that photo, I had a strong feeling that

[18] Also known as 'prārabdha karma,' the part of our past karma that is the cause of our present birth.

Amma was calling me. But still, I didn't take any action. Months passed. Amma might have thought, "My son is not getting subtle clues. Let me send someone to drag him to me" — and she did.

I was doing volunteer work with an American named Daniel whom I had just met that day. While we were chatting, Daniel asked me, "Do you know the hugging saint?" I said, "Yes, I met her in India in 1991." He said, "Amma is coming to Detroit tomorrow (November 27, 2011). Do you want to come with me to see her? I'll give you a ride; we can start early tomorrow morning and return tomorrow night." I agreed.

Early the next day, Daniel picked me up from my home and drove me to Detroit, a four-hour drive from Cincinnati. I had Amma's darśhan and was completely overwhelmed. Amma asked me to sit by her right side. I sat on a stool and Amma spoke to me for quite some time. I told Amma that I had met her in Nagercoil in 1991, at Duthie school. That was my recollection. Amma responded, "Son, I met you in Nagercoil in 1991, at Hindu College not Duthie school." I was shocked. Over these past twenty years, I might have met a few hundred people. Amma met multiple millions across the globe. Yet, she is the one who remembered all the details. Then Amma spoke of the Amrita Vidyalayam schools and many of her other projects.

Later in the day, Daniel introduced me to one of his friends, a lady who was an Amma devotee. Daniel wanted to go home in the evening. I wanted to stay since the next day was the start of a three-day retreat. I tried to convince Daniel to stay as well, but in vain. Then it dawned on me that I could return with him to Cincinnati, pick up my car and some clothes, and go back to Detroit for the retreat immediately. That is what I did. All the craziness for Amma started from there!

After that Detroit program, I attended all of Amma's Midwest and East Coast programs the following year. From then onwards,

I attended Amma's entire North America Tour. But I never saw Daniel in Detroit or anywhere on Amma's North America Tour ever again. I never heard from him after that initial program, and was not able to reach him by any mode. Once, I asked the lady devotee that Daniel had introduced me to if she knew how Daniel was doing, and where he was. She said she didn't even know who I was talking about. That is why I have concluded that Daniel was sent by Amma on a task. He disappeared into thin air as soon as his task was completed.

Once I was at Amma's Boston program walking outside the program venue. A curious hotel customer asked me what was going on inside the hall. As you may know, it can be a daunting task to explain who Amma is to a new person who has never heard of her. I tried my level best to introduce Amma. My intention was just to bring him inside the program hall which was only fifty feet away so he could have a glimpse of Amma. I failed at my task and was upset about missing a great opportunity to bring that person to Amma.

Then I remembered a story which helped me gain some perspective. Once there were two sisters; only one became Amma's devotee. After both sisters had their first darśhan, the new devotee sister kept insisting that the other sister should keep coming for Amma's darśhan. That other sister refused for more than ten years. Finally, one year she relented and went for Amma's darśhan. Afterwards, she was so angry at herself for missing the opportunity to see Amma in all those intervening years. So, she asked Amma during her next darśhan, "Amma, my sister kept asking me to come for darśhan for more than ten years. Why did I waste all these years before meeting you again?" Amma said, "Daughter, it is not you, but I who decide when you come and meet me." So, it is Amma who decides if we can be here. Otherwise, even if we are next door to the āśhram, we cannot come in.

***

All human beings desire to be happy, always. But the objects of desire keep changing over time, place, circumstances, and other factors. The mind wants to keep expanding. It always wants more, better, and different. Since we limit our identity within the boundaries of our human form, and within the confines of the senses, we often restrict our capabilities. We impose the same limitations on mahātmās and on avatārs — incarnations of God, like Amma. This is a huge mistake. As Amma says, we are not small kittens, we are roaring lions!

Amma once mentioned that one can move the Himālayas easier than moving one's ego. When I first heard that, it really put the task at hand into perspective. I also wondered about removing misconceptions in reaching life's goal of realizing one's true nature. Since everything is understood through this body-mind-intellect complex, it is important that we understand its nature clearly.

Amṛitabindu Upaniṣhad, verse 2 says:

> *mana ēva manuṣhyāṇāṁ kāraṇaṁ bandhamōkṣhayōḥ*
> 'The mind alone is the cause of bondage and freedom for human beings.'

Desires are what bind the mind. If the root cause of desire is discovered, there won't be any bondage. The root cause of desire is ignorance. Ignorance can be overcome once we know our real nature which is the Self. With Self-realization, desires may come and go without causing any harm.

First one sees the Self as an object to be desired and obtained; then one sees the Self as the void, or emptiness. Finally, one recognises the Self to be one's own Self. Attaining this at last, there is no seeing because seeing is being. There is no seer and seen, only being.

However, as long as the ego is in the driver's seat, our understanding is flawed and skewed. That is because everything we understand is based on knowledge previously obtained. Past experiences are stored as memory. When encountering new experiences, the ego tries to understand by combining memory and sensory information. As a result, the ego never meets the present moment as it really is without the burden of past knowledge. This raises the question of how to meet the present moment as it is. This "how" question is a big challenge since it introduces time into the mix and also implies observer and observed duality. One thinks, "I will do something over a period of time, and I will achieve the desired result after that time." This is how the mind escapes the present moment. And it all happens in a split second without our awareness.

The essence of karma, or action, is to know the truth of oneself by enquiring, "Who am I, the doer, the one who initiates karmas?" Unless the doer of karmas, the ego, is annihilated through enquiry, the supreme bliss of perfect peace, which is the result of karma yōga, cannot be achieved.

Everything we see, hear, and say is relative. We say the sun rises in the east even though we all know the sun neither rises nor sets. What is east or west to planet Earth floating in space? Of course, a reference point is needed for such things and for many day-to-day practical applications. What is this point of reference? It is the ego. But do we need this point of reference for the inward journey? To realize what is permanent? No. This is not denying the usefulness and utility of relative knowledge. It has its own place. This is where the Upaniṣhadic dictum 'nēti, nēti' comes in handy. Keep rejecting the unreal as 'not this, not this.' And, like Amma says, we should be able to turn the mind on and off like a fan. We should be able to let go of thoughts when we choose to go inward.

I have mentioned all this so that the challenge at hand is clear. When we are fixed on the goal and committed to it, the rest is mere perseverance, continuous effort with patience and without expectation. That is easier said than done.

***

Though I only met Amma in 1991, she was helping me and guiding me even from childhood, though I didn't realize it at that time. Growing up during my school and college days, I always felt very lucky. I didn't have the concepts or maturity to recognize the hidden hand of Amma. Not that I have reached maturity now, but at least I know that Amma's grace is in operation — and I only know that much by her grace as well. After all, we can block the rays of a bright sun by merely closing our two little eyelids.

When I was in sixth grade, I was ill with brain fever. I was admitted to the hospital ICU. The doctors told my parents they didn't know if I would survive. Even if I did survive, they said I would either be paralyzed, or have major brain damage. None of that happened. I remember very well being so weak; my youngest sister used to tease me by placing a coin on my finger. I couldn't even lift it, so the coin would drop. She would laugh. She was seven years old at that time. Later, I walked out of the hospital without any disability. It was purely by Amma's grace.

A few years back I planned to join Amma's Europe Tour. I had all the required visas except for the visa to Ireland. The UK program was the last one scheduled on the Europe Tour. So, I started the tour in Barcelona without the Irish visa. Then, someone informed me that if I could get a UK stamp right away,

I could travel to Ireland. So, I decided to fly to London for the night, get the UK entry stamp at the airport, crash at a friend's place, and return to Barcelona the next morning. It sounded like a perfect plan.

I went to ask Amma's permission to fly to London for the night to get the UK stamp. As soon as the question was asked by the interpreter, Amma turned to me and gestured, "Shhhh," keeping one finger across her lips. It was very clear to me that Amma was saying no. But she didn't say any words. Since the Malayāḷam interpreter didn't see Amma's hand gesture, he probably thought her silence meant yes. He said, "Yes, you can go." My prārabdha came through his words. I got off the stage and booked a ticket to London.

I stayed in London for the night and returned to Barcelona the next morning, but at the airport, someone stole a pouch from my backpack which contained my passport, my money for the entire Europe tour, and my bank cheque book. I noticed it was gone after reaching the Barcelona program venue. At Amma's direction, I filed a police report, obtained a new passport in Madrid, and had to get all the visa stamps again. I missed most of the tour. I could only join the last two programs in Milan and London. Amma tried to save me from that impending pain and suffering, but in my greed not to miss a single program I missed almost 75% of the Europe Tour that year. Upon my return to the Milan program, I went to Amma and apologized for not listening to her. Amma said that when prārabdha karma is strong, it will pull you relentlessly in a certain direction.

I learned a very important and costly lesson. When the Mother of the Universe, who creates multiple universes with the blink of an eye, tries to save you, it can happen only if you are open to it. When prārabdha karma pulls us strongly towards one direction, we need absolute śhraddhā, full attention and unwavering faith in the Guru's words, to recognize it and resist that pull. Why aren't we often able to do that? Because of our saṁskāras, our past impressions, and because we have considered the unreal to be real for many, many births.

Swāmī Amṛitaswarūpānandajī once mentioned that if one follows Amma's instructions, one can reach life's goal in three years. Later, Amma said, "Why three years, it can even be achieved in less than a year. All that is needed is intensity." "How does one get that intensity," another devotee asked. Amma replied, "Just pray."

All it takes is a split-second glance from a mahātmā, then a person's life is set. Those who have come within the ambit of the Guru's gracious glance will be saved and will not get lost. Still, each person should make the effort to pursue the path shown by the Guru. We all are very lucky to be saved by our Guru, Amma.

It is said in the *Kaṭha Upaniṣhad,* 'The Self can be attained only by one who seeks to know it. To that one, the Self reveals its true nature.' (1.2.23) But in order to reach that state, one must have exhausted all possible efforts sincerely.

***

One year, at the end of Amma's North America Tour in mid-July, I was really upset. Amma was about to return to India. Her sixtieth birthday would be in late September. I could not visit Amritapuri to attend Amma's birthday celebration, because of visa and green card restrictions. I didn't have a green card at that time, but I was in the queue. Like most people, I had been meticulously following the rules and regulations related to obtaining one. I calculated I would get the green card in another eighteen months based on the priority processing schedule. I kept thinking, "How can I arrange to go to Amma's birthday?" At that stage of my green card application, I could not travel abroad. Then on September 13, I got an email notification stating that my processing date was current. All of a sudden, the whole system had moved forward by exactly eighteen months.

I was thrilled and couldn't believe what I was seeing. On September 18, I got another notification stating my green card application was approved. On Friday, September 20, I was given the FedEx tracking number of the package where the physical green card was shipped. On Tuesday, September 24, I received the green card and booked the flight to Kochi for the next day, September 25th. I reached Amritapuri on Friday, September 27 in the morning, and returned to the U.S. on Sunday, September 29. I'm so happy and grateful to have been able to attend Amma's birthday program. A few days later, just out of curiosity, I checked the priority green card processing dates. They had gone back to eighteen months waiting time, just as they had been three weeks earlier.

Once, I asked Swāmī Amṛitaswarūpānandajī how to surrender completely. Swāmījī replied, "Surrender is a single-step journey, like jumping into a river. You take the leap, and then you are in the river. You can't plan, or strategize to make it happen. Just prepare yourself and wait for that moment of surrender to happen."

For most, life is like a house of cards. If you take out any single card, the entire structure can collapse. But if that single card is an instruction from Amma which is followed completely, faithfully, and with absolute intensity, the only thing that will collapse is the false notion that "I am the body/mind/intellect," the notion that "I am the doer," — the structure built by the ego. Our entire life is usually focused on 'doing' and 'having.' But pure 'being' doesn't require anything. Just be.

By the time one really understands the name of the game, one may be already quite old and not able to do much. Amma's līlā, her divine play, is analogous to a soccer game, played on the turf of life. If one understands that it's all Amma's līlā, one can enjoy the game of life. Then, the movement in a particular direction makes sense. Otherwise, it is just random wandering or running endlessly and aimlessly without knowing the rules of the game. One might mistakenly think that random wanderings are progress.

A few years back, I had three major car accidents within two years. None of them were my fault. In two of them, I was rear-ended, and in all of them, my car was totaled. I emerged unharmed in all cases purely by Amma's grace. Those were some close calls. I can only pray that when the life force leaves this body, it will be in full awareness, thinking of Amma's lotus feet and chanting Amma's divine name.

I do not know what is the best way to reach the goal. Amma knows what is best for her child. May all of Amma's children be finely tuned instruments in her hands. Amma, I offer my infinite gratitude for everything you have bestowed upon me, even though I am the least deserving child.

17

Compassionate Amma Comes Down to Our Level to Teach

Priya – USA

I first met Amma in 1997 at the San Ramon āśhram when I was eight years old. Amma often mentions how the Guru comes down to the disciple's level of understanding in order to guide them on the spiritual path. As an eight-year old, my level of understanding was that all goodness resided in things that sparkled, specifically crystals. I was obsessed with crystals: big crystals, small crystals, sugar crystals — any crystals.

So you can imagine my joy when, on that first day in the āśhram, before meeting Amma, I stumbled upon a beautiful little crystal while roaming the āśhram grounds. I was absolutely elated to find this little treasure. Later that day, it was time for my first darśhan. While waiting in the darśhan queue, I held on tightly to my new beloved crystal.Then a funny thing happened. When it was my turn to receive Amma's darśhan, I immediately forgot about my love for the crystal in my hand. I found myself completely transfixed by Amma's divine presence and there was no longer any trace of desire for the little rock I had held so dear just moments before. While in Amma's arms, I felt the desire to offer the crystal to her and she accepted it.

The next morning when I arrived at the program, I hopped out of the car and to my astonishment, I saw something glinting in the sunlight on the ground nearby. Imagine my surprise when I picked up another crystal! This one was at least double the size and far more beautiful than the crystal from the day before. I could hardly contain my excitement. At the time, I thought, "Oh, Amma must have given me this bigger and better crystal because I gave her my smaller crystal yesterday." Then it dawned on me...Amma is magic!

As time went on and my relationship with Amma evolved over the years, I gradually learned that the real magic is Amma's unconditional love which tirelessly transforms her children's lives day after day. I am always and forever grateful that Amma firmly took hold of my hand and came down to the level of a crystal obsessed eight-year-old, so many years ago.

Learning IAM

In the past I felt a bit embarrassed because although I was very lucky to meet Amma at a young age, I struggled with depression – which I thought was a 'non-spiritual' person's problem. I eventually learned that depression, or suffering, can in fact be a gift in that it can deepen our relationship with Amma. When stuck in a hole and clawing our way out towards the sunlight we're forced to surrender to something greater than our own will, in other words, to Amma.

My depression became more disruptive during my teenage years. I often felt like I was trapped inside a dark cloud; the sun was shining just outside where I could neither see its light nor feel its warmth. Seeing Amma on her U.S. tour and in Amritapuri became like an oasis in a desert for me. My entire year revolved around seeing Amma. I started with the San Ramon program and then went to a few summer tour stops. But the culmination was one month of pure joy in Amritapuri. I lived for that precious time with Amma. It kept me going for the rest of the months when I had to be away from her. While spending time in her physical presence, I felt like I could finally glimpse rays of sunlight peeking through the cloudiness of my mind. The only problem was that I didn't know how to carry that optimism into the rest of the year.

To make matters worse, when I was fourteen years old and living in Los Angeles, my mental wellbeing was tightly wound up with my appearance. If I looked in the mirror and didn't like what I saw that day, my mind would sink further into a depressive state. I recently found one of my old journals. It had a page that summed up my mindset in those days. The heading of the journal page read: 'Goals for This Year.' That was followed by a list of three things I wanted to achieve in the coming months:

1. Learn to rollerblade
2. Lose five pounds
3. Get enlightened

Needless to say, I had some work to do on sorting out my priorities. At that age, I hadn't had much practice with meditation except during Amma's programs. In 2003, in San Ramon, I was invited to take part in Amma's IAM (Integrated Amrita Meditation Technique) classes. Although I wasn't very interested and would have rather hung out with my friends, thanks to Amma's grace, I attended the introductory session. The instructor explained the many benefits of IAM meditation: "Less stress, more happiness, inner peace..." It all sounded great but I was still unmotivated. Then the instructor continued, "It gives you a glowing complexion..."

Cha-ching! Those were the magic words for my teenage ears. What I didn't understand then was that 'a glowing complexion' referred to the inner light that shines forth from doing spiritual practices. At the time, I translated 'a glowing complexion' to mean it would make me more physically attractive, with nice smooth skin. Therefore, when the instructor mentioned this as a side benefit to doing IAM every day, I was immediately on board.

From that point onward, I made sure I always did IAM every day before school without exception. I would wake up extra early, my dad would bring me a cup of chai, and I would plop myself down in front of the altar to begin. I soon noticed that the more I practiced IAM, the happier and more connected to Amma I felt throughout the day. The clouds of my depressive mind became lighter, and I felt like I could start to glimpse the sun. This brings to mind Amma's example of taking a sleeping pill unknowingly and still feeling its effects. Even though my initial intention for starting a meditation practice was having a 'glowing complexion,' the actual effects were, and still are, profoundly life-altering.

Facing Anxiety

In my experience, depression often comes hand-in-hand with fear or anxiety. And, as many of us know, the only remedy for anxiety is to surrender things we can't control at Amma's lotus feet.

Once the pandemic began, my dance with anxiety became especially active. When the travel bans first came into effect and I learned that I would not be able to see my Amma, I realized my worst fears had come true. I felt utterly helpless. Anxiety started to increase in my daily life. For example, even when I went out to run a small errand like grocery shopping, my thoughts would go on a rampage the moment I left the house, "Did I turn the oven off? What if I didn't, and the whole house burns down? Did I lock the door? What if I forgot, and a thief breaks in. Did I feed the cat? Wait, I don't even have a cat. What if I actually do have a cat and I just somehow forgot?" This nonsensical stream of thought continued until I drove back home and confirmed that the oven was off, the door was locked, and indeed, I did not have a cat.

Each time I let fearful thoughts grab hold of my mind, I reinforced those thought pathways more and more. Then, during one of Swāmī Dayāmṛitānandajī's satsangs, he explained one of Amma's teachings that struck a chord with me. He said, "Fear is the absence of love." After hearing that, I made a promise to tackle my fear thoughts by imagining I was in Amma's embrace and bathed in her anxiety-vanquishing love. I may have a long way to go, but I pray that Amma's love conquers all of our fears and anxieties in life, so we can experience the sweet surrender to her lotus feet.

Fear of Death

One of the most impactful lessons Amma has taught me about facing fear happened in 2012. My father passed away that year, following a difficult illness. The day he passed, it felt like the world stopped turning on its axis. I thought, "How could someone who was so important to me just disappear forever?" One moment he was a living, breathing, talking person and the next moment, he was a silent, motionless form in an ICU bed. That was a very difficult time, and soon after my father's death (I'm not proud to admit it), I started praying that Amma would let me die so I wouldn't have to ever experience that kind of pain again — the pain of losing someone I love.

I had struggled for years with the concept of death. It was too abstract for my stubborn mind to grasp. Amma says, "Death is not the end; it's rather like the period at the end of a sentence." Although this teaching repeated itself in my mind over and over again, I still could not grasp its meaning on a deeper level.

As I mentioned before, out of her compassion, Amma comes to the level of understanding of each person in order to guide them on the path. A couple of nights following my father's passing, I had a vivid dream in which Amma helped me understand her teaching about death. I'll give a little background. While taking a design class in college, I struggled with the concept of perspective drawing of geometric shapes, like cubes. I had been studying the subject intensely and still couldn't quite understand how it worked. The professor would try to teach me how to draw the sides of a cube in a mathematically correct way, but my attempts always ended up looking more like a shape monster had sneezed a pile of lines onto the paper.

So, during my dream, I saw the sides of a cube being drawn. I saw the lines converge at their vanishing point – the point in space where lines meet and appear to end, but in reality, they just continue beyond the capabilities of our limited visual perspective. The same phenomenon presents itself when we look down a long road, and it seems to disappear in the distance. In the dream, I finally understood the concept I had been studying, and far more importantly, I grasped Amma's teaching about death. I understood that death was like a vanishing point; life continues beyond death. It's only our flawed perception that causes suffering. By using a context I was familiar with, Amma showed me a concrete way to think about death, and better understand her precious teachings on the subject.

This new understanding provided a lot of relief at the time of my father's death, but still, the fear of losing loved ones persists, and drains my mental energy. For example, if a loved one doesn't reply to my text message right away, my mind spirals out of control and I come close to tears, thinking that something terrible has happened to them. If they report having a headache or symptom of any sort, I immediately become Dr. Google and try to find out what could be wrong. Worse yet, in the middle of the night, I will frequently shake my husband, Akhilesh, to make sure he is still breathing – even though I am still asleep myself and have no recollection of having done that in the morning. Needless to say, I am still quite a slave to the fear of death. Thankfully, Amma has helped me chip away at this negative mental pattern during these past few weeks here in Amritapuri.

Quarantine

When the Covid-19 travel ban finally lifted and Akhilesh and I were able to book our flights to Amritapuri, I was extremely anxious and determined to do everything in my power to make sure *nothing* prevented us from being with Amma this time. After almost three years of being away from the āśhram, and two and a half years away from Amma, we arrived here in beautiful Amritapuri, the home of our hearts. Since our trip was limited to three weeks due to visa and work constraints, I was determined not to let *anything* stand in the way of spending the maximum amount of time with our Amma. This meant that we were extra happy that there was no longer a required quarantine period, as long as we tested negative upon arrival, which luckily, we did. But as most of you can already guess, things didn't go exactly as we had planned.

A few days later, Akhilesh was feeling a bit off and tested positive for Covid, and immediately went to begin his eleven day quarantine. Two days later, I ended up testing positive as well, and was informed that I would need to quarantine for thirteen days. The thought of being away from Amma for thirteen days out of our twenty-one day trip was devastating. Through my sadness, I was unable to see that Amma was already creating circumstances so that I could feel closer to her than ever before. Before I continue I'd like to express my deepest gratitude to our Amritapuri family for all of the support and help they gave us during that time. Their love and kindness touched both of our hearts, and we will be forever grateful.

For the first five days of quarantine, my mindset was pretty solid. When people would ask how it's going, I would answer,

"It's really nice. Such a great opportunity for sādhanā." After about nine days of quarantine, my attitude shifted a bit. I would say, "It's not ideal. But at least we'll be out of here in three days after we test negative tomorrow." On the tenth day, when I again tested positive, my attitude was not optimal. I thought, "Ok, I've had enough. This is too much." At that point, when it became clear that I'd only get out of quarantine on day fifteen, I couldn't hold back the tears any longer. As the days went by I remembered the world outside of our quarantine room less and less, and I would awaken in the mornings from a night of vivid dreams only to be confused about which world was real. Were the dreams real, or was this waking world real? Was I really in this flat away from Amma, or was this just a dream created in my mind overnight? Or...maybe I'm just going crazy during quarantine!

The theme of Amma coming down to my level of understanding to help me grasp her teachings has been an ongoing gift in my life for which I am profoundly grateful. During those quarantine days she showered some extra compassion on me.

I remembered one dream I had in particular in which I found an old lamp. It was very beautiful and I was excited to take it home with me. I was planning how to transport it to my house, where to put it when I got there, etc. But when I woke up, I was confused as to why I didn't have the lamp with me. It felt so real and my attachment to the lamp was so strong. How could I form such an attachment to something that was not even real? I then recalled what Amma says about life being like a dream, and God-realization being like waking up from that dream. As Amma says, the dream we create is exactly that; a product of our own creation, our own mind.

For me, this dream and subsequent understanding from it was yet another gift from Amma, pointing out another precious teaching about death and the fact that ultimately nothing in this life is permanent. I'm reminded of a verse from one of Amma's *bhajans* titled *'Manassē Nin Svantamāyi'* ('Remember, O mind, this supreme truth that nobody is your own!'):

> *dayāmayiyākum dēvī bhayarūpam eṭuttālum*
> *padatārilkkiṭakkuvōr dhanyarāṇavar*
> 'Even if the compassionate Dēvī takes on a fearful form, those who lie at her feet are blessed.'

During my invaluable time in quarantine, I started thinking that maybe sometimes, out of her compassion, Amma needs to take on a fearful form in order to shake our minds out of their sticky patterns and show us that the only true refuge in the end is her lotus feet. In my case, the 'fearful form' seemed to come as a fifteen-day quarantine and I will always be grateful for it.

Distractions

Being in Amritapuri is a rare blessing in itself, especially since living in the world has so many distractions – especially nowadays with so many screens constantly vying for our attention. Some time back while in the U.S., I was writing notes on my phone about what to say in today's talk. Suddenly an email notification appeared at the top of my phone screen. The preview of the email read, 'Save Big on Spring Essentials.' Without a second thought, I clicked the email notification and was transported away from thoughts of Amma's teachings and inner contemplation, and plopped into the hands of shopping māyā. As I scrolled through product advertisements, I had the familiar upsurge of dopamine that comes with the possibility of consuming new toys. Then I saw a notification for Instagram and opened a message to see a funny video. Then, I received a text message, which of course again I opened. Several minutes later, I became bored and decided to return to what I was doing before all of these notifications came.

But, what was I doing before? It took several moments before I could recall what my original task had been. I felt like Nārada who leaves to retrieve water for Kṛiṣhṇa, forgets his original task, and becomes ensnared in the world of māyā. In my case, instead of being distracted by a spouse, children, and a devastating flood like in the story, my focus was derailed by advertisements and funny cat videos.

Recently during one of Amma's beach meditations, a six-year-old French girl spoke with Amma on the topic of the eternal and the non-eternal. Amma asked her if she was able to differentiate between the eternal and non-eternal during the time she spent in the West. The little girl spoke about going through shops and closing her eyes so that she wouldn't see the toys and become attracted to them. Amma then said that if you chase after toys, then you miss the diamonds, but if you focus on the real diamonds, then everything else comes. This little girl was practicing Amma's teachings in a very concrete way, even at such a young age.

While witnessing this special interaction, I thought to myself, "If a girl who's so young can imbibe Amma's teachings and shut her eyes to the temptations of worldly desires, then at the very least, I should be able to stop being so easily distracted by all the screens and the 'worthless shimmering seashells that glitter like precious gems' in my life, in order to focus on what is truly real. I pray that we all find the strength to avert our eyes from those shimmering seashells and focus on the only true source of permanence in this life — Amma's love.

18

Living in the Garden of Amma's Grace

Leena – Mauritius

The last two years have been quite challenging for everyone who has been away from Amma. Since 2007 I have been in Amma's physical presence at least once a year almost every year. It has always been my primary objective to carry out my responsibilities at home and simultaneously plan trips to see Amma and join her tours wherever and whenever possible. Out of her compassion, Amma has extended the daily webcast to all her children outside Amritapuri. This has indeed been a way to continue to focus on Amma and be part of the Amritapuri family. I am so grateful to Amma and the entire webcast team for bringing Amritapuri to our homes. These daily programs have not only enabled me to see Amma every day, but have also helped me to organize my daily activities in an effective way. I plan all my tasks, be it going to work, cooking, or doing my archana in such a way that I can be free to participate in the daily program with Amma which is live-streamed in the evening in Mauritius.

My employer offered one day of telework per week for all employees... it goes without saying that I selected Tuesdays to work from home. This gave me the opportunity to watch Amma give prasād on Tuesdays while attending to my other duties and responsibilities. The daily webcasts have also helped us to be safe at home, as we all are glued to our television screens instead of going out to socialize. Without the daily programs, we would surely use our time in unnecessary thoughts and actions. Amma is guiding us in our daily activities even though we are far away from her physical presence. We listen to bhajans, satsangs, we meditate, and we hear all of Amma's young kids offer their lively talks and songs. We also get glimpses of Amma's dog Śhakti during ārati, and we see images of all the blooming flowers, and all the birds and animals in the āśhram every day. This has all become part and parcel of our daily life.

I have always been attracted to nature and enjoy spending time in the garden. I wanted to create a greenhouse and a vegetable garden at my home. During my last visit to Amritapuri in 2019 Amma blessed the idea. Amma says, "Children, nature stands before us as a symbol of renunciation. Like mountains, rivers and trees, every single object in nature is teaching us lessons on selflessness. Look at a tree — it gives fruit, shade and imparts cool air. Even as it is being felled, it offers shade to the person cutting it down. Similarly, every being and organism in nature practices renunciation in some way or the other."

Once Amma gave her blessings for the greenhouse and garden, most of our endeavors to create them started in March 2020 during the pandemic lockdown period. With Amma's grace we seized the opportunity of the lockdown to use our free time to undergo training for this project. The first seeds in our large garden were sown in 2020 on Guru Pūrṇimā. We planted 1008 plants. Our first harvest was used in the preparation of Mahāprasād, a blessed meal for devotees, at the Mauritius āśhram. Currently, our tomatoes are purchased by Amma's devotees, as well as other vegetable sellers at the market. Some of the devotees even order vegetables for their family and friends. We pray that the money gained from the cultivation of these crops contributes to supporting the humanitarian projects of Embracing the World.

During the last two years, like all of Amma's children around the world, I have missed being physically close to Amma very much. Almost every day before going to sleep I would imagine that I was swimming from Mauritius to Amritapuri – specifically from Mauritius at the southern end of the Indian Ocean, to the seashore in front of the Amrita Sāgar building in Amritapuri. At other times, to make it more realistic, I would even imagine passing through Sri Lanka and arrive on the coast next to the āśhram. Then I would walk my way to the āśhram.

My second imagination would be that I would arrive at the main gate of the āśhram and it would always be closed. I would yearn for only Amma to welcome me at the gate, not anyone else. All this sounds crazy. These are some things that for sure will never come true, whether it's swimming to Amritapuri or having Amma welcome me at the gate. But Amma says, "Innocent prayer is a very powerful way to please the Lord. You don't need to be a scholar to do that." Amma knows each of our desires, whether they are big or small.

***

I finally arrived in Amritapuri on January 19th, 2022. I did not swim, I flew! I was housed in the Amrita Sāgar building, facing the seashore. Upon seeing the ocean I felt I had reached my destination by Amma's grace. Traveling from Mauritius to Amritapuri had been a smooth journey. My deepest gratitude goes to Amma, the quarantine team, and to the international office staff for assisting devotees from different countries to arrive at the āśhram, and to finally receive Amma's darśhan. They all are indeed instruments in Amma's hands.

As I mentioned, my second daily imagination included the desire for Amma to welcome me at the gate. And so I thought to myself, this desire would surely remain unrealized. However, when walking to attend the evening program while in quarantine, we as a group, were stuck behind a closed gate. It was the gate to Amma's pathway and it was closed to us because it was time for Amma to walk to the stage. She needed clear, unobstructed access to do that. Upon seeing the quarantine group, Amma stopped and asked for the gate to be opened. We spread out in front of Amma, looking at her, all the while maintaining proper social distancing. Amma enquired whether everything was going well and let us know that there was a dedicated space at the back of the hall for the quarantine people. She also told us to come take prasād the next day. That was a wonderful welcome for me. Amma had fulfilled the desire which at first seemed crazy and not so significant. Amma says that if we take one step towards God, God will take one hundred steps towards us. When we are far away from Amma physically, we should always contemplate that Amma is already with us, and we will soon be graced with her physical presence.

In one of Swāmī Pūrṇāmṛitānandajī's weekly talks he said that we need to do our sādhanā regularly and activate the Dēvī within. Swāmījī said, "Amma's children have experienced directly from Amma love from the Divine Mother. These memories sustain confidence and inspire us. The seeker's thirst for his inner deity will lead Dēvī, or Amma, to send invisible hands to help. Dēvī's invisible hand is there around the sādhak (spiritual seeker), protecting him, and comforting him."

As a child, I was always attracted to the goddess Durgā. I would imagine how beautiful she would be in real life, given that as an idol or in photos she always appears to be very beautiful. Once I had a dream in which I heard a loud noise outside. As I went out to see what was happening, I could see a dark-hued lady adorned in a beautiful sāri riding an elephant with her curly black hair bouncing in the air. She was queen-like, and behind her there was a chariot full of colorful majestic-looking sāris. I felt she was Durgā Dēvī herself, but I was wondering why she was of dark complexion. This dream was very vivid at the time, but I forgot all about it over the years.

***

I work for an international organization and have had many opportunities to attend overseas training. Somehow the training divinely coincided with Amma's programs in Europe and in the United States. I fondly recall my first two months of overseas training in Washington, at the end of which I had decided to fly to Amma's San Ramon program. It was my first time meeting Amma outside of Mauritius. I was a bit anxious since I was a first-time traveler in the U.S. I did not know anyone, nor did I have any idea how to get to the program. I booked a hotel closest to the āśhram, praying that I would find my way to the program. The night I arrived at the hotel, the fire alarm went off, and everyone had to be evacuated and wait outside. A lady standing next to me started to enquire where I was from and the purpose of my visit. I told her that I was there for a spiritual retreat. The lady told me she was also there for the same program. She said she would go to the program early since she was involved in preparing flower garlands to welcome Amma. She then offered me a ride to and from the program every day for my whole stay. That very night, Amma's invisible hands were already there to help me.

That trip was also the one where I first saw Amma in Dēvī Bhāva. She was adorned in a majestic-looking green sāri and as she stood up, with her beautiful hair bouncing in the air, I immediately recalled my dream from long ago. Hence, I felt my wish of seeing Durgā Dēvī in person was fulfilled. In a book by Swami Paramātmānandajī someone asked him if dreams of Amma are real. Was Amma really appearing to the dreamer, or was it just a figment of the dreamer's imagination? Swāmījī stated that such dreams of Amma are real. In fact, it is traditionally accepted that when you dream of a mahātmā, a saint, a god, or a deity, it is due to grace — it is a blessing. Dreaming of them happens not just because you are thinking about that being. It's due to the saṅkalpa, the divine resolve of that being that you are able to dream about them. Swāmījī also says that the dream from a mahātmā will be vivid, and that there will be a kind of thrilling or blissful feeling in it, a feeling of great love.

It was indeed by such grace that Amma came to see me, even before I met her. Amma says, "Nothing in this universe is accidental, not even creation. If it were, the whole universe would be chaotic. But the inherent order in nature and its extraordinary beauty indicate that behind the workings of the universe are an expansive heart and an intellectual power that the human mind can never fathom." Sometimes situations unfold without us being aware of the end result. Self-effort is important, but Guru's grace is more important. Amma says, "the light of Guru's grace helps us see and remove obstacles in our path."

***

Let me recall an incident to illustrate this point. I traveled from Mauritius to Japan in 2016 to be able to experience my first Guru Pūrṇimā celebration with Amma. Some friends and I arrived in Japan the day before the program began. In our excitement, we went to the program venue hoping we could assist in any way, knowing there was always a lot to be done before Amma's arrival. To our dismay we were told that the venue would only be opened on the day of the program. Quite disappointed, my friends and I decided to return to the hotel. However, even at the hotel, we were restless and could not shake off the idea of joining the Japanese devotees to assist with sēvā.

We found the āśhram address online and put it into Google Maps. We headed towards the āśhram not knowing exactly where we were going. With the help of local people we took two trains and one bus to reach the station nearest the āśhram. Once there, we could see the āśhram on the map, however, it could not be found in real life. We were lost. My friends and I started to ask people for assistance. We were amazed at how the Japanese people were so nice and helpful. One lady agreed to walk with us to help us find the āśhram. But despite her great efforts, she could not find the way and asked another person in a shop if he could help us. That person just left his shop open and walked with us to assist us again. It was amazing how they did not speak much English but were willing to go to any extent to help us. We walked through several streets for another twenty minutes. It seemed like we were very near the āśhram but still could not find it. Finally, our guide kindly told us that he had to take leave of us, as he had to go back to his shop. We were grateful to him for his help. After an hour of searching to no avail we decided to head back to the station.

We turned the corner and just then, we smelled the fragrance of 'Guru Kṛipā' ('Guru's grace') sandalwood incense, a special variety that you can get only in Amritapuri. We thought we might be having an olfactory hallucination. We followed the fragrance and reached a junction where we were amazed to see an Indian man wearing a dhōti[19] standing on the street. My friends and I walked up to him and spontaneously said, "Ōm Namaḥ Śhivāya."[20] To our disbelief he replied, "Ōm Namaḥ

---

[19] Traditional outer garment worn by Indian men.

[20] 'Salutations to Śhiva, the auspicious one, the inner Self,' a famous mantra that is also used as a greeting in Amma's āśhrams.

Śhivāya. Get inside, Amma is coming." What a divine surprise! Inside the strong fragrance of 'Guru Kṛipā' intensified. It was a wonder how indeed our Guru's grace had reached us through a Guru Kṛipā incense stick!

Everything was ready to welcome Amma and after a short while she arrived. My friends and I were asked to hold a curtain aside for Amma to enter the hallway. Later that night Amma gave a beautiful short satsang in which she said in this day and age it is easy to develop the same bhakti (devotion) as the gōpīs of Vṛindāvan who were the milkmaid devotees of Lord Kṛiṣhṇa. Amma also mentioned how her darśhan has become quicker over the years. Amma said she would love to spend more time with each of her children, but due to the increasing number of people wanting to see Amma, the time spent with each one had to be reduced. Amma then compared the quick darśhan with getting prasād at a temple. She said no matter how little we get, we feel content and cherish the sweetness of the prasād. Similarly, I believe we should feel grateful and cherish every moment we have with Amma. After the trip, when discussing that satsang with my friends, our hearts felt so full. We could not understand why Amma said all that when she had already given us so much.

***

During the pandemic Amma's words came to mind especially when we could not be in her physical presence. Moments with Amma are so precious, we should not take them for granted. We must cherish all our memories with Amma and keep them alive in our hearts. Amma says, "You cannot predict when grace takes place, you can only wait. Relax." Behind every small action, behind every piece of advice and encouragement that you get from friends, relatives, and even from strangers; from our Amma dreams, from divine contemplation, and from our personal Amma experiences; Amma's grace is there. Amma's invisible hands are always there to support us, whether we recognize it or not. In the first volume of the book *Dust of Her Feet,* Swāmī Paramātmānandajī recounts having experienced grace from Amma. Then swāmījī asked Amma how he could get more of that grace. Amma replied, "Son, it is not something that you can buy in a shop, you just have to long for it. That's all." Swāmījī then asked, "Do I have to deserve it?" Amma replied, "You can't deserve it, grace is not something that you deserve. It just flows. Go on doing your sādhanā and when it strikes Amma's mind, then the grace will flow to you." I offer all my heartfelt gratitude to Amma for all the grace she has showered on me.

19

"Be Strong, Be Positive, Be Hopeful"

Manusri - Germany

In this lifetime my journey with Amma started after my medical studies. I was working in a hospital during my specialist training for internal medicine. From a materialistic point of view I had everything at that time. I had a good job and career in front of me, a beautiful flat, a lot of money, etc. But something unknown and fundamental was missing. I was raised as an atheist. I thought if there is a God, I don't want to deal with him because there is so much suffering in the world. I was very sad and empty. I was drinking and smoking a lot.

All through my childhood I had a strange feeling; I felt very old. I felt as if I had already lived in many places and had thousands and thousands of children. I thought, "At least in this lifetime I will not have children." Until I met Amma, I thought something was wrong with me. I always had the feeling I did not fit into the so-called "normal" world.

At some point I bought a CD containing parts of the book *The Gospel of Sri Ramakrishna*. I listened to this CD on my way to work at the hospital and on my way home. It was the only time of the day when I felt happy and peaceful inside. On the CD, Śhrī Rāmakṛiṣhṇa[21]said, "The Mother doesn't bother about her child as long as it is busy with its toys. But when it throws away the toys and cries the Mother will come running." I started crying and praying to Mother Kāḷī along with Śhrī Rāmakṛiṣhṇa on my way to work: "Oh Mother, I don't want name, nor fame. I

[21] The great spiritual master (1836 – 1886) from West Bengal, hailed as the apostle of religious harmony.

don't want occult powers. I don't want physical comfort. Please Mother, give me only pure love for you." Even though I didn't understand much of what Śhrī Rāmakṛiṣhṇa was talking about, this incident shows the greatness of satsang and how it can transform a life. The Mother hears the cry of the little ones. Regardless of where she is, she will come running to us. That's what Śhrī Rāmakṛiṣhṇa said, and that's what Amma did.

My father told me about Amma and said she would come to Munich in October 2009. I was interested but was so overworked that I forgot to make travel arrangements. Finally when the time arrived, I realized I had to work a twenty-four-hour shift at the hospital during Amma's three-day program and therefore could not attend. But Amma already had her hand in the matter and I was asked to change the twenty-four-hour shift to one day earlier. Thus I could go to the program after my shift.

With hardly any sleep and exhausted from the work week I boarded a train in the early morning after my shift for a five-hour ride to Munich. I arrived on the third day at the end of the morning program before Dēvī Bhāva. I was totally crushed because that night during my shift a patient had died unexpectedly, and throughout that night I had been very busy. I sat in the hall on the floor and could not see Amma. My body pleaded for rest. The program ended and Amma walked across a high balcony over the crowd back to her room. The first time I saw her was from far away. I immediately knew I had never seen anyone like that before. The way she walked — with such a presence — I was totally stunned.

After Amma left, I thought of resting on the floor, but no... my tapas (austerities, penance) had no end. Everyone had to leave the hall and go out into the cold winter evening. At that point I did my first sēvā, not out of selflessness, but for survival! I went to the warm dish washing tent. At least I could do that much with my tired body and mind. When I look back I can see this was the perfect preparation for my first darśhan.

My first darśhan was during Dēvī Bhāva. Amma wore a beautiful red sāri. I didn't know what to expect. But I definitely wanted a mantra. Arriving at Amma's feet I said, "Amma, mantra." But Amma didn't react and simply put my head into her lap. I thought she didn't hear me. People were talking to her and the music was loud. So, I looked up again and said, "Amma, mantra." This time she pushed my head down. I got the message to just be quiet. While I was still in her lap, out of nowhere a question arose in my mind, "Are You God?" At that very moment I felt like my heart exploded, and the next thing I remember, I was sitting in the mantra line totally shocked. I could not get over what just happened. Here was God, and she hugged me! There was only love, and a huge burden from my heart and shoulders was removed. When I arrived back on stage, still in line for a mantra, Amma looked at me, her eyes piercing my inner core.

Later, I roamed around the bookstore area at the program. I was very shy and thought, "If this is God, who are the people traveling with her? Angels? Enlightened beings? Yōga masters? Can they read my thoughts?" Everyone behind the bookstall tables smiled at me and gave me a lot of attention. I was scared of them, partly because they only spoke English. That was my worst subject in school, and school had been a long time ago! Today, I know the devotees at the bookstall were just happy that somebody came along late at night whom they could help and serve.

Like a shepherd Amma gathers us from all over the world, at all stages of life, and at all ages. She knows where to find each one of us at the right time. Actually she is never separate from us. From that day onward there was an invisible hand in my life guiding me and arranging everything for the best.

Traveling with Amma

The following February in 2010, I came to this holy place, Amritapuri, for the first time. My first sēvā? Dishwashing, of course! Amma had just left for the North India Tour. Following her was not an option because I was afraid of traveling. I was so happy just to have reached Amritapuri! Every day I cried. Every day conveyed a lesson for me. I saw that everything I had learned previously about the world and about myself was wrong. After a few weeks Amma departed for her Australia Tour. I was scared to the bones to travel alone. But Amma blessed me with the sēvā of assisting and traveling with one of Amma's wheelchair-bound devotees. Thus, I went on my first tour with Amma to Malaysia and Australia.

That was my honeymoon time with Amma. She lured me into her courtyard and bound me with her love. On a daily basis she gave me glances and smiles, sometimes she even called me directly for darśhan a second time! I was in bliss!

A few weeks later Amma left Australia and went back to India. I was unable to follow her due to visa restrictions. I was left alone in Australia — devastated. Every day I walked on the shoreline, crying and listening to her bhajans. I felt worse than a teenager abandoned by her first great love. Whenever Amma sings the bhajan *'Jai Jai Jananī Jai Hō Tērī'* ('Victory to you, Mother') I see the dark blue waves of the vast ocean through my tears and pain of separation. Going back to my previous way of life was impossible.

Since that Australia tour, by Amma's grace alone, I have been able to do every Europe and U.S. Tour until the pandemic started. I have been a staff member on many of Amma's tours in India, Malaysia and Japan; and I have been able to call Amritapuri my home as well. Thank you Amma, for this unimaginably big blessing!

One time I felt beaten down by my ignorance and sadness and I went to Amma to seek help. I thought Amma would give in and cheer me up a little bit, perhaps as the disciple Arjuna had expected from Śhrī Kṛiṣhṇa in the *Bhagavad Gītā,* a little consoling...but we all know how it is with Amma and our expectations. She mentioned three points which I initially could not grasp in my sadness. Upon contemplating them, however, they started to unfold like a magic box. I now think of these three points as 'my little Amma Gītā.' Let me explain what I have learned from Amma's words.

"Be strong."

The first thing Amma said to me was: "Be strong." The instruction to be strong can be understood on different levels: mentally as well as physically. Being strong mentally means being equipoised in all circumstances. Often on Amma's tours in India, the night before the program starts, I would go to the stage for sēvā. Sometimes when I looked out across the huge venue and imagined the crowd the next day I would immediately feel weak and exhausted. I would say to Amma in my mind: "Amma, if you were to take the backdoor and go to the airport tonight, I would totally understand!" But as you all know, Amma never left.

Amma comes on stage and looks at the crowd — an ocean of humanity stretching to the horizon — and greets all the people with an expression of inner peace and immense strength on her face. She is calm and fully present in the here and now... She just starts the program. Thinking of Amma's face in that situation always gives me a lot of inner strength. Of course the real strength lies in knowing ourselves, our true nature, being the all-powerful Ātman, the Self. Amma shows the way for all of us, her little lion cubs, to awaken to this inner strength. Until we reach that point Amma tells us again and again to "have the strong conviction that whatever comes my way, I will be happy, I will be strong. Amma is always with me."

I remember an incident that happened after a Dēvī Bhāva. We had been very busy for three days and nights in a huge hall. I was staying at a place that was quite a long walking distance from the hall. The Dēvī Bhāva program went very late. As usual I hadn't slept. Normally I like to say goodbye to Amma's caravan, which drives off immediately to the next program location. But after this Dēvī Bhāva I could hardly walk. Amma made her way from the stage to the car outside and I started slowly walking the long distance to the exit at the back of the huge hall. I didn't know what to do. I hardly had the power to walk out of sheer exhaustion. I thought, "How will I get to the hotel, have a shower, pack, and come back with my heavy bag in just one hour to catch the tour bus?" — I had no idea. I took one step at a time.

On the floor I saw a trail of flower petals; they were even outside on the street. They had fallen off the devotees as they left. Suddenly a pain went through my heart. I thought, "Amma is gone and I cannot follow her. How lucky are the swāmīs..." At that moment I looked up and there they were! The van full of swāmīs stopped next to me at a red traffic light. And behind the van? Amma's car was right there. Amma opened the window and stretched out her hand to me. She was glowing. Softly, I touched her hand. The light turned green and all the cars drove off. I started crossing the street. To my astonishment, I could walk again! All my energy had returned! I ran to the hotel, took a shower, packed my bag and returned in plenty of time. Amma is our inner strength, the real power behind all our actions.

"Be positive."

The second thing Amma said to me was: "Be positive." In the *Bhagavad Gītā*, chapter 6, verse 5, Śhrī Kṛiṣhṇa says:

> *uddharēd ātmanātmānaṁ nātmānam avasādayēt*
> *ātmaiva hyātmanō bandhur ātmaiva ripur ātmanaḥ*
> 'Let a man raise himself by his own mind, let him not debase himself; he alone, indeed, is his own friend, he alone is his own enemy.'

Amma says: "Our mind always tries to take us down. It is like water — always flowing down. We should watch the mind with awareness of our thoughts. Awareness is like fire. However you hold a flame, it will always point upwards." Of course this is not an easy task. Constant effort is needed and often we fail due to wrong attachment to our thoughts. It is like falling into a pit again and again. We can conquer these downfalls by having a positive outlook. Ultimately we are responsible for our life and our mental state. Our mind is our best friend when we fill it with godly and positive thoughts about ourselves and others. It becomes our worst enemy when one of the inner enemies (anger, jealousy, lust, greed, etc.) takes over and pulls us down. With awareness we can see a negative thought and nip it in the bud before it can grow and become stronger.

Life gives us many lessons in awareness, even in the simplest ways. In my room I have what I call "awareness police." I bet everyone has them in their home. Who are they? Imagine you're eating a tasty cookie in your room (or even worse — in your bed). If you are not aware and even a single tiny crumb falls through your fingers, within a few hours the 'ant police' will definitely arrive! They will crawl all over you and sting, reminding you of your lack of awareness. Similarly, constant alertness and awareness is needed to make our mind a good servant, and not let it be our bad master.

The mind is a God-given tool and we should use it to uplift ourselves, as well as others. Amma says, giving somebody a smile and a kind word can save their day, or even their life. It is free of cost and everyone can do it. Wearing masks during this Coronavirus time makes it hard to see each other's smiles. The lack of smiles might have made some people unconsciously sadder. However, let's try to be optimistic and see the good in all circumstances. Similarly, many of us may dislike washing our hands so often during the pandemic. But instead of getting upset, we can choose to be positive. For example, we can think, "At least I only have two hands!"

"Be hopeful."

The third thing Amma said to me was: "Be hopeful."

In the *Bhagavad Gītā* Śhrī Kṛiṣhṇa says in chapter 2, verse 14:

> *mātrā-sparśhās tu kauntēya śhītōṣhṇa-sukha-duḥkha-dāḥ*
> *āgamāpāyinō 'nityās tāns-titikṣhasva bhārata*
> 'Contact of the senses with their objects, o son of Kuntī, gives rise to experiences of cold and heat, pleasure and pain. Transient, they come and go. Bear them patiently.'

The nature of the world is impermanence. It is always changing. If we face difficult times we should remember, 'This too shall pass.' After winter comes the spring. After night comes the day. Just recently I went to Germany to deal with some family matters, but for a long time I didn't receive my visa for India. I was stressed out for a few weeks as the day of my flight to Amritapuri was fast approaching while my visa still had not come. I said to Amma internally, "Ok Amma, this is a hard time for me, but this too shall pass." This knowledge helped me at once in accepting the situation, as well as in keeping a positive outlook and not drowning in my own mental negativity. Of course my visa issue was eventually resolved in time and I could return to Amritapuri.

Being hopeful also means never giving up. As a toddler learns to walk it falls down many times but always gets up and enthusiastically tries again. It is the same when children learn to ride a bike. Likewise, we may fall repeatedly into the pit of negativity in our minds, but we should just get up and try again, no matter how many times we fall. Because when Amma says, "Be hopeful," she not only means to have an optimistic outlook, but also that there is hope to reach the highest goal. We just have to keep trying to the best of our ability.

Amma tells a story about a herd of baby goats who wanted to eat the grapes on a mountain top. They all started enthusiastically running up the mountain. Yet as they climbed higher and higher, they gradually lost hope and confidence, and one by one they dropped out. They said to each other, "This is impossible, we'd better return." But one baby goat kept going upwards. The others tried to call him back and made fun of him. In the end this one goat baby reached the top and had all the grapes. When he finally returned, he was asked, "How did you make it all the way?" But he didn't answer. His mother said, "My son is deaf. He can't hear you or the others." Because he did not get discouraged by the others, he proceeded and attained the fruits. Similarly, we should neither listen to our own minds nor to others when they try to discourage us from the spiritual path. We are all sitting in the Mata Amritanandamayi Devi Express buses headed straight to the goal! Just don't get off the bus!

Be strong!

Be positive!

Be hopeful!

To conclude I want to share an Amma dream with you. I had this dream in the early years after meeting Amma. At that time there was a lot of fear in my life because everything was uncertain. I wondered if I could really be with Amma, or would she send me back to the world.

In the dream I was standing to the side with many other devotees, waiting for Amma to pass. As she approached us she held her hand up to touch everyone as she walked by. I did not hold my hand up to touch hers, and I let Amma pass. After she passed me, she stopped and turned around to touch my hand. As she turned, Amma hurt her hand by scraping a piece of broken glass, and the back of her hand started bleeding. We went to the hospital and finally we were alone in a treatment room. Amma was lying on a treatment chair. Her injured hand was on a metal table and I started to clean the wound. Because I was nervous, I spilled too much disinfectant over her hand. Knowing that Amma does not like to waste anything – even dream disinfectant – I apologized and said, "I'm sorry Amma. I have not done this for a long time because I have been on tour with you."

At that moment the smile on Amma's face disappeared and a voice spoke. It was strong and deep and pierced me to the bone, "WHAT DO YOU WANT?" It echoed through my whole being. I knew this was life-changing. I said: "I only want to be with *you*. I want nothing else." Amma said, "It will not be easy. It will be painful." I said, "It does not matter, I only want to be with *you*." Then I woke up. I was sleeping that night wearing an anklet. As I woke up, the anklet broke.

Amma's words, "What do you want?" come back to me often. Whenever it is difficult and I struggle a lot, I hear that deep strong voice. And then I ask myself the question again and again. And to this day the answer has not changed. "I only want to be with *you*, nothing else." I pray that all Amma's children have the inner strength and love to stay on the path until the goal is reached.

20

Finding Success with Amma

Danny Johnston – USA

What would make any one of us leap out of the water of our familiar lives into the unknown? The poet Mary Oliver beautifully describes the magic of a fish jumping out of water, its appearance changing from black to silver when struck by starlight. She thinks, this is holiness: 'the natural world, where every moment is full of the passion to keep moving.'[22]

What would make any one of us leap out of the water of our familiar lives into the unknown? What would motivate us to take such a leap? Did we have any idea there was something above us? Did we even know there were stars and night air and a world beyond the one we knew? Did we have any idea that the starlight could ever touch us and change us? Somehow everyone here made that leap out of the water into the night air, to be touched and changed by the starlight of our Amma. We've all had the direct experience of that, and we will never be the same.

When I think back to the transformative moment when my life took a more spiritual turn, I want to say it was my first darśhan. But with deeper introspection I must say it was an incident that happened two years prior.

I was twenty-two years old and walking home from work in New York City late one evening. Two youngsters came out of a park and beat me up, stabbed me, took all my money and ran off. I share this story as an example of how light and holiness can be present even in the darkest of moments. Because this story has a happy ending. It was from this incident that the

[22] From the poem, *At the Lake* by Mary Oliver.

entire focus of my life changed. I didn't care about anything anymore. Not my dance career, my New York connections, my accomplishments, nothing. At that point, I only cared about going to yōga class. Yōga was the only thing that made me feel better. It was in the practice of yōga that I could be my real self. All my emotions and confusion, all the newfound anxiousness and fear, they all flowed through the āsanas, the yōga postures. I had to go to yōga class every day; I couldn't miss it. Gradually the practice worked its magic and I felt better — less confused, less anxious, and less fearful.

I met my first meditation teacher at my yōga studio. She would come every few months to lead workshops on meditation. I fell in love with meditation. I could feel its healing power from the beginning. I loved the silence and I loved going to the retreat center for week-long silent retreats.

Two years after the park incident I was at the yōga studio looking at a poster of a very cute smiling Indian woman. Someone passed by and said, "That's Amma! She is holding a program here in a few days, you should go! She gives you a hug! It's so nice!"

And somehow I found myself sitting in the program hall at 8:45 a.m., waiting for Amma to arrive. I honestly don't know how I got there or what drew me there. It just seemed to happen. I was so confused. (Confusion might be a theme you'll notice throughout this talk.) I was raised in an atheistic family, there was no God or religion allowed. So, for me the program was already weird — the white clothes, the crowds, and the whole thing.

Amma arrived. I instantly liked her, and I loved Mā-Ōm meditation. I waited patiently for darśhan, very skeptical of the scene around me, but being drawn to Amma and the silence I felt around her amidst all the chaos. I can't say I remember anything about the first darśhan. I immediately left the hall and walked to meet a friend. We met after I had just walked about twenty blocks in New York City and realized I hadn't heard a single sound. I exclaimed to my friend, "I met a saint!"

***

Not long after that, I found myself on my first India tour with Amma. The whole tour was a blur. I couldn't believe that people slept on the ground without beds! The crowds, Amma giving darśhan to thousands and thousands of people, not sleeping, the pot washing, the long bus rides, the Brahmasthānam temple festivals, again I found myself confused, but also quite happy.

One time we had a long drive between two cities and had to stop overnight before continuing the next day. I can't remember exactly where we stopped but there was a Sikh temple on a cliff and a lake nearby. In the morning we were told we wouldn't leave till lunch, so I took a walk. I saw in the distance a bright orange statue and I decided to walk towards it. When I got to the statue, I saw it was Hanumān.

I didn't know much about Hinduism or deities, or what even to do at a temple like this. It had a very modest fence around it and there were some goats inside. I was hesitating to go any closer when suddenly a woman appeared. She opened the fence and beckoned me inside. I prostrated to the statue and thought, "Well, Hanumān isn't my deity, I'm more of a Dēvī devotee, but how nice is this?" After a little time I wanted to offer something to the woman to say thank you. But I didn't have any money with me, only a bag of peanuts I'd brought as a snack. I felt I couldn't offer her peanuts because in America there is this saying, "It's just peanuts." It means: it's nothing, it's worthless. I was embarrassed but felt I had to give something, so I walked uphill to where the woman sat next to a man. They were cooking something. I approached them and offered the peanuts saying, "Namaḥ Śhivāya." The woman looked at the peanuts happily and received them.

The man then gestured to the rock face behind him. There was a small opening in the cliff with some light coming out. He pointed to it, indicating I should go inside. Not wanting to be rude, and being curious, I went inside. I turned a corner and saw a very humble, beautiful statue of Dēvī that had been carved into the rock. It was so beautiful to sit in this small, candlelit cave, gazing at this statue. I learned an important lesson that day. God wants what you have to give, not what you think you need to give. I didn't need to offer a grand amount of money, only whatever item I had. Amma would keep teaching me this lesson many times in the future.

During my first few years with Amma I vacillated between doubt and love. I loved Amma and the wild, other-worldly life of touring and endless service, but I remained confused about spirituality. As I mentioned before, coming from an atheist household, I really didn't know anything about religion or spirituality. I just loved charity work and meditation. Amma had widened my notion of what it was to be happy, that I could think of others and give something back to the world. That was enough to keep me traveling with her and working for the charities.

But I was often confused. Was Amma enlightened? Was this the right thing to be doing with my time? Does Amma really know me? Can I believe in God? I would feel such love for Amma and then doubt for a long while. Yet something kept me bringing me back to the āśhram and to the tours. What was it? Whenever I spent time with Amma, I felt better. I felt like layers were being peeled off me and I could finally breathe.

Finally, one day I was doubting and complaining to a tour staff member who said, "You have to decide for yourself. Is

Amma offering something you want? Does it improve your life? Does it help you? Does it help the world? If you can't answer yes to these questions, maybe it's better not to come on tour and spend your whole time wondering if you should or shouldn't be here." Something changed at that moment and my whole perspective shifted.

Amma was patient and gentle with me during that whole time. She allowed me to adjust to spiritual life and to a spiritual way of thinking. She allowed me to mature at my own pace and discover for myself what God might mean to me. Amma let me experience spirituality rather than telling me what it was. There was no forcing or pushing to believe any particular thing. As an early Buddhist nun put it, "The path isn't a place on the map. It's a great shining world. Enter wherever you like."

Yes, I wanted what Amma was offering. I had received nothing but amazing lessons and knowledge from my time with Amma, and I knew there was much more to discover. Amma's example of service, love, and compassion became the entry point into that shining world, the path of spirituality. Amma's example continues to inspire and encourage me to this day. Initially, meditation drew me in because I could believe in my own experience. But the experience of Amma was so far beyond me that I really needed time to adjust my mind.

A year after that change of perspective I was ready to ask Amma a question about my life and felt open to accepting her answer. It was the dawning of my faith in Amma as my Guru. I was twenty-eight and didn't have a college degree because I started to work as a professional dancer right out of high school. I was nervous about my future. So I asked Amma what I should do. She gave me some really great advice about how to proceed and then said, "Anyway, why try to succeed in the world when you could succeed with Amma?"

Succeed with Amma? Wow! It seemed so clear — I was going to get enlightened! That moment was the beginning of an amazing inquiry. What is success with Amma? I still don't know the answer. But the answer is evolving for me every year as my inner and outer experiences teach me more and more. I love to contemplate Amma's question, and I'll always remember Amma's face when she asked it.

***

Before meeting Amma, I danced professionally. After I met Amma, I dropped my interest in a dance career. I thought serving the world through Amma was the only way to offer myself. Dancing seemed so frivolous and unspiritual, so unhelpful to people in need. Charity work was obviously the only thing to do.

Another thing you should know: I'm really shy around Amma. I don't want to bother her or get in the way of her work in this world. I love being in the back of the hall, or on the sidelines, or in the kitchen. I don't mind being far from Amma. I'm rarely on stage or sitting close to her. But once, I happened to be on stage and a darśhan assistant said to Amma, "Danny is such a good dancer." Amma's face lit up. She looked at me and said," I want to see! Perform on the tour!"

There is a poem by Galway Kinnell that always makes me think of that moment. He describes the flowering of a bud representing 'all things,' even 'those things that don't flower.' This blossoming happens on its own, 'of self-blessing.' And yet he also admits that, 'sometimes it is necessary to reteach a thing its loveliness.'[23]

Amma began the process of opening me up to being 'retaught my own loveliness.'

[23] From the poem, *St. Francis and the Sow* by Galway Kinnell.

***

I prepared a dance to show Amma and when the time came, it was like a dream. Amma stopped the darśhan line and gave me such motherly attention. To be seen in that capacity by a being as great as Amma was perhaps the most healing moment of my entire life. I have no words to describe the feeling of recognition. That moment will live in my heart forever. Afterwards, I shyly went on stage, and Amma said, "Amma loves watching dancing and really respects the arts. You should teach dance in the āśhram!"

My idea of success with Amma evolved once more. Just like with the peanuts, God wants what you have to offer. Your talents and skills are uniquely yours and are your offering back to the world. There's no need to hide them away or think they're too small or useless. Trust that your talents and skills aren't frivolous or that you need to save the whole world in order to be of service. Do what you can, and do what's right when the time comes. Amma makes it so simple sometimes.

Many people came to tell me how the dance affected them. I realized that art isn't just for show as I had previously thought. The dance classes in the ashram were very healing for people, uplifting them emotionally and spiritually, and bringing them closer to their own inner connection to God.

***

On that same tour with Amma, the person who usually gives out darśhan tokens asked Amma if I could be his replacement for one month while he was away. Amma changed her attitude quickly, looked at me sternly and said, "Amma will train you. Don't listen to him, I'm your Guru, not him!" We all laughed but...I was really nervous.

A few weeks later it began. I was terrified. I would have to talk to Amma twice a day to discuss how many tokens to give and who should get them. What a blessing... But I didn't even like to go on stage! It was time to get over my shyness. On the first day Amma told me how many tokens could be given out. Later when I told her how many were actually given out, she just said, "Okay." All right. Day one down!

The second day Amma said smilingly, "Many people no problem. Send them, many people." I had no idea what that meant or what to do and Amma didn't say anything else. So I gave out lots of tokens, many more than the day before. When I told Amma how many tokens I had given out, she looked at me and said, "You didn't listen to me! You didn't listen to me!!!" I mumbled an apology and ran off the stage. I felt horrible! I wanted to listen to Amma, but I had misunderstood something.

From then on Amma was very clear with me and told me the exact numbers of tokens to give out. I slowly learned how Amma likes things to be done, and who should get priority for the tokens: the new people, the people staying for a short while, the very sad people.

A week later during satsang, Amma said something powerful. As she said it, I felt she was looking at me. She said, "The Guru has to scold the disciple sometimes because the Guru sees the disciple as a plant, and the Guru can see the weeds and critters that are on the verge of overtaking the new sapling. The Guru's scolding will remove the weeds and critters before they harm the plant." I began to think long and hard about what it meant to listen to Amma, or anyone else for that matter. Listening is an attunement, an attunement of the mind to the person who is speaking. To attune our minds to Amma's mind we must be silent and allow her in.

In my egocentric rush to do a good job I hadn't attuned my mind to Amma's mind. I blindly followed what I thought were instructions without really thinking. We must also hear with our hearts. I could have listened and observed Amma to get a sense of what she might want, and then try to guide myself in that direction.

I also learned that for Amma, nothing is insignificant. Everything counts, everything matters. Amma knows when too few or too many tokens are given out. She would always catch me if I tried to lie about even one token. It's amazing to see how much attention Amma gives everything. I have had the opportunity to give out tokens a few more times over the years and thankfully, Amma didn't have to scold me like that ever again.

***

During the pandemic I was offered a job teaching yōga and meditation classes to people in recovery from drug and alcohol addiction. When I teach them, I take a psychological approach that I feel is most similar to Amma. It's called 'unconditional positive regard.' It means that you love whoever you are with without judgment. That way the student can feel safe and loved, and their healing can progress. They can have faith that the person helping them is open and willing to be with them no matter what arises.

I feel Amma has done this for all of us to a degree that we can't even understand. As spiritual aspirants we are also in recovery from our egoic addictions, negative tendencies, greed, anger, hatred, and delusion. Amma knows when to relax and give us space, and when to pull us closer. She knows when love is needed, and when a more serious attitude is required. So, I try to offer this tiny fragment of Amma's love and care to those students.

It's been very interesting. Generally after a long period of drug and alcohol abuse people are in a state of extreme restlessness and extreme tiredness at the same time. They're too tired to sleep, too energized to calm down. At first I was surprised to see that these students couldn't meditate without moving for even one minute. They could barely hold a yōga pose for three breaths. They complained of being exhausted but when I asked them to lie down and rest, they couldn't stop moving.

It reminded me of something Amma told me. I once had a disturbing experience in my spiritual practice. When I asked Amma about it she said, laughing, "You can do whatever practices you want, but the point of all these practices is to make you relax." So I try to help the students relax and find a space inside where they can let go for a while. Over time they learn to rest, relax, and be with themselves. We don't usually talk about spirituality unless they ask about it. Then I try to relate the importance of spiritual principles in a simple way. It takes time, but I see students blossom as they find happiness and contentment after the ravages of drug and alcohol addiction. I try to embody a relaxed and calm figure and hopefully impart a little bit of Amma to them. I try to remember back when I first met Amma. I couldn't even say the word God, and I didn't know what spirituality meant. So I allow these students to be themselves, just like Amma did with me. I couldn't be forced into believing anything, I needed to experience it. Through that freedom I discovered discipline, love, and faith in God.

Now what's my idea of success with Amma? I'm still searching for the answer and I may never know. But it is becoming clearer that to succeed with Amma, we have to be open, humble, and willing to learn. We must let Amma's love integrate our hearts and minds, so we can be 'retaught our own loveliness' and find inner self-confidence. So that the lessons we learn are a part of us, and wisdom can start to flow out and benefit everyone around us. We have to serve society, give back what we can, and do our part with a good attitude. Success with Amma might just be a willingness to love this world and treat everyone and everything with compassion.

May all of us be blessed with whatever our personal understanding of success with Amma may be. May all of us have the grace to continue to serve and love, to grow in compassion and understanding of both our inner selves and the outer world. May the starlight of Amma, our greatest treasure and true wealth, be ever present in our lives, hearts, and minds.

21

Amma Takes Care of Us All

Smt. Jayamala – Singapore

In a Tamiḷ bhajan, Amma sings:

> *kaṇṇai imai kāppatupōl,*
> *maṇṇai maram kāppatupōl,*
> *nammaiyellām kāttiṭuvāl, māriammā*
> 'As the eyelid protects the eye, as the tree protects the soil, so does Amma take care of us all!'

Amma spends every moment of her life working for our spiritual progress. She says that her children's happiness is her happiness. But it's difficult to feel ambitious for spiritual progress if Amma is always outwardly friendly towards us. Therefore she sometimes uses the masks of seriousness, sternness, or anger. Amma gives the example of a cow that enters our garden and starts eating the plants. If we say, "Oh my darling cow, my sweety, please do not eat the plants. It took so much effort to raise them. Please go away." The cow will not go away, it will keep eating. But if you take a stick and chase it while yelling, then it will run away. Similarly, if Amma shows us only love and affection we may not be serious in our spiritual practices and our progress can stagnate. So sometimes Amma behaves sternly. Amma says all her outward emotions are only there to guide us on the spiritual path. They can also create bhaya bhakti[24] in us and help us transcend our weaknesses and vāsanās (latent tendencies).

---

[24] Devotion arising from fear of repercussion.

Amma doesn't identify with the emotions she exhibits; she can quickly change moods. Amma says the emotions she shows are like a line drawn in water. Lines drawn in water vanish quickly. A doctor will prescribe liquid medicine for some patients, tablets for others, and perhaps injections for others depending on their illness. Similarly, Amma will instruct us differently depending on our vāsanās and level of maturity, but whatever the instruction, it's all for our benefit.

Initially Amma smiles, laughs, hugs and kisses us during darśhan. But if a mother sees her child playing in dirt, she will carry it to the bathroom for a good scrub. Similarly, once we develop a certain degree of surrender and love towards her, Dēvī starts to clean our inner dirt and get rid of our ego. A more challenging stage begins, with mental friction and lots of internal pushing and pulling involved. It's the equivalent to having a bath with a good scrub; one develops good qualities like patience and tolerance. Amma does this for our own good.

Ten Reasons Why Amma Might Not Look at Us

It's common to hear people complain that Amma doesn't look at them or speak to them, even during darśhan. However, she talks a lot to others, and even jokes with them. Someone told me this a few years ago; my response was to say that I'm also in the same boat. Nevertheless, with Amma's help, I've managed to remain happy through this period. Others should try to be happy too. It's only when one becomes close to Amma that she does this. It indicates that Amma is preparing us for our next level of spiritual progress. This is a serious phase of testing, and if we want to pass the tests, we need to take this separation positively.

Sometimes:

- Amma speaks to us without directly speaking with us.
- Amma sees us without directly seeing us.

- Amma smiles at us without directly smiling at us.
- Amma gives us darśhan without directly giving us darśhan.

At the same time, it can also be helpful to inquire why Amma might not directly be looking at us. Here are 10 possible reasons:

1. To help devotees face calamities.
2. To recognize our ātman (inner Self) in everyone else.
3. To realize Amma in our hearts.
4. To deepen our devotion and kindle the longing for keen meditation on Amma.
5. To manage people with heavy vāsanās.
6. To reduce the ego and negativities within us.
7. To discuss official matters of the āśhram and other institutions run by Amma.
8. To help us appreciate that absence makes the heart grow fonder.
9. To reply to urgent and important letters from devotees all over the world
10. To hold question and answer sessions with devotees

Let us examine each point.

1. To help devotees face calamities.
Amma may spend time talking to someone who is in a difficult situation. Seeing that her child is about to face a potential calamity, Amma takes time to comfort them and give them mental strength. When Amma ignores us it is never done to hurt our feelings. This understanding will help us develop the positivity that we need to make the spiritual progress that Amma has planned for us.

2. To recognize our ātman in everyone else.

Amma sometimes tests us to see if we are happy when she looks and smiles at someone else. In this case we need to be happy by feeling that our ātman is inside the other person, too, and imagining that Amma is in fact smiling at us, or even giving us darśhan. Actually, Amma is smiling at us without directly facing us. There have been many instances when I longed for Amma's darśhan as I watched her hug another child. By imagining that we are the child on Amma's lap, we can pass this testing phase and gain happiness from it.

3. To realize Amma in our hearts.

Here's another possibility: Amma talks with others outwardly, but she is actually closer to us, since she also talks to us inwardly. Amma is indirectly encouraging us to realize the internal link we all have with her. Also, what she says to one person may be applicable to us as well, if we really listen.

During that difficult testing time Amma frequently takes care to provide us with silent messages and indirect darśhans by enabling us to feel her presence in various situations. For example: I sometimes stand at one side of the program stage when Amma walks back to her room. Amma may stop to speak with the person standing just next to me. This usually happens when I am longing for Amma's darśhan. Often on such occasions, the conversation Amma has with the other person provides an answer to my question. It may also be a message I need to hear for my personal spiritual progress.

While Amma is interacting with us physically she is also performing thousands of līlās, actually infinite numbers of divine plays throughout all the worlds. Amma's līlās involve many of her true devotees, everywhere. She showers her compassion and love on them through divine dreams, divine visions, coincidences, and secret messages and communications, depending on their degree of devotion and surrender. So physical outward darśhans are not the only way that Amma interacts with us.

4. To deepen our devotion and kindle the longing for keen meditation on Amma.
In the *Śhrī Lalitā Sahasranāma*, we chant:

> *ōm sahasrākṣhyai namaḥ*
> 'Salutations to Dēvī who has a thousand eyes.' (283)

Amma has an infinite number of eyes watching over all the worlds and performing her līlās. She also has an infinite number of forms to experience all the worlds. She can take any form at any time, anywhere, to help us feel her presence. She looks after us in the dark, in deep sleep, in the dream world, and even in our bathrooms. It's rare to find a great Guru like this.

Every time Amma gives darśhan, she bends her back and neck forward. She bows down to bring her divine head to the level of the person she is hugging, perhaps whispering a mantra into their ear, giving them her full attention. Amma does this for everyone who comes to her, whether they are ill, handicapped, rich, or poor. How much physical pain must Amma endure from giving darśhan thousands of times a day? Somehow, she has the strength to bear it all and still manage our spiritual progress. Even when devotees come to garland her, she bows her divine head with humility to receive the garland, even though she is parāśhakti, the supreme power, the queen of the universe.

5. To manage people with heavy vāsanās.
When guests come to visit with their children, the hostess of the house cannot discipline the guests' children. She can only afford to correct her own children as she has a sense of responsibility for them. She can't ask the guests' children to behave in any certain way. She needs to be cheerful in front of them. Similarly,

it is only after we get a certain degree of affinity or surrender towards Amma that she starts to become strict with us to highlight areas needing our attention for spiritual growth. If Amma were to be strict with people of bad character they may end up staying away and falling deeper into māyā or delusion. By being cheerful with them, Amma gives them the opportunity to remain connected with her. Understanding this, we can see that Amma only works towards the spiritual progress of those who come to her.

6. To reduce the ego and negativities within us.
Amma looks after us without increasing our ego. If she were to praise us in front of others, our ego would inflate since we would think that even Amma appreciates us. Such thinking could be a setback. Amma says, "Be a zero to become a hero in spiritual life." Have the attitude that God, or Amma, is the power behind all our actions. This understanding opens our hearts. Such devotional love enables us to realize Amma within. If Amma praises someone it could be for many reasons we cannot see or understand at the time.

7. To discuss official matters of the āśhram.
Amma talks to some people about official matters. We cannot afford to take this in a negative light and think that she is not looking after us.

8. To help us appreciate that absence makes the heart grow fonder.
In the Telugu bhajan *Sāgara Chēpaku* we sing, 'It's only when a fish comes out of water and gasps desperately in the air that it realizes the value of the sea.' Similarly, when Amma doesn't speak or smile or approach us for some time we come to realize her true value. This encourages us to meditate on her in various ways. Even then she's working on our spiritual progress.

9. To reply to urgent and important letters from devotees all over the world.
The swāmīs and other āśhram staff discuss urgent and important matters with Amma during darśhan. Particularly during this Covid-19 time, Amma has been inundated with phone calls and correspondence from her various institutions and devotees. Amma needs to reply in time to all.

10. To hold question and answer sessions with devotees.
In her overseas programs there is a special queue for devotees who have questions. Amma answers them during darśhan time. We would find it difficult to do even one job with concentration, but Amma manages to perform hundreds if not thousands of jobs perfectly at once.

Amma's 2016 Canada Tour
In Toronto after Dēvī Bhāva, I checked out of the hotel to wait in the lobby since my flight check-in time was at 3:30 a.m. By Amma's grace, a devotee invited me to stay in her room with a small group of ladies. I gratefully accepted her offer. She was also booked on my Tokyo-bound flight the following day. I suggested we leave the room three hours before check-in time but she assured me that two hours was enough. Since she had given me a place to stay I didn't want to argue — we'd leave at her convenience. I thought it was all Amma's līlā.

At the airport, her suitcase exceeded the weight allowance so we repacked our bags and I carried some of her items in my suitcase. Then we went for our security check where my hand luggage was opened. One of the security officers took my yogurt rice packets and gave them to another officer. They examined them and had a discussion for a long time. Finally they returned the packets to me. I needed them due to health issues. Since 1997

I have flown many times with yogurt rice packets, but never before had they prompted such an extensive investigation!

I looked ahead and saw my roommate heading to the waiting area for boarding, but I faced a long queue at the immigration and customs check. In a hurry now, I repeatedly asked those in front to let me through. When I reached the customs officer, he was on the phone. He stubbornly ignored my requests to speed up the process and asked me, "Who am I?" I replied, "You are the *great* customs officer." He immediately told me, "I am the *senior* customs officer." After that he just continued his call before attending to me and giving me customs clearance.

After all the delays I rushed to the gate only to learn that the flight had departed without me. I panicked about my luggage, but found out it was retained at the airline counter, and with Amma's grace, I managed to collect it. The airline also helped me reschedule my flight.

Surprisingly, my new flight was non-stop to Tokyo instead of having a layover in Los Angeles. Even better, despite its later departure, my new flight would land two hours before the original one. I checked in smoothly, passed through security and customs, and walked to the gate.

Suddenly I saw two of Amma's tour staff. They said Amma was booked on the same flight! Within a few minutes, Amma, her swāmīs, and the entourage arrived. In that waiting area, Amma spoke to us for a long time and gave chocolate prasād to everyone.

In the *Śhrī Lalitā Sahasranāma* is the name:

> *ōm mahā buddhyai namaḥ*
> 'Salutations to Dēvī who is supreme in intelligence.' (223)

I realized it had been Amma's līlā all along: Taking the form of my roommate, we left too late for the flight and had to repack the luggage during check-in. Taking the form of the security officer, Amma had my yogurt rice packets taken away for a lengthy examination. Taking the form of the stubborn customs officer, Amma taught me patience while making me miss my previous flight. — All those hurdles were good things. Amma helped me develop patience, and by her grace, my itinerary was rearranged to travel on her flight.

Amma's House Visit in 2006

In April 2006 Amma visited our Singapore house. We performed Amma's pāda pūjā. After that Amma did a pūjā, sang a bhajan, and distributed prasād to everyone. Then Amma took our family members aside. Amma asked my husband, Kumar, "What is your job?" He replied, "Safety officer." Actually he was an Environmental Control Officer. Because the designation was too long, he shortened it to Safety Officer. After Amma left the house, I scolded him asking why he lied to Amma. Every word we say must be true. It was only then that he realized his mistake. Surprisingly, the very next day after Amma's visit, he was promoted to Safety Officer. It was all Amma's grace: she knew his ambition for that job and blessed him. Now he is working as Safety Manager.

Amma's 2007 Japan Visit

Amma helps us overcome our prārabdha karma in three ways:

1. She totally removes it if we are fit for that.
2. She partially reduces it so we can easily overcome it.
3. She does not remove the prārabdha, but she gives us strength to overcome it.

I'll share an incident of how Amma reduced my prārabdha.

My son and I wanted to join Amma's program in Japan. But three weeks beforehand I suffered from severe headaches, dizziness and nausea. Visiting the doctor twice and taking prescribed medicines did not help. With just a week to go, my son and I were doubtful about traveling. One morning I bought some flowers for puja and laid them on a newspaper. To my surprise I saw the words, 'Follow me to Japan' printed in bold letters. It seemed like a message from Amma. We booked our tickets to Japan without giving it a second thought.

The next day I had a dream in which Amma said, "Go and check your eyes." I went to the optician for a checkup. My near vision had changed and Amma had alerted me through the dream. My new spectacles were ready the day before we departed. It was purely Amma's grace that when the doctor was unable to diagnose the actual reason for my illness, Amma — the best doctor in the world — helped me identify the cause and blessed me with the cure, through a dream!

The third day of the program in Japan was Dēvī Bhāva. My son and I had Amma's darśhan. Afterwards, we sat down and one of the stage monitors told me to move back towards the rear of the stage. Due to my carelessness, I kept moving back without realizing I had reached the edge of the stage. I fell off the back of the stage and landed next to a pile of iron rods. It was purely Amma's grace that I escaped without a head injury with so much metal lying below the stage. Seeing me fall, my son rushed to help me up and took me to Amma. I felt pain in my right wrist and started massaging it. Amma took a look at my hand and said, "Don't massage, it's a fracture," so I stopped. Luckily there was a devotee on the stage who was a doctor. Amma called him immediately and told him to help with first aid for my injury. It was perfect planning by Amma to save me from what could have been a big accident, and to have a doctor ready to help without delay. At a nearby hospital, an x-ray showed it was only a hairline fracture. Only by Amma's grace did I escape major injury.

A few months before the accident, I had a dream where Amma had a stethoscope, like a doctor, and she said she would give me medicine. At that time I didn't understand the meaning of the dream. But after the accident, I realized through Amma's dream that she gave me the medicine of courage to endure the whole experience.

After Amma's tour group reached America, on the first day of the program, I got a phone call from Swami Rāmakṛiṣhnānanda-jī who said Amma was enquiring about my fracture. I mentioned how Amma had given me the courage to face the situation.

We visited Amma in Amritapuri to offer our heartfelt gratitude for my speedy recovery. Amma had taken good care of me and saved me from major peril. When I look back, all I can see is her well-planned līlā to protect me during a bad time. She reduced the severity of the injury from a major to a minor fracture, and ensured her protection at every step. We all know that Amma has been protecting millions of devotees all over the world like this.

In the *Bhagavad Gītā* Chapter 12, verse 8, Lord Kṛiṣhṇa says:

> *mayyēva mana ādhatsva mayi buddhiṁ nivēśhaya*
> *nivasiṣhyasi mayyēva ata ūrdhvaṁ na saṁśhayaḥ*
> 'Fix your mind on me and establish your intellect in me alone. Thereafter, you will abide solely in me. There is no doubt about it.'

Likewise, if we always think of Amma and perform good actions with surrender, Amma will definitely protect us. Thinking of Amma is a very good meditation. Amma's love and compassion knows no bounds when it comes to the protection of her children. We have read about Rāma, Kṛiṣhṇa, Saraswatī, Kāḷī and Māriamma, and other deities as well, but we have never seen them. Now we have Amma, who is all of them. We have a golden opportunity to live with her and see her every day.

Amma is the:

- God of the Universe!
- Queen of the Universe!
- Divine Mother of the Universe!
- Heart of the Universe!

22

Amma is Within You

Lakshmi – Finland

Having the grace to know that you are Amma's child is the most precious and mystical feeling in the world. There is nothing greater to achieve in life than her grace. What could be more divine than hearing her speech which flows like honey, or seeing her blissful glances whose beauty alone can lead us to the eternal? What could be more divine than seeing the miracle of how Amma endlessly serves her children?

Being attached to the world is like being in a storm, alone and wandering, with fear as our only company. But the darśhan token is like a lighted window that glows in the dark of the storm. We start running with tears in our eyes saying, "I finally found my home!"

During this pandemic time many of us were not able to see Amma. By Amma's grace, the physical distance from her was not as hard for me as I first imagined it would be. My experience has shown me that we can be with Amma wherever we are. Amma says repeatedly, "Amma is always with you!"

One of my first experiences of guidance from my inner Amma happened in 2017 when I was about to go to the holy land of Amritapuri for the first time. A few days before leaving I remembered the rent... I needed an extra 500 euros from somewhere. Immediately inner Amma came along and said, "Don't worry. You will get it." I replied to my inner Amma, "Are you sure? Amma, I only have three days?" Was this just my ego's voice inside my head trying to avoid the payment, or was it really Amma guiding me from inside? I decided to trust

Amma and not worry about the payment. After two days I got a message from my grandfather saying he was thinking about me and was sending me five hundred euros. Happy Christmas! My grandfather had never sent me money like this before, and actually he didn't even know that I was going to India. I just said, "O Amma, I trust you and I better stop questioning you."

During these last few years this inner Amma has become my daily guide. How can I rely on her? How can I know it is Amma and not my ego? Well, I probably can't, but humans have the power of intuition. Sometimes we just feel and know things without further investigation. For example, when I met Amma I started loving her and feeling her beauty immediately, even before my first darśhan and getting to know her teachings. Of course this was only because of Amma's grace, but to be honest I was not excited about meeting Amma at first.

I had left Christ behind a year earlier for many reasons. I felt I was not worthy of God's love and that God is beautiful and I am ugly because of my actions. I felt ashamed and thought, "God is better off without me." How silly! As Amma says, " The sun doesn't need anything from us to shine." God always loves us no matter what. Every moment is a new beginning, a new chance to change our course and take refuge in God.

***

In 2013 when I was sixteen years old and in high school, I took a world religions course. The teacher started talking about Gurus and showed a picture of Amma. My grandmother had been following Amma since I was born in 1996, so I said to my teacher, "My grandmother is into these Amma things." My teacher replied, "Really? Amma is coming to Finland in a few days. You should go see her and then interview your grandmother. Go see Amma. On Monday I want a presentation about Amma!" I called my grandmother and told her I would accompany her to see Amma.

When I arrived at the program Amma was already giving darśhan. I had a pen and journal with me. Why did this Indian woman hug people? I went to the program feeling really skeptical. I thought I would sit and look at what Amma does for forty-five minutes and then return to my worldly ways of spending the weekend.

Within fifteen minutes I felt like I was floating. Something inside of me opened up. What? God was sitting on the stage so close and so easy to reach? Was everyone seeing this miracle? I used to believe that we are composed of physical, mental, and spiritual aspects, but in this moment, it felt as if all those had stepped aside, revealing something greater. I am not just my physical, mental, or spiritual self; I am something more profound — I am the Eternal.

Whenever I seem to have forgotten my true Self it is actually never totally forgotten and never not present. It is just like I am an actor putting on a costume and starting to act in different roles on the stage of māyā, the cosmic drama. Hopefully I'll soon remember who I truly am, take the costume off, and get some fresh air. Then all the dēvas (demi-gods) in the audience will clap and say, "Finally this play has ended! Now we can all go home!"

After my darśhan I sat on the stage. Once an hour had passed, I thought it would be good to get up for a while — in reality, I had been sitting for several hours. Time stood still and there was nothing to ask, tell or explain. There was only the Divine Mother. The only language was the language of the heart, where there was no intellectual thinking or verbalization. There was only deep silence which calmed down all the vāsanās and all the questions and wanderings of the mind. Thus, when we get close to Amma, we begin to remember who we truly are. This is something that māyā can't touch or manipulate. We do our sādhanā so that we can remember that we always remain in our true nature.

I learned a beautiful teaching about water from a Buddhist monk. Take a glass full of water and shake it. The water starts to spill, and the waves in the water are trembling. Then put the glass of water aside. What happens when the external stimuli stop manipulating the water? In a few seconds the water goes back to its calm, natural state. Similarly, when the waves of thoughts in our minds subside, like the waves in the glass of water, we can see a clear reflection of who we really are. We also see what is happening around us without compelling us to get involved in or react to every situation. We stop being shaken.

One time in meditation I felt the desire to travel to Amma. Amma says that we pay a lot of money to travel around the world, but we never travel to the Self, even though it is right within us all the time and requires no money or visa. I was praying, "O Amma, let me see you!" I enjoy imagining myself in the Kāḷī temple wherever I am meditating, and this time I was lucky. Amma appeared there with a few brahmachārīs. When I saw Amma, naturally I started to cry. Amma sat next to me. Everytime she looked at me I cried more and she started laughing more, and we played this beautiful game for a while. The Divine Mother found this game very funny, and the brahmachārīs did too. Finally, Amma had to leave. I stayed there in the Kāḷī temple amazed by what just happened, until I remembered to open my eyes and realized I was in Finland, thousands of kilometers away from her! How do we know what is actually God's manifestation and what is our imagination? I wonder, "Amma, does it really make a difference to know if it is God's manifestation in front of us rather than our minds steeped in devotion?" Then again, isn't everything before us God's manifestation?

My mother's husband is not spiritual at all. He is an atheist but he always serves everyone with love and awareness. He respects my love for God even though he has no belief in God. He gets many of the benefits of a hard working spiritual aspirant through his actions. This reminds me that we should not label people. We should just try to see everyone as our beloved Amma, or God. Amma says that someone who truly loves Amma, will love all of creation in the same way. Through this understanding and practice we can reach the state of samādhi.[25]

Here I wish to mention that people are easily influenced by each other. If one person sees that life can actually be lived with peace and happiness, others will also believe they can attain those states. When we do a good deed for someone, it often inspires that person to do some good for others. When this snowball starts rolling down the hill, the effect grows bigger and bigger, and soon nothing can stop it. Doing good eliminates our bad habits. And when all our negative vāsanās or tendencies have been cleansed, we will attain God realization.

So, whether we play with God in our devotional mind or with the physical manifestation of God, won't it have the same effect? I don't know if I was really in the Kāḷī temple with Amma, or if I was just in my mind. Anyhow, it doesn't matter to me. I felt devotion and great gratitude for Amma, which gives me more strength to be less identified with my mind, to refrain from saying a mean word, and instead to breathe and wait for a while before speaking. When I find myself doing something that I know isn't nice, I can take refuge in Amma, and from there, gain more awareness. This ability gives me more faith that Amma is with me and within me.

***

[25] Transcendental meditative union with the ultimate reality.

When I meet older Amma devotees I am always surprised to learn their ages. Once I met this old Finnish couple — I don't know if they were in their fifties or their eighties — but their eyes were like the eyes of children who were in their favorite game or play with their mother. I guess they had realized the nature of māyā and understood that their mother, Amma, is the director. No matter what happens, Amma will help us take the next step in the play. Of course, it's easier if you know your lines.

In acting I have learned that you cannot really immerse yourself in a role until you have memorized your lines. Once you know your lines you can relax, surrender, and have more awareness while working on a scene. The director, the one who helps everyone individually and who also serves the whole production, is extremely important. In a spiritual context, the director is the all-knowing Self. The other actors in the play are the people we meet in our lives. Our close relationships are the great vāsanā cleansers. Studying the script and its secrets could mean studying spiritual texts and divine words by avatārs, divine incarnations, like Amma. This kind of spiritual understanding can connect us so that our actions are done through the heart and not the brain. So what could learning our lines mean? Doing our sādhanā, our spiritual practices, of course! When we do our sādhanā don't we feel more relaxed, surrendered and aware? In the theater in Finland we say that you need to know your lines like they're part of your backbone. Similarly, Amma teaches that our sādhanā should become our second nature.

Amma also says that even if a light is switched on accidently, it will still give light. Likewise, if we sometimes do our sādhanā with less devotion than we hoped, we are still making the effort and evolving. Like in a play, the most important thing is that the actors show up. Not having the actors is the worst case scenario. If an actor is not present, the whole scene changes and everything previously rehearsed must be thrown out the window. Therefore, even if an actor doesn't know the lines, they should still show up. It always benefits the play. Even if we're not in the mood, or are angry with Amma, let's have the strength to show up for archana, sēvā, meditation, satsangs, and bhajans. Let's pray for Amma's grace to have the strength to do our sādhanā for the benefit of the whole play.

Through spirituality we gain sincerity. On the path of surrender to God we realize how small we are and how great God is. We gain some humility which allows us to surrender to life and to the knowledge that physical death is unavoidable. Of course death is an illusion. There is no death, only God. But we are so attached to our bodies that the mystery of death is not easily understood.

***

Christ said, "I tell you the truth: unless you change and become like little children, you will never enter the kingdom of heaven. Therefore, whoever humbles himself like this child is the greatest in the kingdom of heaven." And as Amma simply says, "Only a child can grow."

Here in Amritapuri we have seen some inspiring little souls, Amma's little āśhram children. Their eyes are full of devotion and sincerity. If they do something wrong, they tell Amma openly. For example, they say, "O Amma, pride took me and that's why I forgot the words to the song." Or, "Amma in front of you I am an angel, but for everyone else I am a demon." And when one of these children sings to Amma, everyone in the audience is either crying or laughing. The children say everything openly, not just in front of the Divine Mother, but also in front of everyone else in Amritapuri and those who are watching online! As adults we usually feel afraid to share our shame and fears openly. We should learn from these children. Become a child, then there is no shame, no hiding, just openness!

Meeting Amma as a teenager and understanding that Amma knew everything made me feel afraid. I wanted to do a lot of spiritual practices and be more strict with myself. When I could not do enough practice, I felt sad and I punished myself. At first, I thought being mean to myself when I didn't do my spiritual practices was part of spiritual life. But being mean actually made me feel even more sad and tired. I started telling myself, "Tomorrow I will do my practices." Later on, by Amma's grace, I discovered that the one who is punishing me is my ego. Being mean to myself does not help me. Nor will being mean to anyone else give them more strength and belief in themselves.

A lotus can only bloom through the nurturing care of Mother Earth. Let us nurture our Self and others with love. Allow for others what we allow for ourselves. If we stop blaming and punishing ourselves, we save a lot of time and energy. It is just the ego wanting attention.

When I became more loving towards myself, I actually got more motivation to do spiritual practices. What was I afraid of, that Amma will see how weak I am? She knows everything anyway. As we live in our homes, no matter how clean or dirty we keep them, the locks still work and the floors don't complain. In the same way, God is always welcoming us. We are all actors who just need to show up. When we remove our costumes, we will see that there really is no difference between us.

Amma is our mother, and we should let ourselves be her children. A child doesn't do anything before asking for mother's blessing and permission. We should look at all our actions and seek the inner Amma to appear to us and give her blessings for all of our decisions. God has manifested in the purest form in our lifetime! God is not from some distant place or a time in the past. God is right here. Have some courage and talk to Amma who is connected to the universal computer! Courageously ask Amma what actions you should take to attain what you want in life. Close your eyes and wait for guidance.

***

I want to share a recent experience. I teach theater, and in one of my groups there are three little children. They always ask to play hide and seek. The school has many places to hide. One Monday morning as soon as I opened my eyes, my inner Amma gave me a message not to let the children play hide and seek. When class started, the kids asked carefully if they could play the game. It actually felt like they had known that today they were not supposed to play. I said no, gently but strictly.

I went with the kids to the corridor for a moment. It was already dark outside because it was wintertime. In the corridor the lights were off. Suddenly I saw someone running on the second floor. He turned, looked at me, and ran out the door. Someone had broken into the school or come inside secretly. I took the kids back to our room, and thanks to Amma's grace, I saw one teacher walking with a flashlight. I told her the situation and we sent the kids home because I had a feeling that someone was still in the school. We called security and left. The next day I heard there had been two other intruders. The cameras showed them when they came out from their hiding places. Think if I had found these intruders while playing hide and seek with the children? I would probably have had a heart attack! Thank you, dear Amma, for helping me avoid that unpleasant situation!

No matter where we are, Amma loves and cares for her children. Even if we are physically as far away from her as Finland, Amma takes care of our journeys in the world. Animals don't speak and that's why their intuition is so sensitive. Let's practice silence to better feel our true Self and hear Amma's guidance.

Recently I was in a hotel room. There was a sign on top of the phone that said to press 0 for everything and anything. It reminded me of Amma. Why? Because Amma teaches that when you become a zero you become a hero. When we (our egos) become zeros, God's grace flows to us and we can get everything and anything. But the beauty is that with God's continuous presence in our hearts nothing else satisfies anymore. We don't need to have everything and anything. Instead we become heroes. We give everything to others in need and help them in any way we can. In this way we are always in Amma's embrace, and others benefit from it too. Dear Amma, how can we thank you for this grace?

Let me conclude with this prayer from Amma's bhajan *Īśhvar Tumhi Dayā Karō*:

> *O Lord, please show us mercy. Other than you, who is here to look after us?*
> *You are the creator and the destroyer of the world. Problems are solved by you alone. Other than you, who is here for us?*
> *You are our mother, father, benefactor and friend. You are our only refuge. Other than you, who is here for us?*
> *We don't know anything. Without our love for you, what would become of us? Other than you, who is here for us?*

23

Lessons in Ahiṁsā

Devika – USA

I have taken on many different roles for earning money in this lifetime; one of them was being a clown for children's parties and events. In the summer of 2005 in New York City, I had to leave Amma's program early for a job or 'gig' as they say. So, I had brought my clown costume with me in a small bag, and when it was time, I dashed downstairs to change in the women's restroom. Although my costume was colorful, it did not compare to the beautiful sāris and Punjabi outfits that surrounded me, but on the other hand, no one else was going to wear a funny red nose!

Before leaving, I went upstairs to catch my last glimpse of Amma giving darśhan. I stationed myself in the back of the hall as I was self-conscious and, believe it or not, in some weird way, I did not want to attract attention. As I was standing there, devotees encouraged me to get Amma's darśhan. But I thought, no way, I was too nervous about it. As I stood there, people kept bumping into me in a way that forced me to step forward so they could walk past me. Before I knew it, I was getting closer and closer to Amma. And then it happened. By her grace, there I was, standing so very close to the Divine Mother. I had blown up a red heart balloon and gave it to Amma. She kissed the red heart balloon as she gave me darśhan.

One year later, I had a dream. It was the evening of September 10, 2006, the night before the fifth anniversary of the fatal 9/11 attack in New York City. That was the attack that occurred on September 11, 2001, killing thousands of innocent people. Two airplanes flew directly into the tallest skyscrapers in New York City, the World Trade Center Towers, and two other planes crashed, one on the way to the Pentagon in Washington D.C., and one in a Pennsylvania field on the way to the U.S. Capitol. In the dream, Amma said to me, "The only thing that is real is Dēvī."

I woke up from that dream the next morning, on September 11, 2006. For some reason, what began to work in my mind was the thought that I should go to the 9/11 memorial that had been created to help those who had lost loved ones. The suffering was so deep and prevalent. I thought maybe I should go with my clown costume and red heart balloons. My courage wavered as I thought it would be crazy to do that. But the message from Amma in my dream fortified me without me really knowing it. At that point, there was only a simple stone wall with plaques of the names of all those that had died. I took the train into Manhattan carrying my clown costume with me in a small bag. When I arrived downtown, I found a local department store down the street from the 9/11 memorial and dashed in to change into my costume in the restroom.

Now, in New York City it's not uncommon to see anyone doing just about anything. So dressed as a simple clown, I walked over slowly to the 9/11 memorial site without much notice from anyone. I felt a little self-conscious but I also felt I had to continue. I carried with me some red heart balloons. The memorial site was actually a small platform. A few people were there looking at the names on the wall. I didn't know what to do. I began to blow up one red heart balloon at a time and just held them in my hand, trying to stay in the present moment.

For some people, the pain of seeing their loved one's name on the plaque was too much for them to even look up. Their heads lay low and their hearts were heavy. Others looked at me with such deep grief and received a red heart balloon with a moment of pause, and without words. The silence was impenetrable and yet I told myself to stay. I prayed to Amma to guide me. As I played the role of a quiet clown, my heart began to open more and more and a kind of stillness became apparent. There was nothing to say. Being present was the only thing I could do.

My dream of Amma telling me that, "The only thing that is real is Dēvī." was planted in my heart, but my senses could not forsake what I was experiencing emotionally. And yet I was grateful. For in this divine play, this māyā, in all the roles we all play for each other, Dēvī, Amma, brings us to her, to pierce through the suffering again and again, in order to realize the Supreme Truth.

Recently one of our sisters who gave a satsang said, "The ultimate grief or suffering is our perception or belief that we are separate from God." Amma has come to guide us home. She shows us the path and holds our hands and heals our hearts. With Amma, who is the living scripture of all scriptures, there is no end or beginning to the illumination. There must be infinite threads that nurture the awakening that we are not separate from God.

***

Amma has mentioned the importance of knowing the yamas and niyamas, which are moral restraints and observances. I would like to briefly touch upon the first yama today which is ahiṁsā or nonviolence. I chose to introspect on ahimsā as I have struggled terribly with anger throughout my life. I have a volcanic heart of emotion and therefore have been deeply challenged with the practice of creating a gap before I speak. My struggle has caused harm to people. I have even been known to throw things. Once I threw a bag of coffee, once a small jar of tiger balm, and that rage was scary. A blindness takes over.

After meeting Amma, through her grace, this suffering began to change.

When I first met Amma in 1999 at Dēvī Bhāva in New York, I immediately took a mantra not really knowing its spiritual significance. Also, my mother had fallen ill that year, so meeting the Divine Mother seemed perfectly timed. Amma's grace allowed me to pour my heart out in a letter to Amma about all the troubles in my life. A few years later in 2002, as I was watching Amma give darśhan, I felt Amma reach my heart through the tenderness of the bhajans. My heart opened in a way I had never felt before.

And now through Amma's grace, over twenty years later, Amma has cradled me to gradually help me become a little calmer. I am deeply grateful for all the sādhanās I have been taught, all the golden opportunities of sēvā, the transformative panchakarma[26] treatments, the powerful pūjās, my immersion into the sādhanā retreats, my marriage, my friendships, Mother Nature, Amritapuri, every tour with Amma, and most of all, every precious darśhan.

I seek the forgiveness of all those who have been exposed to my anger and negativity, known and unknown to me, in any way, ever. Forgive me Amma. May I never take anything for granted and please keep me bound to your most holy lotus feet.

Ahiṁsā is the opposite of the word hiṁsā which can mean destruction. That is just one of many possible meanings. The first letter 'a' negates the meaning of hiṁsā, so ahiṁsā means non-destruction, noninjury, or nonviolence. If I am not destroying something, not causing pain to someone or something in thought, word or deed, then what am I doing?

---

[26] A set of five traditional Āyurvēdic therapies for detoxification and rejuvenation.

Amma said recently, "We should understand the fundamental principle of yōga. Here, the focus is not merely on physical beauty but on the beauty of the mind. When our focus changes to increasing the beauty of the mind, we become people who give beauty to the world and make the entire world beautiful. We should be able to touch people around us with our love and compassion. It is only then that one becomes a true yōgī."

The beauty of ahiṁsā is in giving life its full expression. As Amma tells us, it is a good attitude to collect flowers only after they have fallen to the ground, so that they have had the chance to give their full expression of beauty. And if we must pluck a flower, then doing so towards the end of the day is better, for at least the flower will have had the whole day to reveal and share its beauty and fragrance.

One can imagine the conversation of flowers, as they wave in the wind at us, as they smile through their colors and comfort through their fragrance. "Psst.... You too will blossom like me," said the bird of paradise. "Yeah," chimed in the desert rose, "and don't worry about the rain, it helps us grow and you get to splash in the mud!" "For sure," laughed the hibiscus, "and the monsoon is even better!" "Well," said the jasmine, "I prefer to hide under the violet when it rains, she protects me so nicely." But silently they all wonder, "Will I be plucked for Amma? Will I sit in her garland, will I rest in her hand? Will I adorn her altar, will I land on her head?"

Ahiṁsā is a creative and spiritual force for good. Just as the artist finds those moments of freedom in their art form or as the spiritual aspirant may find those moments of freedom as the instrument of God's grace, or Amma's grace, ahiṁsā attunes to the highest creative powers for adding beauty to the world instead of destruction. Ahiṁsā is adding love and compassion to the world, instead of hate and negativity. Even if we do get angry, we can try to practice ahiṁsā on ourselves by not judging or punishing ourselves. It's very hard when we are really tired or in pain, hungry or scared, agitated, traumatized, or in deep grief. Yet with Amma directing our battlefield within, we have everything we need to overcome these challenges. She will never leave us until there is total victory. Ahiṁsā tells us to be patient, but to act as well. Amma is ever encouraging us in our worthiness to express our spiritual beauty and express that beauty to others, to forgive ourselves and others.

The act of forgiveness and foregoing retaliation is a huge spiritual step. Deep in the psyche, or in our saṁskāras, our past impressions, is the habit of thinking 'an eye for an eye,' 'a tooth for a tooth' — the other deserves to suffer as they made me suffer. It has taken me decades with Amma to pause, reflect, and meditate on the harm felt or caused, and transform it into seeing the destructive acts or words for what they are, actions of the ego, ignorance, and pain. How many countless times did I say things that I regret, trying to get the last word in to be right, which only escalates anger and drains my spiritual energy?

Jesus said in showing mercy to a sinner, "Let he who has not sinned cast the first stone." In other words, how can I possibly judge another's actions when my own are so far from perfect? And when Jesus was asked by his disciple, "How many times should I forgive someone, seven?" probably thinking that was a pretty high number, Jesus replied, "I say not seven times, but seventy times seven." We need to keep forgiving until we have really forgiven, completely, meaning that there is no replay of the hurt in our mind, we have really let it go and moved on. The spiritual principle of ahiṁsā reveres all beings as expressions of the one divine energy, knowing that harm caused to others unfailingly returns to oneself. It is based on the eternal truth that Amma tells us, "The creator and creation are one."

***

In ancient Greece, Socrates was reputed to hold knowledge in high esteem. One day an acquaintance came to meet the great philosopher and said, "Do you know what I just heard about your friend?" Socrates immediately stopped him saying, "Wait a minute. Before you talk to me about my friend, have you made absolutely sure that what you are about to tell me is true?"

"Well, no," the man said, "actually I just heard about it and..."

"Oh! I see," said Socrates. "So, you don't really know if it's true or not. Is what you are about to tell me about my friend something good?"

"Umm, no, on the contrary."

"So," Socrates continued, "you want to tell me something bad about my friend, but you're not certain it's true. Is what you want to tell me about my friend going to be useful to me?"

"No, not really."

"Well," concluded Socrates, "If what you want to tell me about my friend is neither true, nor good, nor even useful, why tell it to me at all?"

As ahiṁsā guides us to be careful with our words, it also guides us, to relieve another's pain, as even to neglect another person in distress is a kind of hiṁsā or violence. Over the years, I have learned that not acting is also an action, and in this case, it can be viewed as an action of omission, not helping someone who needs help. As we evolve, everything, as always, depends on context. We need high levels of discernment. Violence may be justified in order to prevent further harm to oneself or others. And sometimes we have to be forceful with our voice to stop someone from getting hurt, or discipline with love to correct adharma or unrighteousness.

To cultivate ahiṁsā in our day to day lives, it helps to be lighthearted. As I recently read, "Laugh every day, it's like inner jogging." Many years ago in San Ramon, when I asked Amma about comedy and spirituality, she explained that there are different levels, but the highest is the ability to laugh at oneself. Of course, when Amma laughs at us, or corrects us with her love, there is only bliss.

Years ago I was asked to hold an umbrella behind Amma on the beach during meditation to keep the sun out of her eyes. Standing behind Amma's chair, holding a small black umbrella, I tried to shield the sun's rays from Amma's eyes. Within a few minutes Amma swiped the umbrella back towards me, indicating she didn't want it. I am sure that I was not really shielding Amma from the sunlight. But her action made me giggle, and I felt my innocence arise, an inner smile, a baby in the hands of the Divine Mother who was telling me, "Śhraddhā! Have awareness, little one!"

***

Silence helps me to let my emotions cool down, to allow softness inside me before speaking again. Time seems to be a great healer as it can nurture the discernment to question myself and my own emotions. For example, if I have an issue with someone, should I discuss it with that person tomorrow, next week, in a month, a year, or maybe never? With grace, the big inner Self tells the little egoic self the solution.

Chanting one's mantra must be the highest state of peace to offer oneself in our day-to-day life, and especially in times of deep inner conflict. I pray I can begin to have that experience. Sometimes I notice if I do something totally different than the situation that upset me, my mind can reset and find some space. With inner space comes the ability to observe the situation with compassion; that seems to open my heart. That allows me to see that others are trying their best, as I am trying my best. Ahiṁsā cultivates sensitivity, empathy, and compassion towards others and all forms of life. We need only watch Amma, and this truth is easily revealed.

In this Kali Yuga, the current age where discord and unrighteousness predominate, we are greatly challenged. What can we do? Amma tells us to express our love for creation by planting a tree, raising vegetables, caring for each other and Mother Nature, feeding the hungry, and helping those in need. Every act of kindness, no matter how small, a smile or laugh shared, a warm meal, a bed to sleep in, a shoulder to cry on, is an offering to bring the beauty of human hearts together.

In the face of extreme hiṁsā or destruction, I am inspired by the Ukrainians who captured a Russian soldier and gave him tea and food because he was starving. Then they helped him call home to tell his mother he was safe. This is similar to the actions of countless brave people who hid Jews in basements, attics, and trucks during World War II to help them escape death. These are people who chose the high road of care and kindness for our fellow sisters and brothers. They perform heroic deeds every day, in war-torn areas such as Afghanistan, Yemen, Iraq, and Syria, to name a few. Amma's humanitarian projects, implemented through the Embracing the World network, are the perfect and most beautiful examples of ahiṁsā in action. Never before has the world seen the hands and hearts of Dēvī spread her love across the world, to help people in such an everlasting way.

Amma has shown me to seek expansion, as it is our true nature. The ever-expansive embrace of the entire creation, to recognize all as part of oneself, is to realize there is no other, there is only unity, only the One. For that expansion, growth is required with the application of force or pressure at times. This force can also be highly transformational. Amma can create intense circumstances that internally squeeze us so tightly into a corner with our ego, that we have no choice but to finally surrender our mind to her. Why? Because we don't have the answers to our pain, confusion, or ignorance.

Only Amma can heal us. When we give up our wall of defense, which is our denial, we will inevitably feel the release of a greater Self unfoldment. Tension dissolves and peace prevails, even if only for a moment. These endless cycles of growth with Amma's grace, bring us ever closer to ahiṁsā as our hearts become more tender and open, overflowing with love and compassion. I offer my heartfelt prayers to Amma that we all flower fully in the Divine Mother's heart of ahiṁsā.

24

A New Outlook on Life

Valery – Belgium

Today I am six years old. You will understand why later on. You cannot imagine how happy I am to be here. It is an immense joy to see all of you here, and to be with you to share my experiences with Amma.

My wife Sophie, our three children — Youri, Calvin, and Flora — and I had the immense grace to meet Amma on Mauritius Island in April 2016. So now you understand why I am six years old. Since then, as you can imagine, our lives have changed considerably. I can never thank Amma enough for allowing us to meet her in this lifetime.

Our story begins in November, 2015, in Belgium. We had good jobs, a house, and we were healthy; so all the conditions were met for a happy life in the West. We were happy overall, but deep inside, we felt something was missing. Something absolutely fundamental and essential was missing from our lives. So my wife and I secluded ourselves in our living room, for hours on end, in order to think, and to figure out what we were missing. Should we move? Is there a problem with work? Is it a psychological problem? Is it an issue regarding the children? We enquired meticulously about every aspect of our lives, but we couldn't figure out anything specific. After hours of discussion, we came to the conclusion that we had to leave Belgium.

That truth imposed itself on us: the solution to our dissatisfaction was not to be found here. We had to leave. Within a month and a half everything fell into place as if by magic. The only problem remaining was that we just didn't know where to go! We had no preconceived idea of where to travel, but very soon at a school party, we met people who had been traveling around the world and they advised us to go to Mauritius Island. Three days later our daughter Flora, who was five years old at the time, came home from school singing a song about Mauritius. We told ourselves, that might have been a sign. That night I watched a video about Mauritius where I saw people playing drums on the beach of Flic en Flac. I thought the name was funny and I laughed with my wife in the morning before going to work, saying that we would go to Flic en Flac. I was joking!

In the evening, Sophie said to me, "Everything is settled, I booked us for Flic en Flac." I told her, "But wait, I don't even know where Flic en Flac actually is. I don't know if it's a nice place, we don't even have a travel guide." But that's how within three weeks time, we moved with our children to the other side of the world, to Flic en Flac, in Mauritius. We started living as Mauritians. We were part of the local life. We lived in a Tamil village and we participated in the spiritual festivals with all our friends and neighbors. We celebrated *Kāvadi Āttam, Hōli,* and even *Śhivarātri;* these are all Hindu festivals.

Then, after a few months, in April, I became obsessed with the idea of going to Kerala. I told my wife, "We have seen Mauritius inside and out, I want to go to Kerala now. Kerala, Kerala, Kerala." Suddenly, all five of us fell ill with the seasonal flu. Once recovered, we came across a small poster with a photo of our beloved Amma, indicating that she would be in Mauritius from April 26 – 28.

Two years earlier, I told my wife about Amma after seeing a short video of Amma giving darśhan. I told Sophie, "On the internet, I saw a lady saint from India, a woman who gives hugs to thousands of people, and after watching her, I feel an immense sweetness inside me. Her name is Amma." And that was it. Sophie, without ever having seen the face of our beloved Amma, remembered this conversation and said to me, "Look who's coming to Mauritius. We should go see her." Upon returning to our little house, we discovered a huge poster nearby announcing that Amma was coming to the village of Quatre Bornes, not far from our house! All five of us went there.

When we arrived and were seated on our chairs about twenty meters from Amma, the five of us were completely charmed by her. Strong emotions ran through us. We received darśhan for the first time. We were overwhelmed with emotions and cried. Before returning home, we came across a friend who, with immense kindness, took the time to explain everything to us. He told us we could come back the next day and enjoy Amma's presence by sitting close to her. He even went so far as to tell us that we could go and see her in India. To reassure us, he described Amritapuri at great length without forgetting to mention that there was a swimming pool, pizza, extraordinary juices, and milkshakes! I think the milkshakes finally won us over.

While taking the bus home from the program, we discussed the idea of going back the next day. We were a little tired and told the children we would think about it. The children's reaction was immediate, "No, we're going back tomorrow! Sophie and I looked at each other. "All right, we'll go back tomorrow." The next day, in the program hall, we received the divine grace of darśhan, and when it was over and time to move away from Amma, someone caught up with us and told us that Amma wanted us to sit next to her on the stage. Surprised by this, we went there. Once settled near Amma with our three children, Amma kept turning to us making funny faces, each one funnier than the last! We were dumbfounded. I began to understand that I had just met God, incarnated as Amma, and she was making faces at me while relieving the suffering of the people she took in her arms. The moment was quite extraordinary.

Shortly afterward, Sophie turned to me holding a tiny piece of cake and said, "It seems that we have to eat this." Almost mechanically, I swallowed the little piece of cake. Suddenly my face was gripped by intense shivers. Then, my whole head was overcome by shivers. I was overwhelmed with emotion. I burst into tears. I turned to Amma who was looking at me. And that was the tipping point for me. I understood in my heart, "God is in front of me and she is looking at me. I am safe forever. I am living a miracle." Later, before heading home, I was irresistibly drawn to a small green book. We discovered it was an archana book. It would become so precious to us.

We decided to return to the site of the program three weeks after Amma's visit. We were so moved by nostalgia, remembering the experiences we had there. Once we arrived, we discovered... a parking lot; it was a very nice, simple parking lot. That's where the public program had been held. But a little further on, we discovered a small sign that said 'Āshram.'

We went inside this magical Mauritian temple dedicated to Amma. We were ignorant of Indian customs, but we visited the place by looking at different explanatory panels of information about Amma's work. There was a man dressed in yellow seated in a corner. He looked at us kindly and asked us about our presence. We were so excited about our recent meeting with Amma that we naively told him about her visit from a few weeks earlier. We said that meeting Amma had been an extraordinary moment for all of us. We asked him if he had ever had the opportunity to meet Amma. If not, we strongly encouraged him to do so. I said that I didn't want to speculate too much, but I believed Amma was really divine. Suddenly, a couple arrived. They bent down to touch our friend's feet. We understood our mistake. Brahmachārī Sadāśhivāmṛita Chaitanya was so kind to us. He truly welcomed us, as did the whole Mauritian Amma community.

***

We started going to the āśhram two or three times a week. We would hold a satsang group every week at a different devotee's house. It was so welcoming, kind and touching. Everyone brought food. It was a real party.

After five and a half months spent in Mauritius we planned to leave for Montreal, Canada. Shortly before leaving I wondered, "Now that we are attached to these practices, and to Amma, I hope there are other devotees in the world who pray to Amma. Are there any in Montreal?" I looked on the internet and found an Amma center there. It looked like an apartment in the photo. I had fears. Coming from Mauritius and this superb āśhram, with the memories of our devout friends there, what did Montreal have in store for us? I called the number and reached a man who had a beautiful Parisian accent. I asked him if he organized Amma satsangs there. He said yes, satsangs were held in his apartment. Yes, I could bring my family, and yes, I would find it to be a very relaxed setting.

Once there, we discovered a whole group of Quebec devotees. They were so kind to us. Everyone embraced each other and us. That was it, we were adopted again. What a joy to find devotees on the other side of the world who, like us, prayed to Amma. That same day they said, "Did you know Amma is coming in two weeks? Come with us to see Amma in Boston, and we'll go to Toronto for Amma's retreat! We found it hard to believe. Barely after leaving Mauritius, we found our beloved Amma again. We were overflowing with joy and gratitude. All of this could not be a coincidence.

In Toronto we had the great blessing of singing and dancing in front of Amma with our devotee friends. When they asked us if we wanted to do the ārati by waving the lamp in front of Amma, we replied: "The ārati? Which ārati? Yes, why not, we can do the ārati if you want." How innocent we were, and what a great blessing it was!

Once we left Toronto my wife and I began to doubt the idea of settling as expatriates in Montreal as we had planned. Our devotee friends told us that we could ask Amma about it. Ask Amma a question? Here was something new again. Incredible! Ask God a question! In our lifetime! We'd be asking about a subject that may seem trivial, but in our eyes it mattered a lot: 'Where should we settle with our children?' Without really consulting each other, my wife and I asked Amma the same question individually during darśhan. For my part, I listed a dozen places in the world on paper. Belgium, the United States, Australia, France, and so on. As I got closer to Amma, I trembled, as always. I arrived on my knees with my little paper in my hands. It was then that Amma said to me, "Sit there and meditate on your question."

I was so freaked out and my ego was rising to the surface. I replied, "What, sorry, I didn't understand." Three times she had to repeat it. Disconcerted and slightly disappointed, I sat down and began to meditate. After three minutes, I experienced a very intense white flash of light in my head, accompanied by a word that resonated with extraordinary force. Belgiuuuuuuum!!! Later I learned that Sophie had had exactly the same experience, and we both burst into tears.

After the last program we returned to Montreal. On the way home, driving over a Montreal bridge overlooking the city, I said to my wife, "I'm so happy to be moving to Montreal. We'll be so happy here." Yeah, right... A few days later the administrative requirements and procedures for our move to Montreal were blocked and we realized that something was wrong. Sophie and I remembered what Amma had told us. Two weeks later we were back in Belgium. We then found out how important this decision was for the five of us. Sophie's mother was diagnosed with Alzheimer's disease. Very quickly we met with Belgian devotees who sympathized with us. They told us, "Did you know that Amma will be here in three weeks for her European Tour?" We couldn't believe our ears! What a blessing.

With our three children back in school, we were able to join a few stops on the tour. To be able to see Amma, this time only three hours by car from our house, was incredible. It touched us so much to know that God had come this far to embrace us.

At a program in Holland, our eldest son, Youri, found himself in the line for questions. Only ten people were allowed to ask a question to Amma per program. Since Youri was only eleven years old, I asked him, "Are you sure you have an important question to ask Amma?" Youri said yes he did, but he politely declined to tell me what he was going to ask Amma. "Well, all right," I thought. A few moments after he asked his question, we found Youri with a huge smile on his face. He said, "I asked Amma if we should come to her āśhram in India, and if we could come in December, and she replied, 'Yes, come in December, come in December!'" Sophie and I looked at each other with smiles that said, "I have the impression we will soon leave for India."

***

Our first arrival here in Amritapuri, our true home, was in December 2016. Thank you, Amma, for all these gifts, and for your wonderful hospitality. Since then, we have returned here every year until February 2020, shortly before the Covid-19 pandemic. Amma has always been there, close to all of us, accompanying us every day. Each test, whether small or big, has become a lesson; a prasād or blessed gift from Amma. This is one of Amma's greatest miracles: She showed us how to change our outlook on the world and on our lives. It is so important for all our brothers and sisters around the world to know that there is a place here, Amritapuri, from which light shines on the rest of the world.

***

I would just like to share two more experiences regarding Amma's teachings, or at least how I have interpreted certain experiences in regard to Sanātana Dharma. When we traveled to Amritapuri in 2019 — actually, it's pretty much the same every time we come here — the entire trip takes us around forty hours from our home to the āśhram. We love to travel, the trip is always an exciting adventure. Despite that, it requires a lot of preparation, and traveling with three kids requires us to be constantly very alert.

We took several different means of transportation; first our car, then the bus to reach Paris, then the plane, etc. Finally we arrived here, a little tired, but so relieved to be here, and grateful that everything went well on the trip. We went to the International Office to check in.

I asked the person at the desk, "Today is Wednesday, right?" "Yes, yes," was the reply. "So, it is a darśhan day?" I asked. "Yes, absolutely. Do you want to go to darśhan? Here are the last darśhan tokens. I have five left," he said. Five tokens...

Of the thousands of devotees who came to the program and for darśhan that day, after forty hours of travel where we couldn't miss any of our close connections, we received the last five tokens. Less than two minutes later, a devotee arrived asking if there were any darśhan tokens left, but we had already received the last five. It was another sign from Amma. I associated it with the need that we all have to practice śhraddhā. One must never lose one's attention and alertness.

I should also tell you about my first South India tour with Amma. At that time, I was determined to go on the tour, but Sophie and the children, for logistical reasons, could not accompany me. I was really excited to go, and had been preparing for it for a long time. The moment of departure finally arrived. It was with great emotions that Sophie and the children ran behind the bus taking me away on the tour. That was the first time I traveled with Amma, but without my family.

A few minutes later, a strange thing happened to me, a funny feeling. I no longer felt anything. I felt totally disconnected from Amma, from the tour, and from all my surroundings. What happened to me? Until then, almost everything had been based on my feelings. Amma's love led to the emotional and physical intuitions to follow her, and to follow her teachings. Those feelings had become my barometer. And then, suddenly, for the first time...nothing. Very quickly, I drew a conclusion: It was a sign. Amma was telling me that this was not my *dharma*, not my duty. If I didn't feel anything anymore, it was because I had turned away from Amma's path. Yes, it was clear that I must stay with my family. I immediately called my wife. It had been barely fifteen minutes since I got on the bus; the children hardly had time to dry their tears.

"Hello Sophie," I said, "I don't feel anything anymore." "What? How come you don't feel anything — what do you mean?" she said. "Well, what can I tell you?" I said. "I feel like I'm all alone at a seaside resort in the middle of winter. I feel like I'm in the wrong place. I think Amma is telling me that this is not my dharma. Look, I'm going with the tour to Trivandrum. From there I'll take a taxi and go back to Belgium with you and the kids." "Are you sure?" she said. "What else can I do?" I replied. I went to Trivandrum. There, I shared my anxieties with some of my Amma brothers and sisters who, strangely, were all quite hard on me. I was even scolded by some of them. They said, "No, man, it's your ego." Then a friend who was responsible for the sēvā assignments on the tour came to find me and said, "Finally, I'm putting you on the pot washing team." "Ah, what is pot washing?" I asked. "You'll see, you'll wash away a lot of karma," he replied.

Gulp. I did my first shift, from 10 p.m. until midnight. At midnight, there were people missing. We kept going until around 2 a.m., but there were still some dishes. At 4 a.m. we went to bed. However, people were needed at 7 a.m. for pot loading sēvā. We were there and finished at 11 a.m. At that point, we were all called to get on the buses for the next stop. Once on the bus and back on the road, my Amma brothers asked me, "So, you didn't take the taxi after all?" I answered, "What are you talking about?" — That was a great lesson from Amma about sēvā. I recommend sēvā to all those who, like me, sometimes ask themselves too many questions.

I am so grateful to Amma especially for the wonderful values that she transmitted and taught with patience and love. May Amma's love and teachings live on forever.

25

Learning Spirituality through Selfless Service

Dr. Deepa Straub – Germany

When we worship the Guru's feet, we worship the values and virtues embodied by the Guru. When we bow down to Amma's feet, we worship her for being rooted with both feet in this world, in our lives, and in our hearts.

In the *Śhrī Lalitā Sahasranāma,* one of the names of the Divine Mother is: 'ōm guru mūrtayē namaḥ.'[27] It means, 'Salutations to the Divine Mother who has assumed the form of the Guru.' Amma's presence as the Divine Mother teaches us the essence of the scriptures through the incomparable example of her life. By living our lives with her, and just by observing her, we witness the underlying principles, the very foundation of spirituality. My limited experience and knowledge about spirituality and the scriptures comes only from witnessing Amma's words and actions.

I was a little girl when I met Amma and I have no memory of a life without her. So I can't tell you how Amma changed my life. But I do know that once we have surrendered to Amma and she has taken our hand to guide us, either knowingly or unknowingly, everything will be taken care of in the most perfect way.

I say perhaps 'unknowingly' because only by looking back at my life can I see her great masterplan. Amma walks one step in front of us to show the way. She knows the individual path each one of us will take that ultimately leads to her. Amma says, "The

---

[27] *Lalitā Sahasranāma,* 603.

fulfillment of spirituality is the ability to love and serve others." Amma shows us true spirituality by her example of compassion in action. We can attain spirituality through sēvā, which will be the topic of today's satsang.

My parents' quest for spiritual guidance must have been strong and sincere, because they had the rare opportunity to meet Amma during one of her early visits to Munich in 1994, when my sister and I were little children. I do not exactly remember my first darśhan, but I was told that I wanted another darśhan after having received our family darśhan, and that I was determined to go through the line again by myself. When I reached Amma, she put me on the seat next to her and gave me some more candies. After that, my parents prepared for our departure to India, and from 1996 onwards I would visit Amritapuri regularly.

By that time, Amma had already left a great impression on us. During our first airplane flight when there was some turbulence, my little sister and I started to sing "Ōm Namaḥ Śhivāya"[28] from the bottom of our hearts, singing the fear away. It's important to repeat spiritual practices, songs and mantras, so that in an emergency, we can hold on to them.

My childhood memories of Amritapuri are those of a paradise on Earth: We would sing bhajans with Amma in the Kāḷī Temple, or while Amma was sitting on the pīṭham (Guru's seat) with all the children around her. We would play games with Amma like hopping on one foot while Amma tried to catch us. We traveled with Amma, and bathed with her in rivers during the roadside stops. We did sēvā with Amma and her senior disciples. At Christmas time, Amma would watch from the balcony of the Kāḷī Temple as the āśhram children performed plays for her. I

---

[28] 'Salutations to Śhiva, the auspicious one, the inner Self,' a famous mantra that is also used as a greeting in Amma's āśhrams.

have photos where I am playing an angel one year. These are all memories of my precious childhood with Amma. I can recall and hold onto those memories whenever I'm feeling far from her.

***

As a youth, I realized that having Amma in my life had already helped me for a long time. Amma's principles, her example, and her unconditional love made me a self-confident young girl. I felt that other young people should also be able to learn from Amma's example. This idea became my motivation for engaging in AYUDH[29] meetings. As young people, we start to look for the purpose of life; we look for role models with whom we can identify. By giving purpose to our lives, Amma is like a torchlight guiding us in the darkness.

I was eager to go to the first AYUDH meeting in Europe organized by Swāmī Śhubhāmṛitānandajī in 2004 in Germany. The first year, I went as a participant and was filled with Amma's love. I made new friends and started to play music with them for Amma. The next year, I helped organize the event. The annual AYUDH Europe Summits are designed to make Amma and her teachings accessible to young people. Participating in AYUDH was a wonderful way to strengthen my own relationship with Amma. Even though I grew up with Amma, it was still my responsibility to decide how much time I wanted to spend with her, and what priority to give her in my life.

With Amma's grace and with continuous guidance from Swāmī Amṛitaswarūpānanda, Swāmī Śhubhāmṛitānanda and Swāminī Amṛitajyōti Prāṇā, AYUDH Europe started to grow. Large numbers of young people from all over the continent joined the week-long programs which contained a variety of

[29] 'Amrita Yuva Dharmadhara' or 'Amma's Youth for Unity, Diversity and Humanity' — the youth wing of the Mata Amritanandamayi Math.

inspirational talks, workshops, and opportunities to discuss and propose solutions to the challenges of today's society.

Amma says, "If our youth arise and act, they have the strength to create huge transformation in society. Only through awakening the inner power dormant within us will there be true transformation and a permanent solution to the problems facing society."

For its tenth anniversary in 2014, AYUDH Europe was present at the European Parliament in an event titled 'Strengthening Europe through Youth Empowerment' which engaged nearly 300 young participants from twenty-three countries.

Amma enables us to find our own inner power which grows out of compassion and love in action. Amma's youngsters in AYUDH Europe, and all over the world, have repeatedly shown that they care about the wellbeing of others, and about the environment. They are also touched deeply by the challenges many youth face such as being bullied in school and then losing the enthusiasm for life. In response to those challenges, AYUDH Europe initiated the "RespAct" project against cyberbullying in schools in 2015.

Over the years, AYUDH has engaged in projects such as helping the homeless, collecting garbage, planting trees, distributing food, and assisting the elderly, all activities inspired by Amma's example.

During the pandemic, our Youth Summit titled, 'Act Today for a Better Tomorrow,' was awarded the Best Practice Project by the European Union, stating that Amma's Youth and their way of carrying out projects should be seen as a role model for other youth initiatives.

Many of us suffer because we feel we don't contribute to the world. We feel that the subjects we are studying or the jobs we are doing are not making any difference to the world. Only because I have Amma by my side do I have an education and a profession connected to the service of society.

***

When I finished school, the graduation gift I wanted was a flight to Amritapuri. I made the firm decision that I wanted to live my life as close as possible to Amma. I was determined to make Amma the center of all my decisions in life. So, I asked Amma, "What should I study?" I expected her to tell me the best field to further my education. But Amma answered, "Amma is always with you. You are Amma's daughter. Whatever you do, Amma is with you!" Even today I find it hard to understand the underlying deep message in the reaffirmation that Amma is always with me. I guess the message was to look inside.

But Amma kept her word. My studies brought me to Vienna where I met my future husband who was also a devotee. Amma married us during my second year at university. Our common interest in spirituality made our householder lives fully dedicated to service. I felt closer to home and to Amma.

When I finished my master's degree, I had many options and didn't know which one to pursue. So I asked Amma, "What should I do for work?" Amma again replied, "You can do whatever you want, Amma is always with you!" I went on Amma's North America Tour instead of attending my graduation ceremony, traveled with Amma in India, and started to prepare a research proposal for my PhD. But when I presented it to Amma, she didn't quite approve. She said, "Find a good job and from your experience there, you will write your PhD."

But what was a good job? From the perspective of the world, the criteria would include a good salary, fair working hours in a trusted company, etc. But what was a good job in Amma's eyes? If the job were to meet her criteria, it would definitely have to benefit someone else's life. Amma says that a life spent in service is never a wasted life.

I found a job setting up a mentoring program for marginalized youth financed by the Austrian Bank's charitable foundation. After three years at that job, I drafted a new proposal for my PhD in Social Sciences and showed it to Amma during her Europe Tour. After that, I was immediately admitted to a doctoral program at the University of Vienna with the feedback that my topic was very relevant for social sciences. Ultimately, I even got a job offer as a researcher and lecturer at the same university.

This all happened because I had listened to Amma's words and followed her advice. She knew what would be a good PhD topic, one that would make my research valuable for the upliftment of others, rather than just being pursued for the sake of earning a title. Her university, the Amrita University, functions by her credo, so that all research outcomes serve those less privileged in society.

By leading me through the process of finding a topic for my PhD, I learned that if we include Amma in our life decisions, she is always close to us and watches our every step. She appears in the form of a university professor, as the loving mother of compassion, and as the Guru. In her school we learn the necessary skills to succeed in our profession, and at the same time, her advice is always for our spiritual development and for the benefit of the world.

Amma says, "In today's world people experience two types of poverty; the poverty caused by lack of food, clothing and shelter, and the poverty caused by lack of love and compassion." Through selfless service we can address both aspects of poverty mentioned by Amma. But what makes an action a selfless action, and what makes an action a spiritual practice? I am not talking about this topic because I have any knowledge of sēvā or Karma Yōga — there are more learned people to talk about those subjects in Amma's āśhram. But I am always fascinated by the way Amma creates innumerable sēvā opportunities for her children. I came to the conclusion that this must be part of her plan to uplift both the individual soul and the entire world.

We can look at sēvā as a way of expressing our gratitude towards the Divine Mother for having stepped into our lives to guide us. Amma says, "We must become grateful. We are indebted to this world and all its creatures for raising and nurturing us. This Earth, this nature is our mother. We must never forget our debt to our mother." Sēvā can be a way of saying thank you, but it can also be a spiritual practice that transforms our human habit of taking into our true nature of giving. Thus, sēvā can restore balance in our lives.

Amma doesn't need anything, nor does she ask for anything from us. Getting the chance to serve is a rare gift. Sēvā repays debts accumulated over many lives, and at the same time, it gives us a chance to reduce our egoistic tendencies by thinking of the needs of others.

Anyone who has had a chance to serve in one of Amma's programs, centers, or charitable projects, knows that a group of people working together is always required. For decades, I have helped with various tasks at Amma's programs. Each job is significant. Only by working together can the culmination of our individual actions result in Amma's huge public programs. Some of us take smaller roles, others carry more responsibility. Everyone works according to their current situation and capacity. But what unites us all is the goal of making Amma's visit possible. We pray for God's grace that Amma will be able to travel to visit all her children again soon.

The kitchen is a great place to experience how people can serve together. During Amma's North America Tour, I had the chance to join Amma's kitchen staff and assist with cooking three meals per day. Each meal depends on the efforts of many volunteers including those who purchase large amounts of ingredients at the stores, the delivery team, the people who wash the vegetables, the ones who cut them, the cooks who prepare the vegetables into a meal, those who transport the cooked food from the kitchen to the dining area, the food servers, and finally all the volunteers who clean up everything at the end. This process is repeated for every meal, three times a day. By working for the common goal of ensuring that everyone gets a warm meal, we focus less on our own achievements and respect the group effort more.

Next, we can look at selfless service as a spiritual practice by realizing that there is an all-pervasive power inherent in each one of us and that ultimately we are not separate from each other. When the feeling of doership slowly disappears, we get a glimpse of what's possible if we permit God to act through us. Śhrī Kṛiṣhṇa teaches this to Arjuna in the *Bhagavad Gītā*, Chapter 2, verse 47:

> *karmaṇy-ēvādhikāras tē mā phalēṣhu kadāchana*
> *mā karma-phala-hetur bhūr mā tē saṅgō 'stvakarmaṇi*
> 'You have control over action alone, never over its fruits. Live not for the fruits of action, nor attach yourself to inaction.'

The gist of this verse is that in order to reach the ultimate truth we must always act, but never expect the results of our actions to be under our control, nor claim that we have achieved something by our own power.

Thus, we need to surrender ourselves to the Paramātman, the Supreme Self. By incorporating this truth into our actions we perform sēvā, true spiritual practice with the proper understanding that 'I am not the doer, I am a mere instrument in the hands of God.' Finally, this becomes an offering for the wellbeing of others.

***

Assisting with Amma's darśhan was another sēvā experience that taught me a great lesson. During one long shift, I was unable to focus on Amma's body and her feet at the same time. I was supposed to ensure that no one hurt Amma's feet by kneeling on them, or hurt her body by putting too much pressure on her when they leaned forward for a hug. I had to remind people about these concerns in advance, as they waited in line for darśhan in a nice, gentle way. Unfortunately, I failed. So, Amma started to train me. First she said, "Please take care, people are leaning on Amma. You need to tell them what to do. They don't know." I did as instructed. After some time, Amma told me not to disturb or interrupt anyone's meeting with her. So I stepped back and didn't interfere.

Watching Amma give darśhan made me think that Amma doesn't need my help at all. She just needs to work through me. No one can be of service to Amma without becoming her additional arms and legs. Such an attitude is possible only by tuning into Amma's flow and rhythm and forgetting any preconceptions of what might be the right action to take at any given time. I hope to apply this lesson to all my actions, making it a real way to serve people and God simultaneously.

Ultimately, sēvā can become a way of developing love and compassion through devotion. Amma tells us that love arises when the 'I' decreases; since in love, there is only one.

Doing selfless service for Amma's organization is more than volunteering for a good cause — it is a rare opportunity to learn and grow spiritually with Amma's divine guidance. By putting devotion into our actions, sēvā can become the way to focus our minds.

Once Amma spoke about Hanumān as follows, "The monkey symbolizes the mind that never stops chattering. The easiest way to overcome such a mind and to gain single-pointed focus is to assume 'dāsya bhāva,' the attitude of a servant, in our approach to God."

Hanumān is a great example of a selfless servant. He had no doubts regarding the all-pervading power of his Lord Rāma. Hanumān acted out of love for his Lord without fear. That is why he accomplished every task. Just by uttering Rāma's holy name, Hanumān was able to achieve the impossible. And, he never expected anything for himself in return, due to his unshakable devotion to the Lord.

***

During one of Amma's Munich programs, towards the end of her very busy three-day visit, I was helping with the darśhan line. Amma asked if all the people doing sēvā had already come for darśhan. Amma was in Dēvī Bhāva and wanted to see all her children before she had to leave for the next city. I told her that we gave darśhan tokens to everyone. Amma didn't seem happy. She told me to go through all the departments and tell all the people doing sēvā to come for darśhan. I went through all the departments, inside and outside the hall, and asked if all the sēvā people had gone for darśhan. Everyone said yes. I went back to Amma, but still she was not happy. She asked me whether I had gone to the sleeping area. I had to admit that I hadn't checked there. She said that some of the sēvā people might be sleeping, and to please tell them to come soon. I went to the sleeping area and woke up every single person.

It turned out that indeed some people would have missed Dēvī Bhāva darśhan. They were sleeping in anticipation of having to clean the hall after the program, in the early morning hours. I went back to Amma. Again, she didn't seem totally pleased. She asked me if I had been to the dishwashing area and I said yes. Then Amma said that some of her children were doing sēvā there and hadn't come for darśhan yet, and that she missed them. I went to the dishwashing area but couldn't find anyone who hadn't been for darśhan. Again I reported to Amma and she said, "Daughter, go to the café where there is a little dishwashing area. The people there have not come for darśhan. Please tell them that Amma is waiting for them. Amma had never been to that part of the venue, and yet her heart was there, thinking of the people doing sēvā.

When I went there to tell them that Amma was waiting for them, they didn't believe me. They asked, "Who sent you? We can't go for darśhan now, we will go another time." But I insisted that Amma wanted to see them now. Finally, they came for darśhan and realized that Amma really had been waiting for them.

As Amma says, "In true love there is only one." Even if we feel far away from Amma, she constantly thinks of us. So we can see that selfless service is a way of becoming one with Amma. Amma says, "My children are not separate from me; they are all in me and I am in them."

Glossary

abhyāsa: unrelenting spiritual practice, constant effort.

advaita: not two; non-dual; philosophy that holds that the *jīva* (individual soul) and *jagat* (universe) are essentially one with *Brahman*, the supreme reality.

ahiṁsā: non-injury, non-violence, to refrain from hurting any living creature by thought, word or deed.

AIMS Hospital: Amrita Institute of Medical Sciences, a super-specialty hospital in Kochi, Kerala.

Amma(chi): Malayalam word for 'mother.'

Amṛitānandamayī: 'full of immortal bliss,' the name by which Amma is universally known.

Amritapuri: The international headquarters of Mata Amritanandamayi Math, located at Amma's birthplace in Kerala, India.

AmritaSREE: Amrita Self-Reliance, Employment & Empowerment, a network of self-help groups managed by the Mata Amritanandamayi Math and aimed at empowering unemployed and economically vulnerable women by providing them with skill and vocational training and by encouraging those who are interested to become entrepreneurs.

Amṛitēśhvarī: goddess of immortality, a name of the Divine Mother.

Annapūrnēśhvarī: goddess of food and nourishment.

ārati: a traditional ritual involving the waving of a lighted lamp to the Guru or deity usually done towards the end of *pūjā* or worship. At some of Amma's programs, multiple devotees take turns waving the lighted lamp to Amma as she showers them with flower petals and the ārati song is sung.

archana: chanting of the 108 or 1,000 names of a particular deity (e.g. *'Lalitā Sahasranāma'*).

āsana: physical posture, usually referring to *yōga* postures or sitting postures during meditation. Also, the seat on which one sits for spiritual practice.

āśhram: 'place of striving.' A place where spiritual seekers and aspirants live or visit, in order to lead a spiritual life. It is usually the home of a spiritual master, saint or ascetic, who guides the aspirants.

ātmā (ātman): The true Self. The essential nature of our real existence. One of the fundamental tenets of *Sanātana Dharma* is that we are not the physical body, feelings, mind, intellect, or personality. We are the eternal, pure, unblemished Self.

avatār: from Sanskrit root *'ava-tarati'* — 'to come down.' Divine incarnation.

AYUDH: 'Amrita Yuva Dharmadhara' or 'Amma's Youth for Unity, Diversity and Humanity' — the youth wing of the Mata Amritanandamayi Math.

Bhagavad Gītā: 'Song of the Lord,' it consists of 18 chapters of verses in which Lord Kṛiṣhṇa advises Arjuna. The advice is given on the battlefield of Kurukṣhētra, just before the righteous Pāṇḍavas fight the unrighteous Kauravas. It is a practical guide to overcoming crises in one's personal or social life and is the essence of *Vēdic* wisdom.

bhajan: devotional song or hymn in praise of God.

bhakta: devotee.

bhakti: devotion for God.

bhakti yōga: the path of devotion.

bhāva: divine mood or attitude.

bhaya-bhakti: devotion arising from fear of repercussion.

brahmachārī: celibate male disciple who practices spiritual disciplines under a Guru's guidance; '*brahmachāriṇī*' is the female equivalent.

Brahman: the absolute reality, supreme being; the Whole; that which encompasses and pervades everything, and is One and indivisible.

Brahmasthānam: 'abode of *Brahman*.' The name of the temples Amma consecrated in various parts of India and in Mauritius. The temple shrine features a unique four-faced idol that symbolizes the unity behind the diversity of divine forms.

darśhan: audience with a holy person or a vision of the Divine. Amma's signature darśhan is a hug.

darśhan token: 'token' = a numbered ticket given out to devotees wanting to receive Amma's darshan.

Dēvī: goddess; Divine Mother.

Dēvī Bhāva: 'the divine mood of *Dēvī*;' occasion when Amma reveals her oneness with the Divine Mother.

dharma: 'that which upholds (creation).' Generally refers to the harmony of the universe, a righteous code of conduct, sacred duty or eternal law.

dhōti: traditional Indian outer garment worn around the waist and legs.

dīkṣhā: initiation. Transfer of spiritual power from the *Guru* to the disciple.

Dṛig-Dṛiśhya-Vivēka: Distinction between the Seer and the Seen', a methodology of inquiry as well as the title of a popular *Advaita Vedantic* text.

dṛiṣhṭa phalam: literally 'visible fruit.' Refers to the perceived result of an action.

Embracing the World: Embracing the World® (ETW) is Amma's global network of humanitarian initiatives.

Gaṅgā: most sacred river in India. Known as the Ganges river in English.

guṇa: one of three types of qualities, viz. *sattva*, *rajas* and *tamas.* Human beings express a combination of these qualities. Sāttvic qualities are associated with calmness and wisdom, rājasic with activity and restlessness, and tāmasic with dullness or apathy.

Guru: spiritual teacher.

guru bhāva: attitude of *Guru* to someone who expresses sincerity and yearning for spiritual instruction.

guru kṛipā: Guru's grace.

Guru Pūrṇimā: the full moon ('*pūrṇimā*') day in the Hindu month of Āṣhāḍha (June – July) in which disciples honor the Guru; also, the birthday of Sage Vyāsa, compiler of the *Vēdas*, and author of the *Purāṇas*, *Brahmasūtras*, *Mahābhārata* and the Śhrīmad *Bhāgavatam.*

Hanumān: the *vānara* (monkey) disciple and companion of Rāma and one of the key characters in the *Rāmāyaṇa.*

haṭha yōga: physical exercises or āsanas designed to enhance one's overall well-being by toning the body and opening the various channels of the body to promote the free flow of energy; the science of *prāṇāyama* (breath control), which includes other aspects of *yōga*, including āsanas and *mudras* (esoteric hand gestures that express specific energies or powers).

IAM: Integrated Amrita Meditation Technique® is a meditation practice formulated by Amma that integrates gentle relaxation stretches with an effective and easy-to-practice breathing and concentration technique. It is based on traditional methods and designed for the time constraints of modern life.

īśhvara: God.

japa: repeated chanting of a *mantra.*

-jī: an honorific suffixed to names or titles to show respect.

jīva: individual self or soul.

jñāna yōga: the path of knowledge.

jñānī: a person who has realized God or the Self; one who knows the Truth.

jyōtiṣh: *Vēdic* system of astrology.

Kāḷī: Goddess of fearsome aspect; depicted as dark, wearing a garland of skulls, and a girdle of human hands; feminine of *kāla* (time).

Kali Yuga: the present dark age of materialism and ignorance (see *yuga*).

karma: action; mental, verbal and physical activity; chain of effects produced by our actions.

karma phala: results of previous actions.

karma yōga: the way of action, the path of selfless service.

kṛipā: divine grace.

Kṛiṣhṇa: from *'kṛiṣh,'* meaning 'to draw to oneself' or 'to remove sin;' principal incarnation of Lord Viṣhṇu. He was born into a royal family but raised by foster parents, and lived as a cowherd boy in Vṛindāvan, where he was loved and worshiped by his devoted companions, the *gōpīs* (milkmaids) and *gōpas* (cowherd boys). Kṛiṣhṇa later established the city of Dwāraka. He was a friend and advisor to his cousins, the Pāṇḍavas, especially Arjuna, whom he served as charioteer during the

Mahābhārata War, and to whom he revealed his teachings as the *Bhagavad Gītā*.

Lalitā Sahasranāma: 1,000 names of Śhrī Lalitā Dēvī, a form of the Goddess.

līlā: divine play.

mā: mother.

mahā: great.

Mahābhārata: ancient Indian epic that Sage Vyāsa composed, depicting the war between the righteous Pāṇḍavas and the unrighteous Kauravas.

mahātmā: 'great soul;' term used to describe one who has attained spiritual realization.

Mahiṣhāsura Mardini Stōtram: hymn in praise of the Divine Mother who slayed the buffalo demon.

mālā: garland; rosary, usually made of *rudrākṣha* seeds, *tulasī* wood or sandalwood beads.

Malayāḷam: language spoken in the Indian state of Kerala.

Malayāli: one whose mother-tongue is Malayalam.

mānasa pūjā: worship done mentally.

manasthiti: attitude (lit. 'state of mind'). Often contrasted with *paristhiti* (circumstance).

mantra: a sound, syllable, word or words of spiritual content. According to *Vēdic* commentators, *mantras* are revelations of *ṛiṣhis* arising from deep contemplation.

Matruvani: 'Voice of the Mother.' The āśhram's flagship publication dedicated to disseminating Amma's teachings and chronicling her divine mission. It is currently published in 17 languages (including nine Indian languages).

māyā: cosmic delusion, personified as a temptress; illusion; appearance, as contrasted with reality; the creative power of the Lord.

(Ōm) Namaḥ Śhivāya: 'Salutations to Śhiva, the auspicious one, the inner Self,' a famous *mantra*; greeting used in Amma's āśhrams.

niyama: positive duties or observances (the 'do's'); the second 'limb' of the *aṣhṭāṅga yōga* (eight limbs) formulated by Sage Patañjali, and they include śhaucha (purity), *santōṣha* (contentment), *tapas* (austerity), *svādhyāya* (scriptural study) and īśhvara-praṇidhāna (contemplation of God); often mentioned in association with *yama*.

Ōm: primordial sound in the universe; the seed of creation. The cosmic sound, which can be heard in deep meditation; the Holy Word, taught in the *upaniṣhads*, which signifies *Brahman*, the divine ground of existence.

pāda pūjā: ceremonial washing of the feet as a form of worship.

panchabhūta: The five (pañcha) elements (*bhūtas*) that are the material cause of creation. The five elements are ākāśha (ether), *vāyu* (air), *agni* (fire), *jalam* (water) and *pṛithvī* (earth).

panchakarma: set of five traditional Āyurvēdic therapies for detoxification and rejuvenation aiming to cleanse the body and restore balance.

paramātman: supreme Self, *Brahman*.

paristhiti: circumstance, situation. Often contrasted with *manasthiti* (attitude).

pīṭham: small platform; seat for the Guru; also: a center of learning and power.

prakṛiti: nature; primal matter.

prāṇa: vital force.

prasād: blessed offering or gift from a holy person or temple, often in the form of food.

prēmabhakti: highest form of love of God, comparable to *parābhakti.*

pūjā: ritualistic or ceremonial worship.

pūjāri: one who performs ritualistic or ceremonial worship

pūrṇa (pūrṇam): full or whole / spiritual fullness.

pūrṇimā: full moon.

Rāma: divine hero of the *Rāmāyaṇa*. An incarnation of Lord Vișhṇu, he is considered the ideal man of *dharma* and virtue. 'Ram' means 'to revel;' one who revels in himself; the principle of joy within; one who gladdens the hearts of others.

Rāmakṛiṣhṇa Paramahaṁsa: spiritual master (1836 – 1886) from West Bengal, hailed as the apostle of religious harmony. He generated a spiritual renaissance that continues to touch the lives of millions.

Rāmāyaṇa: 24,000-verse epic poem on the life and times of Rāma.

ṛiṣhi: seer to whom mantras are revealed in deep meditation.

sādhak (sādhaka): Spiritual aspirant or seeker, one dedicated to attaining the spiritual goal, one who practices *sādhanā.*

sādhanā: regimen of disciplined and dedicated spiritual practice that leads to the supreme goal of Self-realization.

sākṣhī: witness, referring to the inner observer of experiences and thoughts.

samādhi: Oneness with God; a state of deep, one-pointed concentration, in which all thoughts subside. The mind enters into a state of complete stillness in which only pure consciousness remains as one abides in the ātman or Self.

samarpaṇam: handing completely over, surrendering.

saṁsāra: cycle of births and deaths; the world of flux; the wheel of birth, decay, death and rebirth.

saṁskāra: imprints or impressions left on the mind as a result of past experiences, actions, and thoughts. These imprints shape an individual's character, tendencies, and reactions in future situations. For this reason, traditional rites in Sanatana Dharma are also called saṁskāras.

Sanātana Dharma: 'Eternal Way of Life,' the original and traditional name of Hinduism.

saṅkalpa: divine resolve, usually used in association with *mahātmās*.

sannyāsin: monk (or nun) who has taken vows of renunciation

sāri: traditional outer garment of Indian women consisting of a long, unstitched piece of cloth wrapped around the body.

sat-chit-ānanda: lit. 'existence-consciousness-bliss,' a description of the subjective experience of the Supreme.

Satguru: 'true master.' All *Satgurus* are *mahātmās*, but not all mahātmās are Satgurus. The Satguru is one who, while still experiencing the bliss of the Self, chooses to come down to the level of ordinary people in order to help them grow spiritually.

satsang: 'communion with the supreme truth.' Also, being in the company of *mahātmās*, studying the scriptures, and listening to the enlightening talks of a mahātmā; a meeting of people to listen to and/or discuss spiritual matters; a spiritual discourse.

sēvā: selfless service, the results of which are dedicated to God.

śhakti: personification of cosmic will and energy; strength; see *māyā*.

Śhiva: the static aspect of *Brahman* as the male principle. Worshiped as the first in the lineage of Gurus, and as the formless substratum of the universe in relationship to the creatrix Śhakti. He is the Lord of destruction in the trinity of Brahmā (Lord of creation), Viṣhṇu (Lord of preservation), and Śhiva. Usually depicted as a mendicant, with ash all over his body, snakes in his hair, wearing only a loincloth and with a begging bowl and a trident in his hands.

śhraddhā: attentiveness; faith.

śhrī: a title of respect originally meaning 'divine,' 'holy' or 'auspicious;' now in modern India, simply a respectful form of address, similar to 'Mr.'

Sudhāmaṇi: Amma's birth name.

sūtra: aphorism.

swāmī: title of one who has taken the vow of *sannyāsa* (see *sannyāsin*); *swāminī* is the female equivalent.

tamas: darkness; inertia; apathy; ignorance. Tamas is one of the three *guṇas* or fundamental qualities of Nature.

tapas (tapasya): austerities, penance.

token: see darśhan token.

upaniṣhad: portions of the *Vēdas* dealing with Self-knowledge.

vairāgya: dispassion.

vāsanā: latent tendency or subtle desire that manifests as thought, motive and action; subconscious impression gained from experience.

Vēdānta: 'end of *Vēda*.' The philosophy of the *upaniṣhads*, the concluding part of the Vēdas, which holds the Ultimate Truth to be "One without a second." A *Vēdāntin* is a follower of Vēdānta.

Vēdāntic: pertaining to Vēdānta.

Vēdas: most ancient of all scriptures, originating from God, the *Vēdas* were not composed by any human author but were 'revealed' in deep meditation to the ancient seers. These sagely revelations came to be known as the *Vēdas*, of which there are four: *Ṛig*, *Yajur*, *Sāma* and *Atharva*.

Vṛindāvan: A region in Mathura district in Uttar Pradesh, celebrated as the place where Kṛiṣhṇa passed his early days as a cowherd.

yama: restraints for proper conduct (the 'don'ts'); the first 'limb' of the *aṣhṭānga yōga* (eight limbs) formulated by Sage *Patañjali*, and they include *ahiṁsā* (non-violence), *satya* (truthfulness), *astēya* (non-stealing), *brahmacharya* (chastity) and *aparigraha* (non-covetousness); often mentioned in association with *niyama*.

yōga: 'to unite.' Union with the Supreme Being. A broad term, it also refers to the various methods of practices through which one can attain oneness with the Divine. A path that leads to Self-realization.

Yōga Sūtras: *Patañjali Yōga Sūtras*,' aphorisms composed by Sage *Patañjali* on the path to purification and transcendence of the mind.

yuga: according to the Hindu worldview, the universe (from origin to dissolution) passes through a cycle made up of four *yugas* or ages. The first is *Kṛita* or *Satya Yuga*, during which *dharma* reigns in society. Each succeeding age sees the progressive decline of dharma. The second age is known as *Trēta Yuga*, the third is *Dvāpara Yuga*, and the fourth and present epoch is known as *Kali Yuga*.

Pronunciation Guide

Vowels can be short or long:

a – as 'u' in but; ā – as 'a' in far
e – as 'a' in may; ē – as 'a' in name
i – as 'i' in pin; ī – as 'ee' in meet
o – as in oh; ō – as 'o' in mole
u – as 'u' in push; ū – as 'oo' in hoot

ṛi – as 'ri' in crisp; ṛu – as 'ru' in Spanish 'Peru'
ḥ – pronounce 'aḥ' like 'aha,' 'iḥ' like 'ihi,' and 'uḥ' like 'uhu.'

Some consonants are aspirated (e.g. kh); others are not (e.g. k). The examples given below are only approximate:
k – as 'k' in 'kite;' kh – as 'ckh' in 'Eckhart'
g – as 'g' in 'give;' gh – as 'g-h' in 'dig-hard'
ch – as 'ch' in 'chat;' chh – as 'ch-h' in 'staunch-heart'
j – as 'j' in 'joy;' jh – as 'dgeh' in 'hedgehog'
p – as 'p' in 'pine;' ph – as 'ph' in 'up-hill'
b – as 'b' in 'bird;' bh – as 'bh' in 'rub-hard'

r – as 'r' in ride
ñ – as 'ny' in 'canyon;' ṅ – as 'ng' in 'sing'

The letters ḍ, ṭ, ṇ are pronounced with the tip of the tongue against the hard palate, the others with the tip against the teeth.
ṭ – as 't' in 'tub;' ṭh – as 'th' in 'lighthouse'
ḍ – as 'd' in 'dove;' ḍh – as 'dh' in 'red-hot'
ṇ – as 'n' in 'naught'
ḷ – as 'l' in 'revelry'
ṣh – as 'sh' in 'shine;' śh – as 's' in German 'sprechen'

With double consonants the sound is pronounced twice:
chch – as 'tc' in 'hot chip'
jj – as 'dj' in 'red jet'

Acknowledgements

This book is the fruit of the collaboration of Amma's children done in the spirit of offering. Behind the scenes Anita Raghavan, Rajani Menon, and Ramana Erickson have provided invaluable support. I further wish to extend my thanks to Jagannath Maas for diligently preparing the layout, as well as to Arun Raj for the captivating cover design. Swāmī Vidyāmṛitānanda was instrumental in crafting the extensive glossary. The unwavering guidance of Swāmī Jñānāmṛitānanda has been our backbone. I am deeply grateful to you all.

Julius Heyne

www.ingramcontent.com/pod-product-compliance
Lightning Source LLC
Chambersburg PA
CBHW071207090426
42736CB00014B/2743
9781680379020